I0793191

IMAGES
of America

WENATCHEE

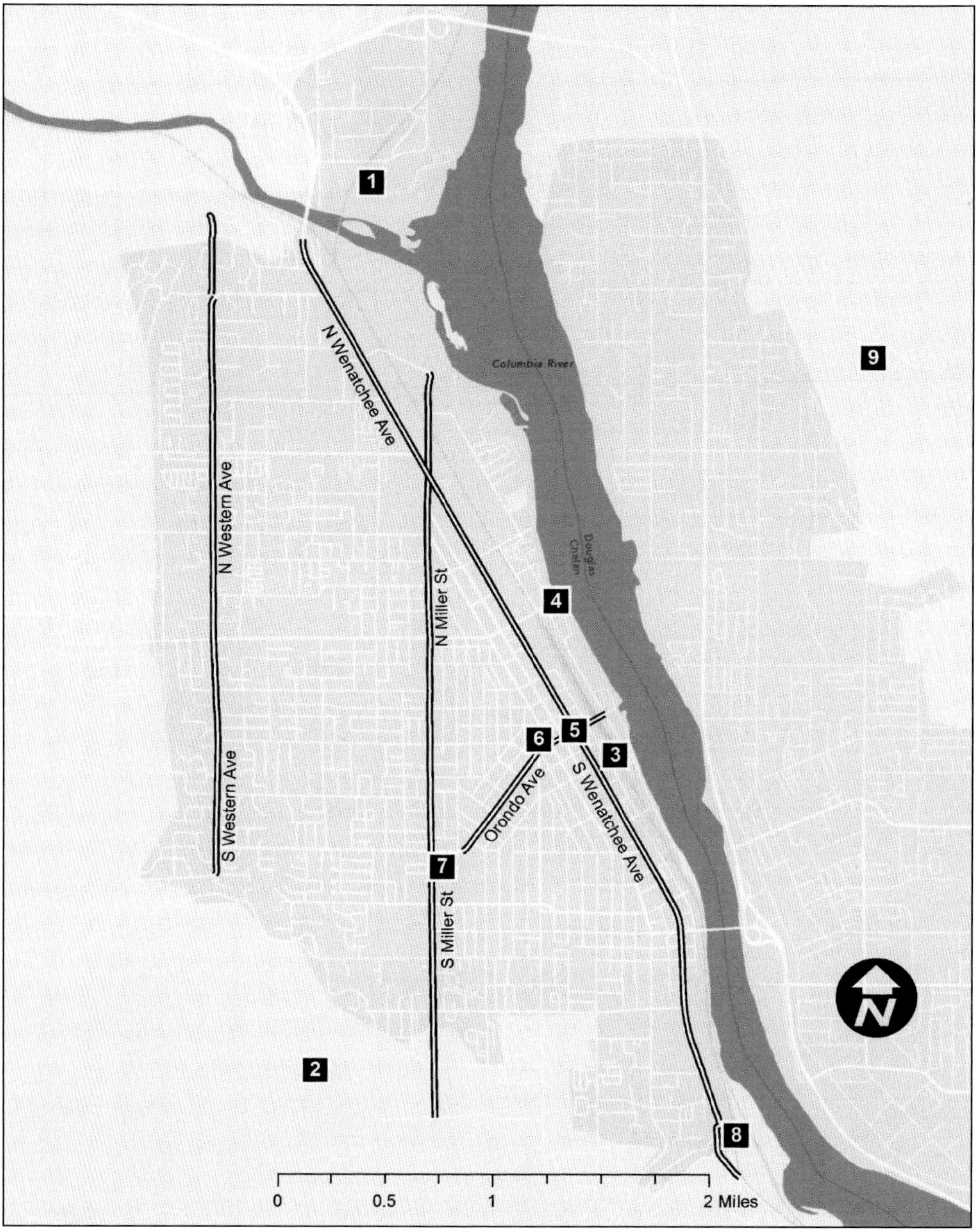

The Columbia River bisects the two-county community of Wenatchee (Chelan County) and East Wenatchee (Douglas County), located in the eastern foothills of the Cascade Mountains of Washington State. Besides a common history, the two cities are linked by the 10-mile Apple Capital Recreational Loop Trail along both sides of the river. Numbers on this map correspond to chapters in the book. Readers are invited to visit each location and imagine the people, businesses, and events of yesteryear that lent significance to this place. (Courtesy of John Ajax, City of Wenatchee.)

On the Cover: Members of the 1922 Birchmount Orchard picking crew pose in the midst of harvesting a 90,000-box apple crop. The large orchard at the foot of Burch Mountain was part of the American Fruit Growers cooperative. (Wenatchee Valley Museum and Cultural Center 83-15-166, donated by Skookum, Inc.)

IMAGES
of America

WENATCHEE

Wenatchee Valley Museum and Cultural Center
Chris Rader and Mark Behler

ARCADIA
PUBLISHING

ISBN 978-0-7385-7446-2

Published by Arcadia Publishing
Charleston, South Carolina

Printed in the United States of America

Library of Congress Control Number: 2010936826

For all general information, please contact Arcadia Publishing:
Telephone 843-853-2070
Fax 843-853-0044
E-mail sales@arcadiapublishing.com
For customer service and orders:
Toll-Free 1-888-313-2665

Visit us on the Internet at www.arcadiapublishing.com

Contents

ACKNOWLEDGMENTS

Since its founding in 1939 by the Columbia River Archaeological Society, the Wenatchee Valley Museum and Cultural Center (formerly North Central Washington Museum) has ignited appreciation for the history, arts, sciences, and rich diversity of this region. Hundreds of people have donated photographs, artifacts, and other mementos of our past to the museum's collection. Thousands of volunteers have contributed tens of thousands of hours to preserve this heritage and to bring it to life through a variety of educational programs and exhibits at our museum, which is housed in two historic buildings in downtown Wenatchee. All are welcome to visit us at 127 South Mission Street or www.wvmcc.org.

We extend our heartfelt gratitude to all whose dedication to our region's cultural enrichment has made this book possible. Special thanks go to Wenatchee Valley Museum and Cultural Center (WVMCC) director Brenda Abney for her encouragement and guidance; John Ajax, Wenatchee Community Development, for creating our map; and registrar Angie Battalio-Bunker, for helping with photographs and the index.

Introduction

Wenatchee has called itself the Apple Capital of the World since the early 1900s. Early settlers recognized that the area's rich volcanic soils, abundant water sources, protection from high winds, and sunny days and cool nights could make it "the Land of Perfect Apples." In a national campaign beginning in 1903 to attract settlers to the region, the Wenatchee Commercial Club (forerunner to the chamber of commerce) focused on orchard opportunities—and apples quickly became the backbone of the regional economy.

The weather was much colder when the first humans visited this region some 12,000 years ago. Evidence of the Ice Age hunter-gatherers known as the Clovis people was discovered in 1987 when a worker digging a ditch for an irrigation pipe in East Wenatchee found a cache of stone and bone tools. Archaeologists excavated the site and termed it one of the most significant Clovis finds in North America. Of the 56 tools and 11 fragments found, five are on permanent display at the Wenatchee Valley Museum and Cultural Center.

The Wenatchi-P'squosa people also inhabited the area. A Salish-speaking, peaceful, seminomadic tribe, they wintered along the Columbia River and moved up the Wenatchee River in spring to dig camas roots, hunt deer, pick berries, and fish for salmon. In late spring each year, they hosted large gatherings of tribes for the plentiful salmon harvest at the Wenatshapam fishery near what is now Leavenworth. Artifacts, mussel shells, and house pits near the headwaters of the river signify Wenatchi habitation about 8,000 years ago. The Wenatchis are now one of the Confederated Tribes of the Colville Reservation.

When fur-trader and surveyor David Thompson canoed down the Columbia River in July 1811, he noted two horsemen at the mouth of the Wenatchee that were probably Wenatchis. (This being the height of the spring Chinook salmon run, the rest of the tribe was probably upriver at the large fishery.) Thompson stopped for several hours at present-day Rock Island, where he reported a village of approximately 120 families living in homes woven from tule rushes.

Chinese placer miners came to the region in the 1850s after the California Gold Rush. They had permanent camps along the Columbia at today's Rock Island, Chelan Falls, Squilchuck Creek, and Wenatchee Confluence State Park. A Chinese village on the east side of the Columbia River near today's Beebe Bridge had log residences, a grocery store, a laundry, gambling houses, and a church. Chinese outnumbered whites in the Wenatchee area until the 1880s.

The coming of the railroad in 1892 was a milestone for Wenatchee. J.J. Hill's Great Northern Railway connected St. Paul, Minnesota, with Seattle and was the lifeblood of all communities in between. Daily train stops brought visitors and new residents to Wenatchee and afforded a nationwide market for the region's apples, pears, and cherries. When Wenatchee incorporated in 1892, it was clear that the town had a rosy future.

Many of Wenatchee's early leaders were tree fruit growers or owned agriculture-related businesses, such as hardware stores or shipping companies. The Wenatchee Commercial Club began in 1903 and soon included many prominent businessmen whose goal was to increase the city's population and industrial development. It published and disseminated throughout the United States brochures that called Wenatchee "the Home of the Big Red Apple, Where Dollars Grow on Trees." By 1910, the town boasted two newspapers, three lumber manufacturers, three solid banking institutions, numerous law and insurance offices, a dozen hotels, and the first vehicle bridge across the Columbia River. The bridge, completed in 1908, carried a large irrigation pipeline to Douglas County to convert some 4,000 acres of sagebrush to fertile orchard land. This provided promoters, such as John Gellatly and Leonard Fowler, with persuasive arguments about the opportunities awaiting people considering a move to the West.

The tree fruit industry thrived for decades and is still a significant part of the local economy, although population growth has transformed many orchards into sites for homes and businesses. A vibrant health-care sector, burgeoning wine industry, retail and wholesale opportunities, and many forms of year-round recreation now draw visitors and new residents to the greater Wenatchee area.

This book examines the development of Wenatchee and East Wenatchee from the standpoint of nine locations. Rather than proceeding in a strict chronological order, we discuss significant people and occurrences tied to each of these places. We invite you to visit each location, in the order you choose, and immerse yourself in its current ambience and historical context.

One

Confluence of Wenatchee and Columbia Rivers

The confluence of the Wenatchee and Columbia Rivers has long been a dwelling place. For thousands of years, the Wenatchi-P'squosa people spent winters along the Columbia River, where the weather was warmer than up the valley. Many large gatherings of First People were held in this general area, including intertribal councils called by Chief Moses, the great leader of the Sinkiuse-Columbias. The spot was easily accessible to the Entiat, Chelan, Methow, and other bands to the north as well as the Columbias, Spokanes, Yakamas, Umatillas, and Walla Wallas to the south. Today, the flat area north and south of the mouth of the Wenatchee River is known as Wenatchee Confluence State Park.

Wenatchee's first permanent business was established at this site in 1872. Early settlers Sam Miller, David Freer, and Franklin Freer purchased the stock of Jack Ingraham and John McBride, who had traded out of a large tent on the other side of the Columbia River before exiting the region after being accused of selling liquor to Indians. Miller and the Freer brothers built a log store, where they stocked rice, canned goods, oil, spices, tobacco, tools, clothing, household goods, and more. Their customers were Native Americans, Chinese miners, white explorers, surveyors traveling the Columbia, and the pioneers who began to settle the Wenatchee Flats.

The Burch family was among the first to acquire land above the confluence. E.C. and Ellen Burch and each of their children filed homestead claims in the early 1880s. This neighborhood, now called Sunnyslope, was known then as Burch Flats; the highest point is still called Burch Mountain. The Fred Olds and Mike Horan families were other early residents of Burch Flats. Many members of the Church of the Brethren emigrated from North Dakota beginning in 1903, further settling the Sunnyslope area.

The green oasis visible on the hillside above the confluence is Ohme Gardens, established in 1929 as a family residence. Herman and Ruth Ohme spent years introducing native plants and building pools and walkways, turning the dry bluff into a beautiful park that now is managed by Chelan County and attracts visitors from around the world.

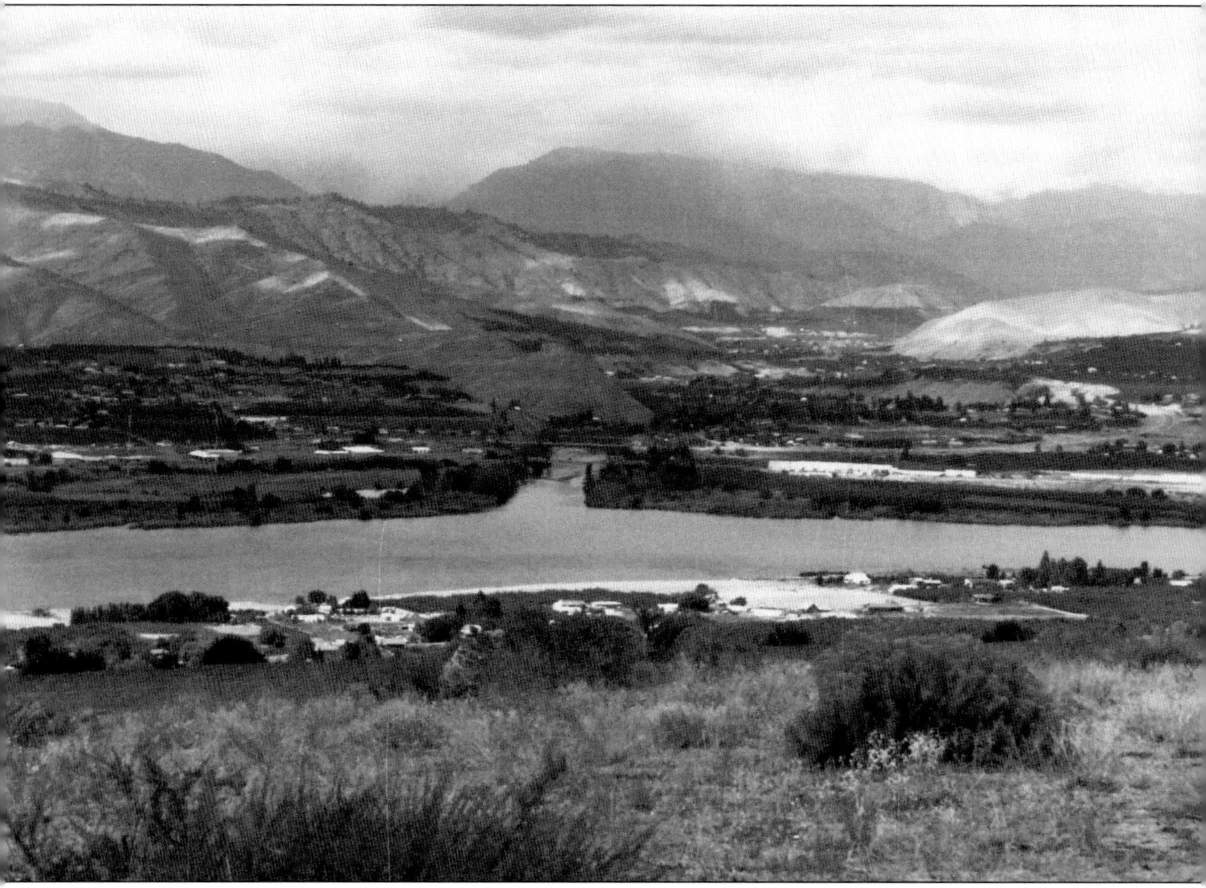

The Columbia River originates near Invermere, British Columbia, and flows southward past Wenatchee (from right) to the Pacific Ocean. The 1,243-mile-long river is the fourth largest in the United States and has the greatest flow of any North American river draining into the Pacific. Explorers Lewis and Clark traveled the lower Columbia River in 1804–1806; fur-trader David Thompson explored and mapped the entire river in 1811. One of its tributaries, the Wenatchee River (center), originates at Lake Wenatchee and flows past present-day Leavenworth and Cashmere. The Wenatchi people lived along this river for thousands of years. Many intertribal gatherings were held near the confluence. (WVMCC 88-108-1423, donated by Ileen Taylor.)

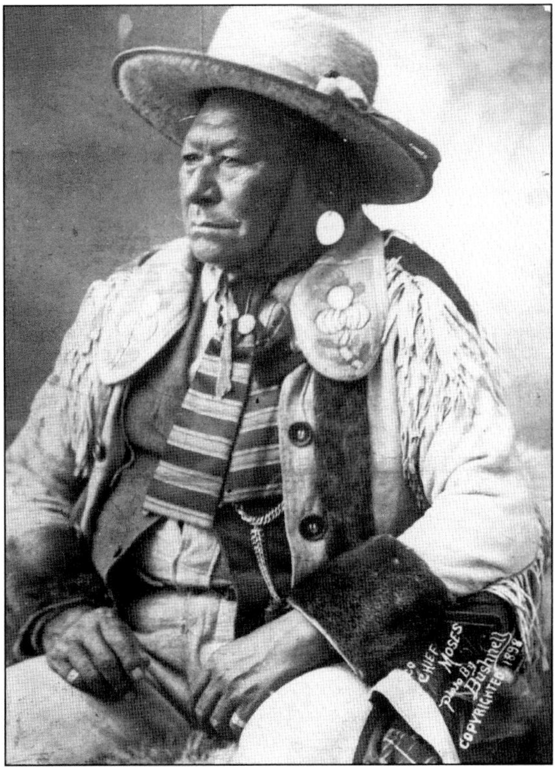

Chief Moses (1829–1899) was the leader of the Columbia-Sinkiuse Indians living on the east side of the Columbia River in today's Douglas County. His tribe also spent time along the Wenatchee River, mingling peacefully with the Wenatchis. Moses represented his people during the 1855 treaty negotiations in Walla Walla that assigned the native peoples of Washington to reservations. He opposed the treaty. In 1879, he convinced Pres. Rutherford B. Hayes to create a large reservation from the Cascades to the Columbia River and from Canada to the south shore of Lake Chelan. Four years later, this order was rescinded, and Moses's people were assigned to the Colville Reservation. Chief Moses had several wives; Mary, shown at a powwow in Cashmere in 1931, was his favorite. (Right, WVMCC 83-84-9, donated by John A. Brown; below, 75-23-66, donated by Bertha Smith.)

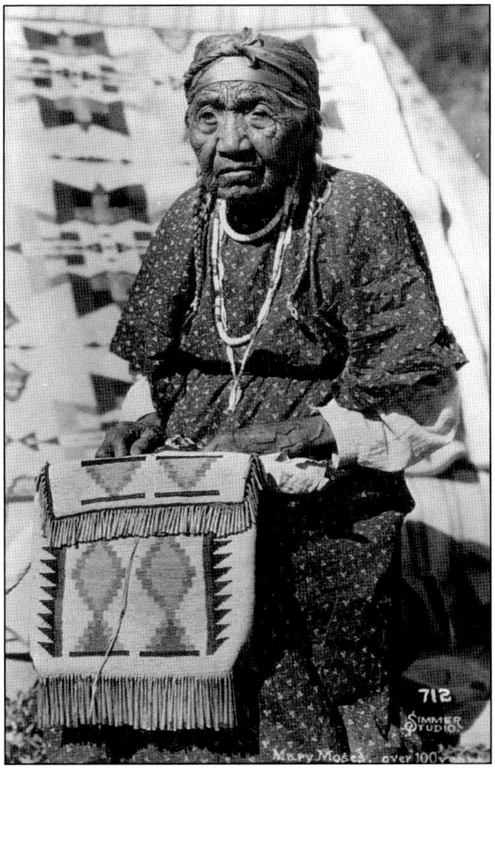

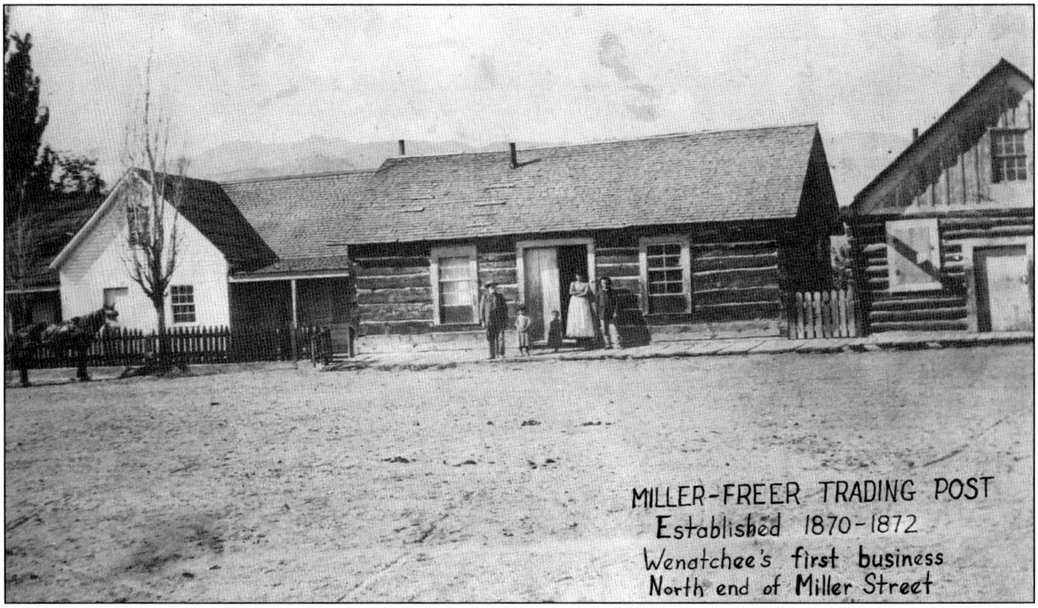

The Miller-Freer Trading Post served travelers, Chinese miners, Native Americans, and Wenatchee settlers from 1872 to the early 1900s. Partners Sam Miller, David Freer, and Franklin Freer accepted cash, gold dust, and items such as chickens or corn for a wide variety of trade goods. Standing in front around 1904 are, from left to right, Sam Miller, Lucy Freer, Hattie Freer, Mattie Freer, and Del Curry. (WVMCC 39-133-1a, donated by Anna M. Smith.)

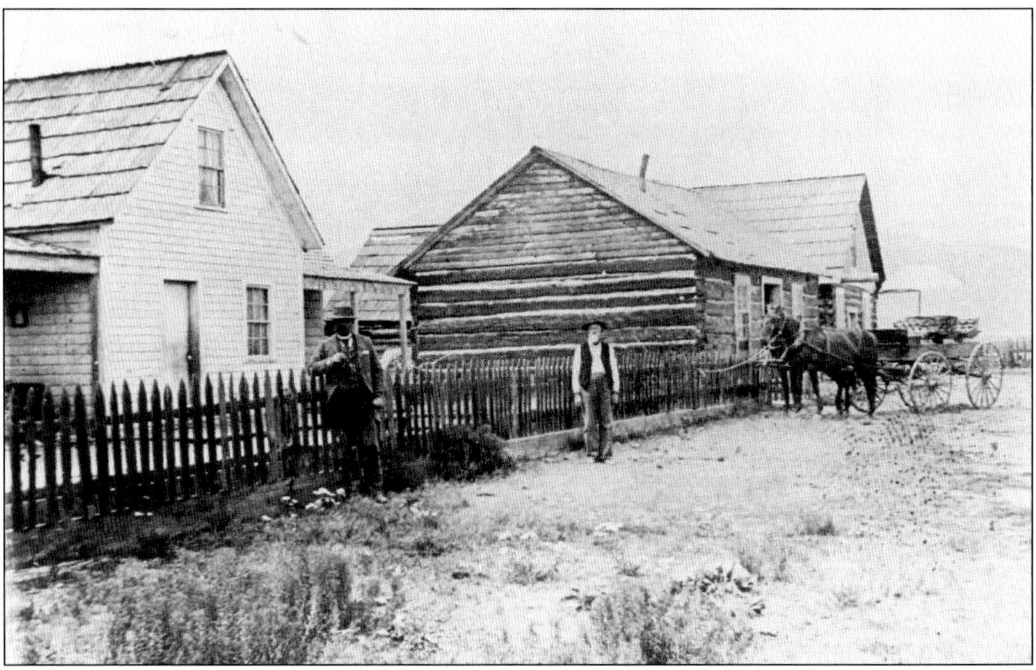

Enoch Morris, left, and Sam Miller stand at the rear of the log trading post around 1895. The store was also Wenatchee's first post office. Morris married David Freer's daughter Mattie; the frame house at left was owned by the Freer family. (WVMCC 78-214-35, donated by Bernice Gellatly Greene.)

The Freer brothers married Indian women. After David died in 1878 and Frank in 1888, Sam Miller adopted their children. Right, Miller holds five of David Freer's grandchildren, from left to right, Bennie Smith, Percy Morris, Leona Smith, Arnold Morris, and (in back) Lawrence Morris. Below, David and Fawn Freer's son Johnny stands with an unidentified man around 1888 in an orchard near the trading post. Miller died in 1906 at the age of 78. The whole town turned out at his funeral to honor "Uncle Sam," a generous and humble man who had extended credit at the store to many of them as they labored to establish their homesteads and businesses. (Right, WVMCC 78-214-97, donated by Bernice Gellatly Greene; below, 83-12-6, donated by Marcelene King.)

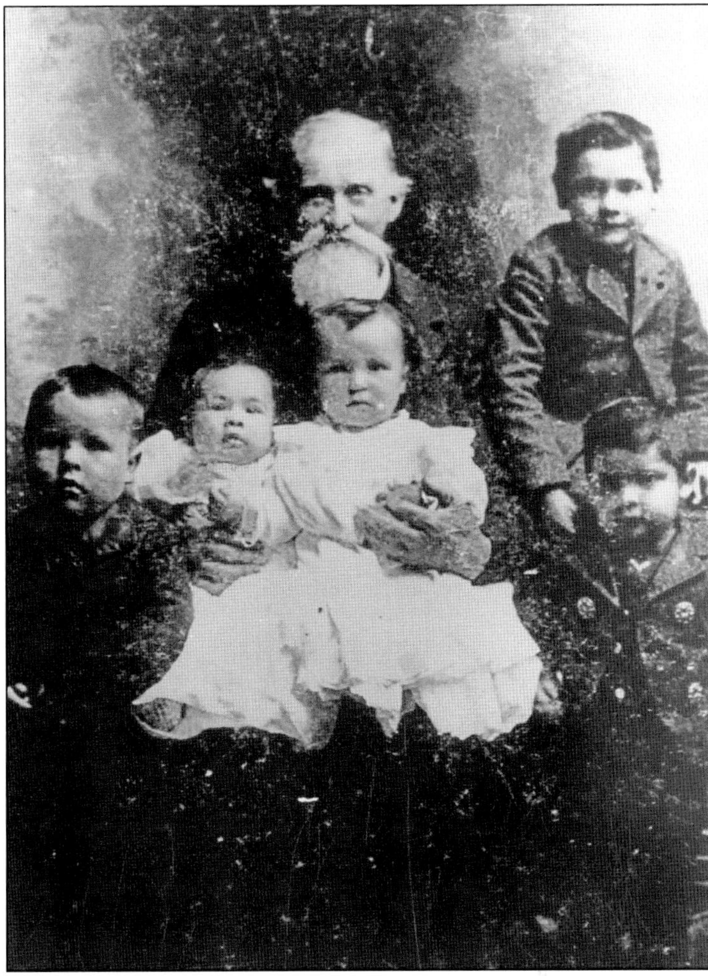

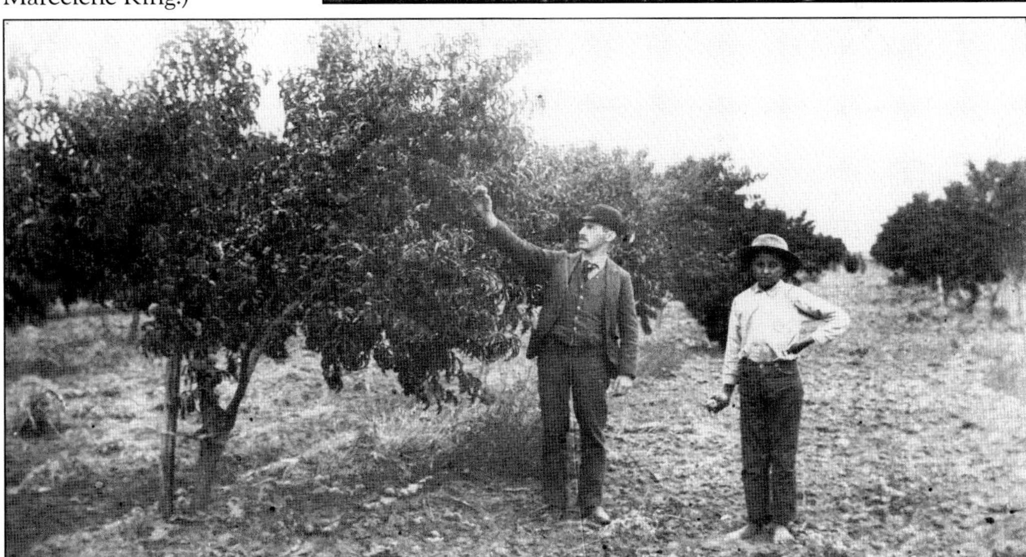

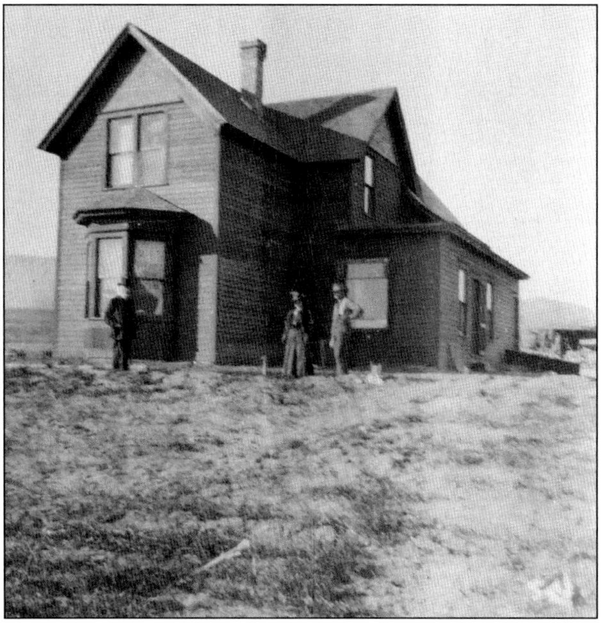

E.C. and Ellen Burch arrived in Wenatchee in the early 1880s with their children—Charles, Etta, Louis, and Frederick—each of whom was old enough to file land claims in accordance with the Homestead Act of 1862. From 1885 to 1889, the Burch family operated a steam ferry across the Columbia River near the Wenatchee confluence. The people in this photograph of the Burch home are unidentified. (WVMCC 94-31-42, donated by Eleanor Spangler.)

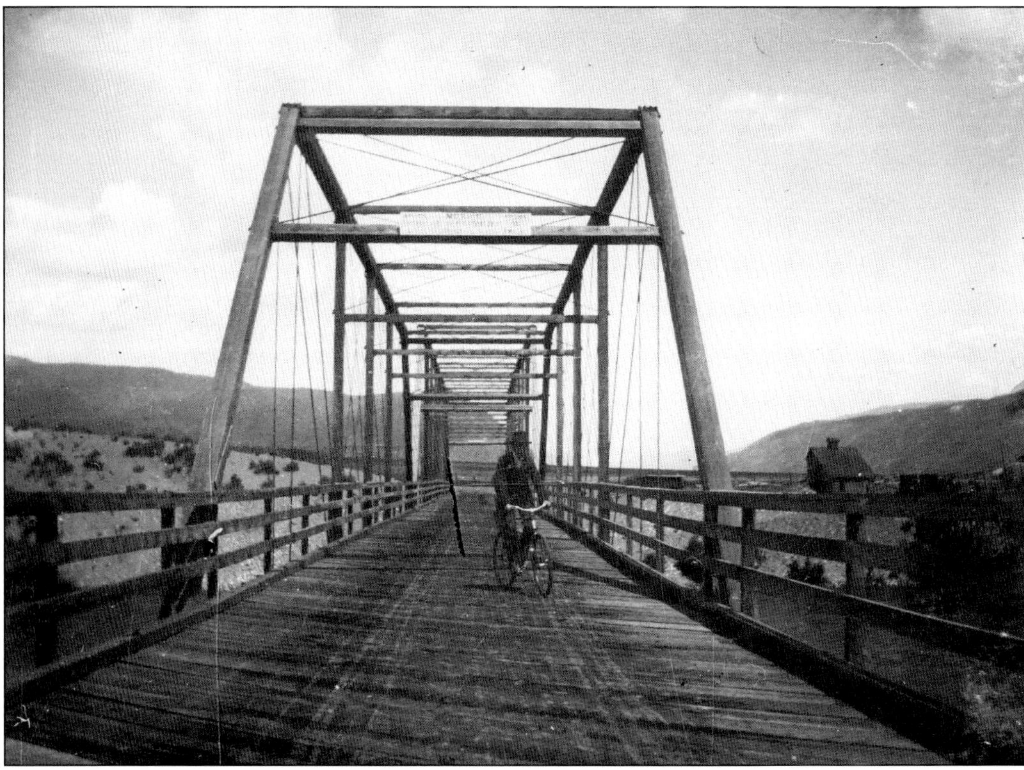

An unidentified man rides a bicycle across the wood and steel bridge over the Wenatchee River just above its confluence with the Columbia River in 1895. This was the second bridge at this location; the first was carried away by high water in 1894. I.J. Bailey built both. The wooden decking of the bridge pictured here was eventually destroyed by fire, but the bridge's two spans were salvaged for a third bridge. (WVMCC 85-0-87.)

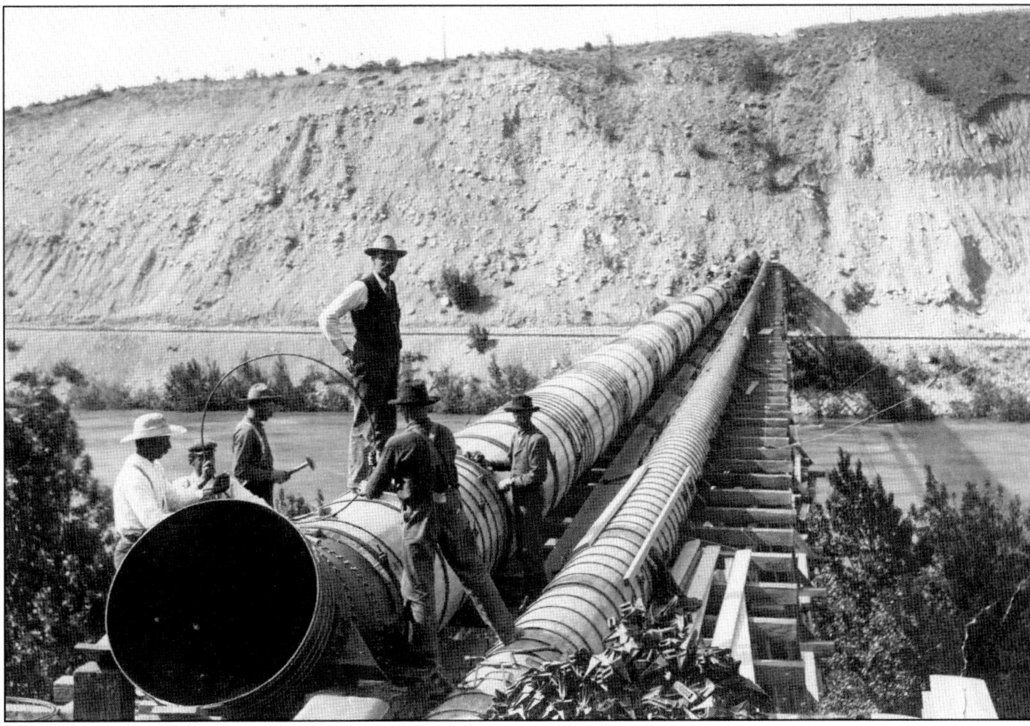

Unidentified men in 1904 are seen building the inverted siphon that carries Highline Canal water downhill, across the Wenatchee River, and then uphill to the Wenatchee Flats. The view is looking south. At right is a pipeline for the Gunn (Shotwell) Ditch. Irrigation water was crucial to the development of Wenatchee. (WVMCC 80-11-36, donated by Edrie Bradbury Davis.)

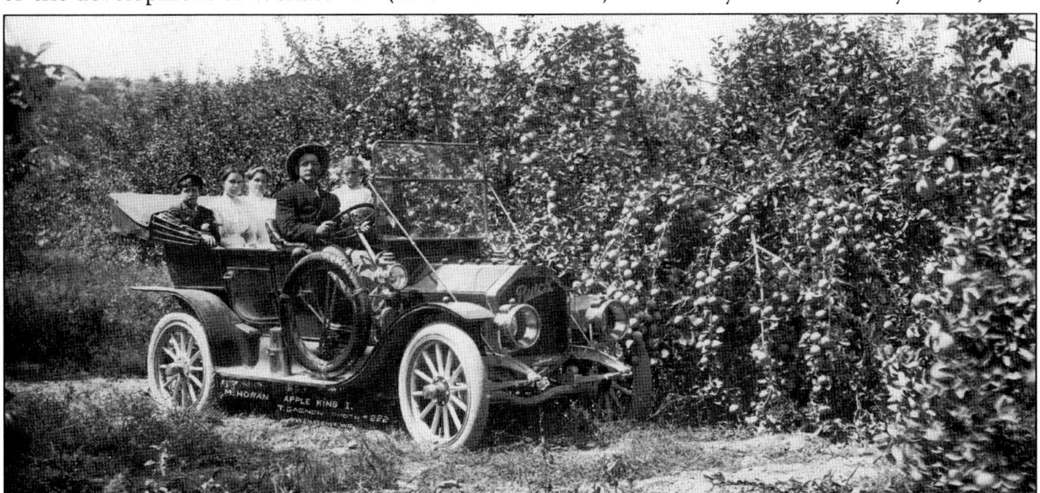

In 1894, Mike Horan (1854–1919) and his wife, Margaret, purchased the Sam Miller homestead, located below Burch Mountain, and planted a large orchard of apples, pears, and apricots. Horan's entry of a full carload of apples in the first National Apple Show in Spokane in 1908 earned him $2,000 and the title of Apple King. In his new Buick around 1910 are, from left to right, (backseat) Walt, Esther, and Margaret; (front seat) Mike, Kathleen, and John Horan. (WVMCC 80-67-126, donated by Madeleine Elliott.)

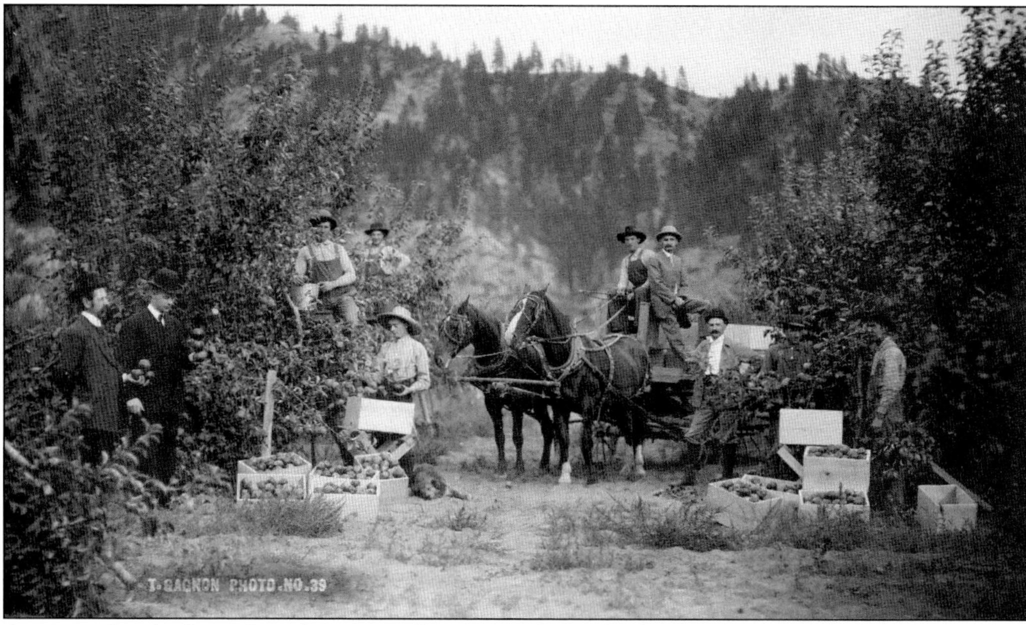

Apple orchards thrived in the Sunnyslope area above the lower Wenatchee River in the early 1900s. Picked apples were placed into buckets and emptied into wooden boxes for horse-drawn wagons to haul away. The people in this undated photograph are not identified, but the men in suit coats and hats probably posed with the apple pickers for a publicity shot aimed at attracting new settlers to the region. (WVMCC 86-24-67, donated by Wenatchee Chamber of Commerce.)

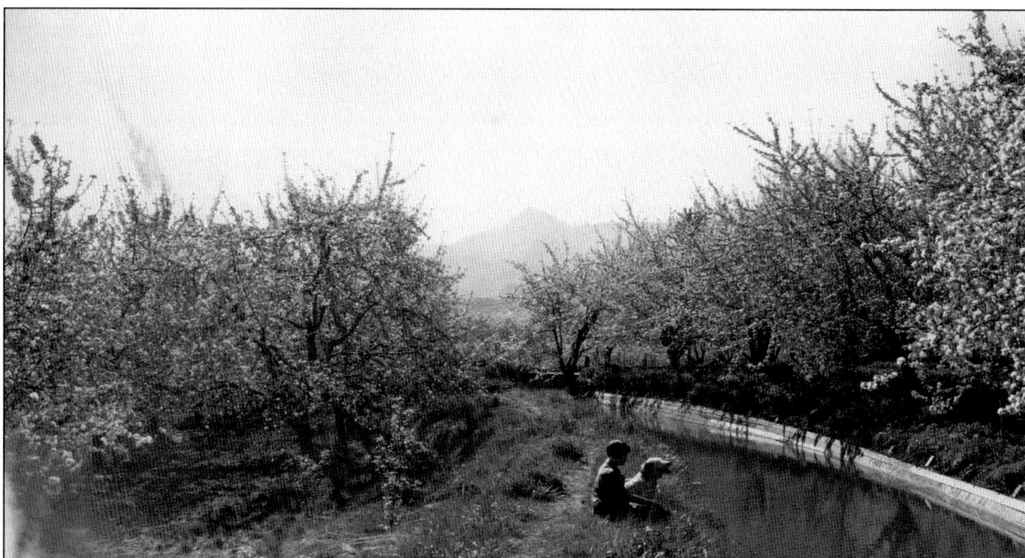

Wenatchee would never have been known as the Apple Capital of the World without irrigation development. The Highline Canal, pictured here, was not the area's first irrigation project but became its largest. Completed in 1904, it carried water taken from the Wenatchee River near Peshastin down the north side of the river to Sunnyslope, across to the Wenatchee Flats, and eventually across the Columbia River to Douglas County (see Chapter Three). (WVMCC 83-15-141, donated by Skookum, Inc.)

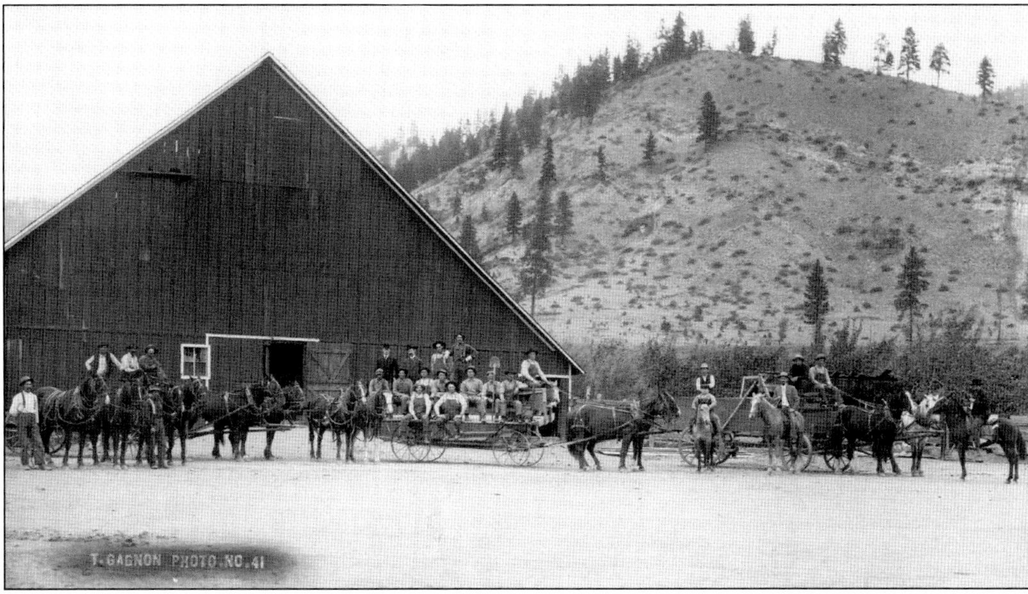

The fruit harvest crew poses in front of a barn in the early 1900s. Horses brought wooden boxes of apples from the field to be checked before lids were nailed to the boxes and colorful labels affixed to the side. Apples were the main cargo shipped from Wenatchee on Great Northern Railway freight cars. (WVMCC 86-24-73, donated by Wenatchee Chamber of Commerce.)

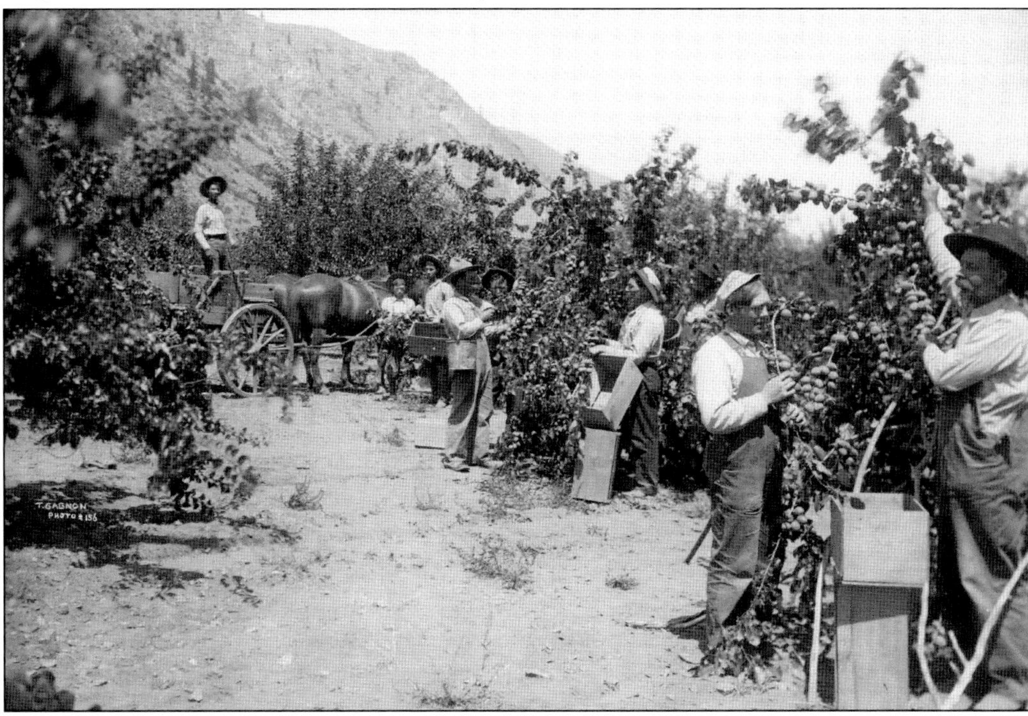

Workers pick apricots in Mike Horan's orchard in the early 1900s. The man at far right appears to be Horan himself. Horan was a county commissioner, member of Wenatchee's first city council and the Wenatchee Commercial Club, and president of the Washington State Horticultural Association. (86-24-339, donated by Wenatchee Chamber of Commerce.)

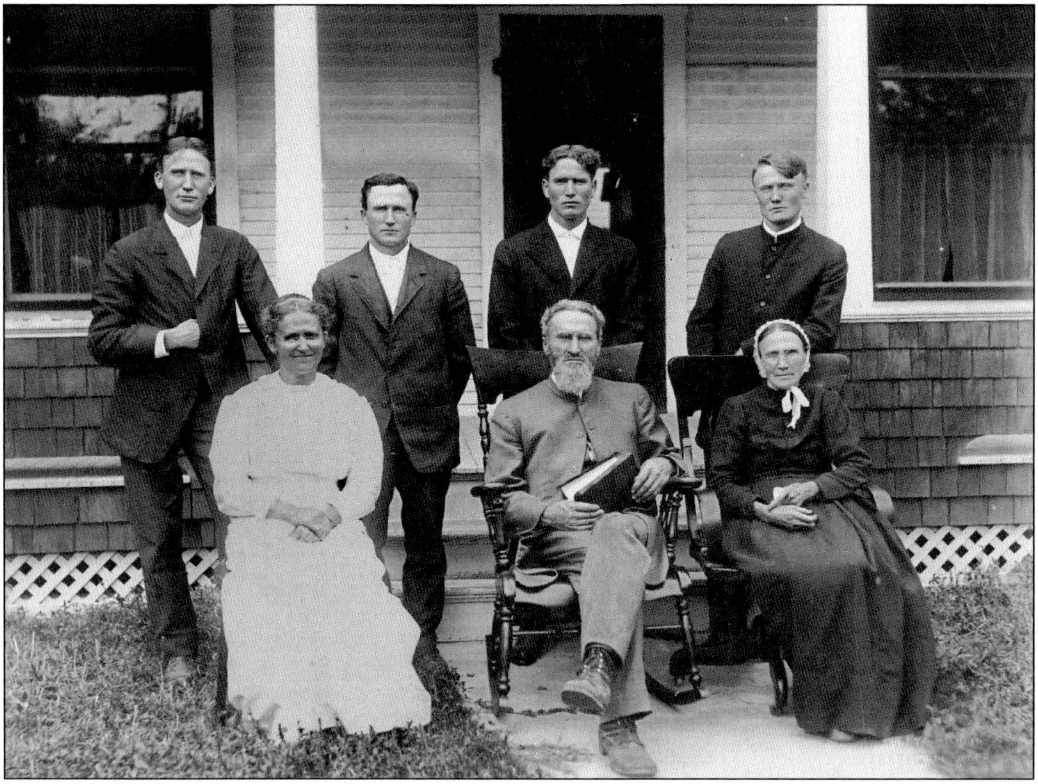

The Reverend Amos Peters was leader of a small colony of Brethren who were "recruited" by Great Northern Railway to emigrate from North Dakota to Wenatchee. After two scouting trips, and despite the so-far-undeveloped landscape of sagebrush and boulders, Peters and his small committee convinced other Brethren to settle in Sunnyslope above the Wenatchee River. In 1902, he purchased 50 acres; the next year, he started a church. With the completion of the Highline Canal in 1904, members of the Brethren colony planted orchards and other crops. Family members pictured above are, from left to right, (first row) Katie, Amos, and Barbara; (second row) Hiram, Marvin, Jim, and John Peters. Below, family members stand in front of the Peters home in Sunnyslope in 1906. (Both, WVMCC 94-69-17 and 94-69-14, donated by George and Hazel Saunders.)

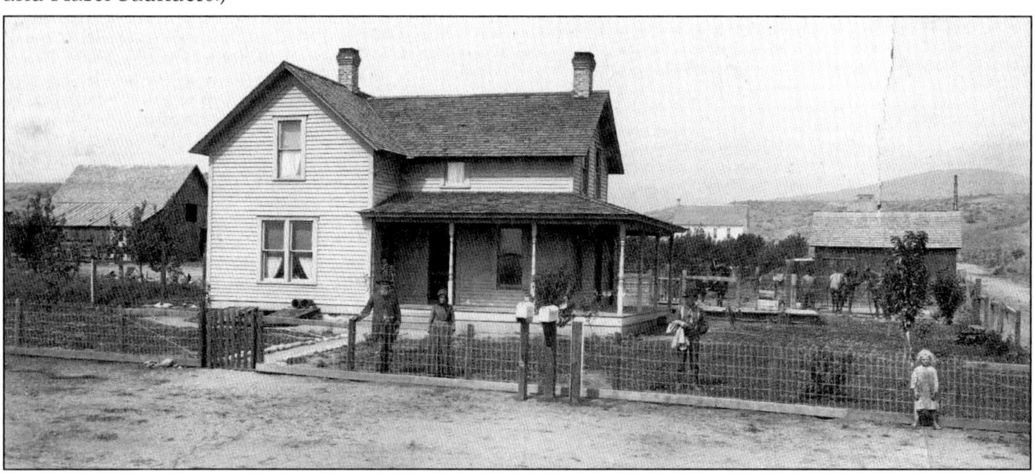

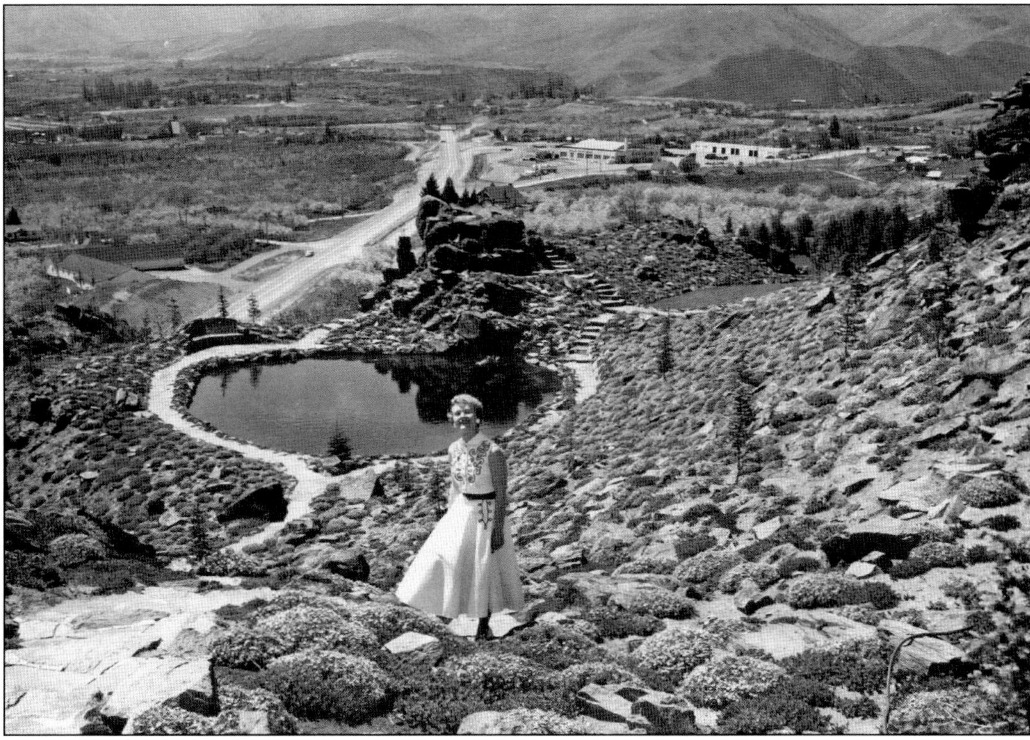

Overlooking the Wenatchee-Columbia confluence is Ohme Gardens, a fertile refuge on the rocky hillside that began as a hobby for Herman (pictured below) and Ruth Ohme. They purchased the 40-acre parcel in 1929 and began to beautify part of it by improving the soil, transplanting evergreen seedlings and ground cover, and moving rock to create pathways and borders. They lovingly watered the plants by hand with buckets of water hauled from the Columbia River before building an irrigation system. After 10 years, they had covered two acres of barren land with flowers, shrubs, trees, shelters, and pools connected by walkways whose flagstone they carried up the hill by hand from the banks of the Columbia. Originally intended as an oasis for their family and friends, Ohme Gardens opened to the public in 1939. (Both, WVMCC 86-24-750 and 86-24-752, donated by Wenatchee Chamber of Commerce.)

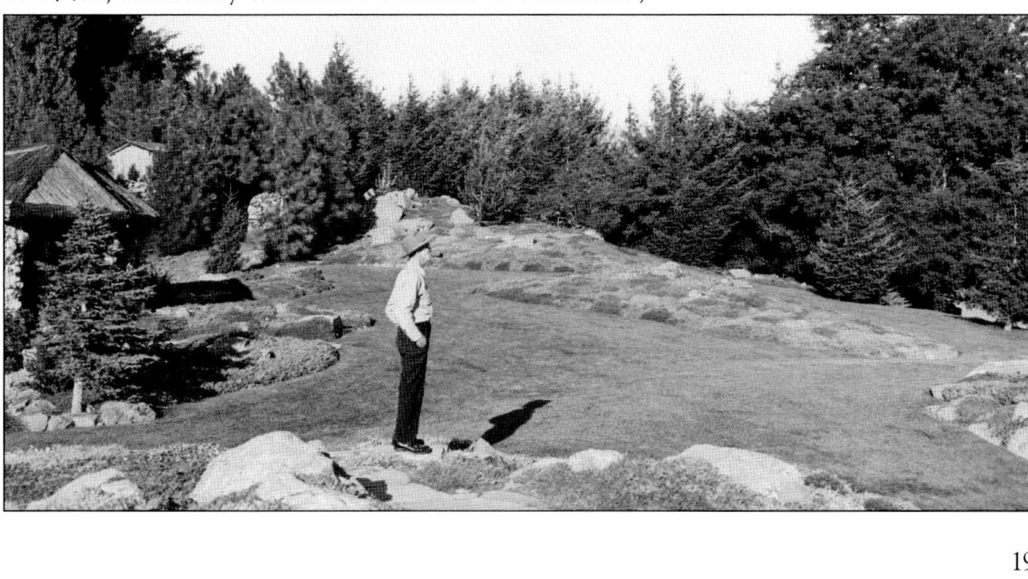

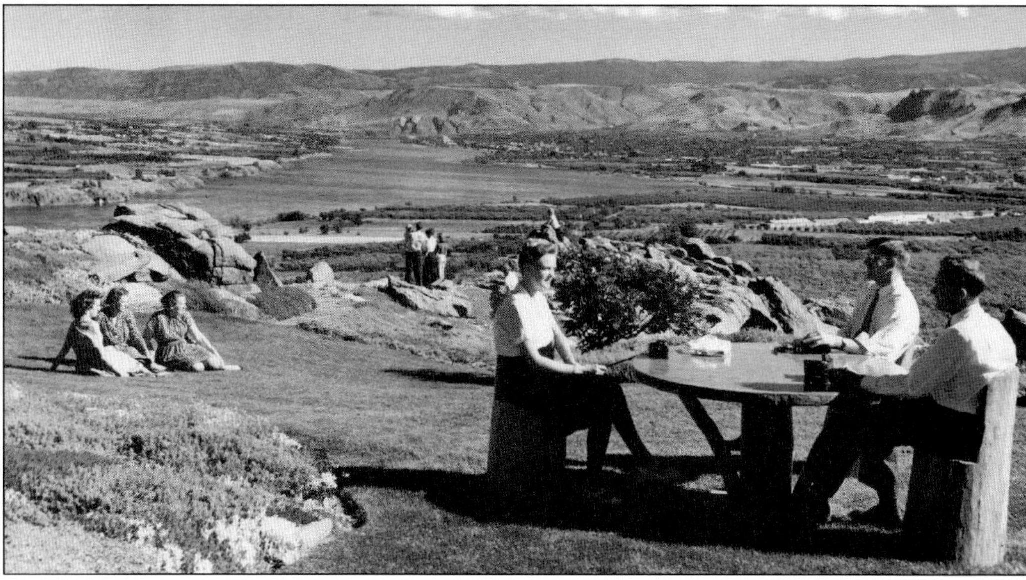

Thousands of guests, like these unidentified people in 1945, enjoyed the panoramic views each year while picnicking at Ohme Gardens. The hand-hewn log seats matched the garden's rustic beauty. After Herman died in 1971, sons Calvin and Gordon and their children continued maintaining the gardens. In 1991, Washington State Parks purchased the gardens and surrounding property; it is now managed by Chelan County. (WVMCC 87-107-1, donated by LaVelle Heideman.)

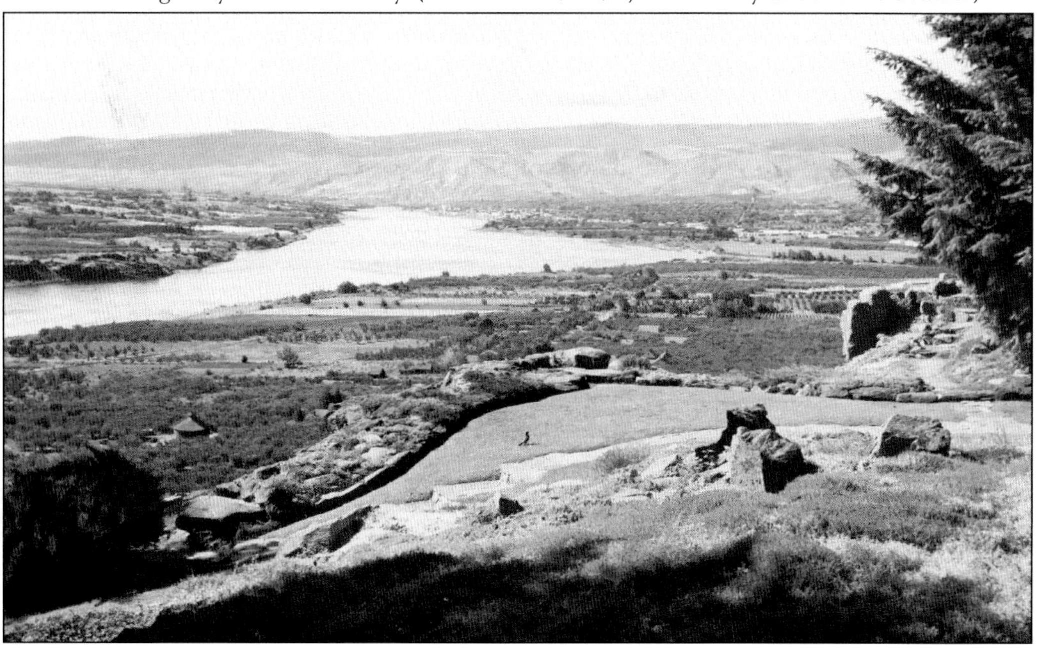

A bird on a grassy terrace seems oblivious to the spectacular view from Ohme Gardens. Visitors can see the snowy Cascade Mountains to the west, the Columbia River and Douglas County to the east, and the mouth of the Wenatchee River and much of Wenatchee to the south. Originally called Burch Flats, the flat ground shown in this 1960 photograph is now known as Olds Station. Higher and out of view to the right is Sunnyslope. (WVMCC 86-24-760, donated by Wenatchee Chamber of Commerce.)

Two

Saddle Rock

Saddle Rock is a well-known Wenatchee landmark. The Wenatchi-P'squosas knew the place as where Black Bear and Grizzly Bear once fought over their husband before being turned to stone for their bickering. The smaller rocks scattered to their sides are variously described as their children or their baskets for gathering roots and berries.

In the late 1800s, white settlers thought the rock formation resembled a saddle. Some called it "Squaw Saddle," a name that appears in newspaper reports of the early 1900s; the unique land feature is now known as Saddle Rock. As early as 1909, Mayor John Gellatly tried to acquire the land around the rock formation for a city park, saying "the view from the top is one of the finest in the valley." Other efforts were made in the 1940s and 1960s to acquire the property, but it was not until 2011 that the Chelan-Douglas Land Trust, City of Wenatchee, and numerous community donors were able to purchase 150 acres from the Washington State Department of Natural Resources and add it to city-owned natural open space. Two popular hiking trails to the top of Saddle Rock may be accessed from the south ends of Miller Street and Western Avenue.

Philip Miller, one of the early pioneers for whom Miller Street is named (the other being Sam, who was not related), arrived in Wenatchee in 1872. He settled below Saddle Rock and began to grow peaches, apples, and grapes, which he watered from a small ditch from Squilchuck Creek. Before the railroad offered access to a large market, Miller turned much of his fruit into wine and brandy for local sale. He also grew alfalfa and ran cattle on his property.

In 1889, he sold 160 of his 530 acres to the Wenatchee Development Company. Another large sale in 1906 to the Wenatchee Realty and Investment Company resulted in the subdivision of many plats of orchard land. Newcomers eager to profit from the lucrative tree fruit market gobbled up these smaller plats in what came to be known as Millerdale.

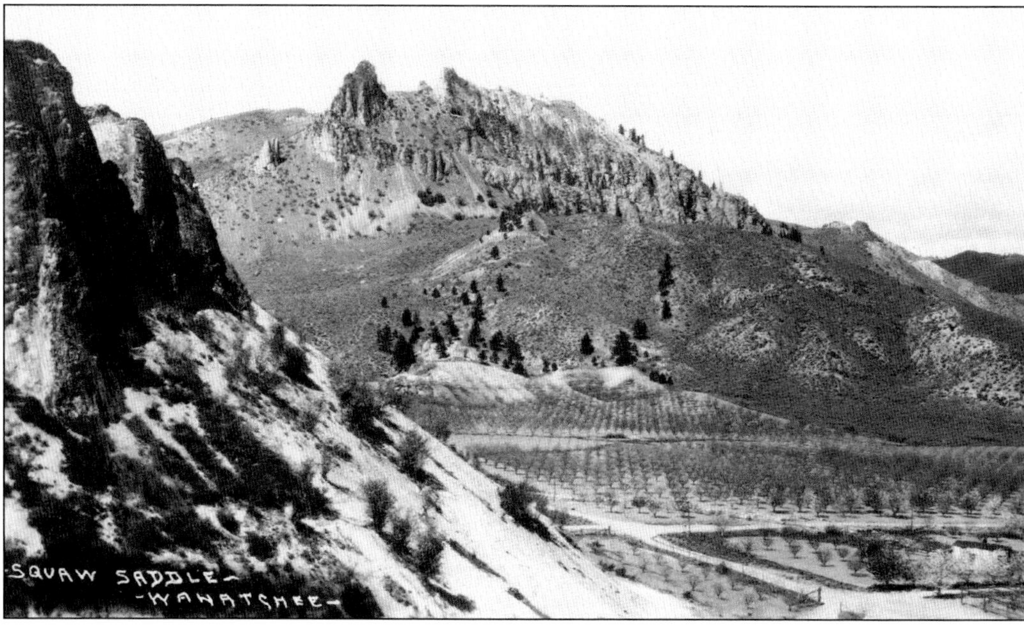

The distinctive rock formation now called Saddle Rock is visible from East Wenatchee and many points in Wenatchee. Its image appears in photographs taken during all seasons and dating back more than a century, including the 1930 postcard above and the wintertime shot taken in 1950. The feature was formed from an ancient intrusion of volcanic magma through the sedimentary rock of the western foothills. (Above, WVMCC 98-26-29, donated by Norm June; below, 88-108-44, donated by Ileen Taylor.)

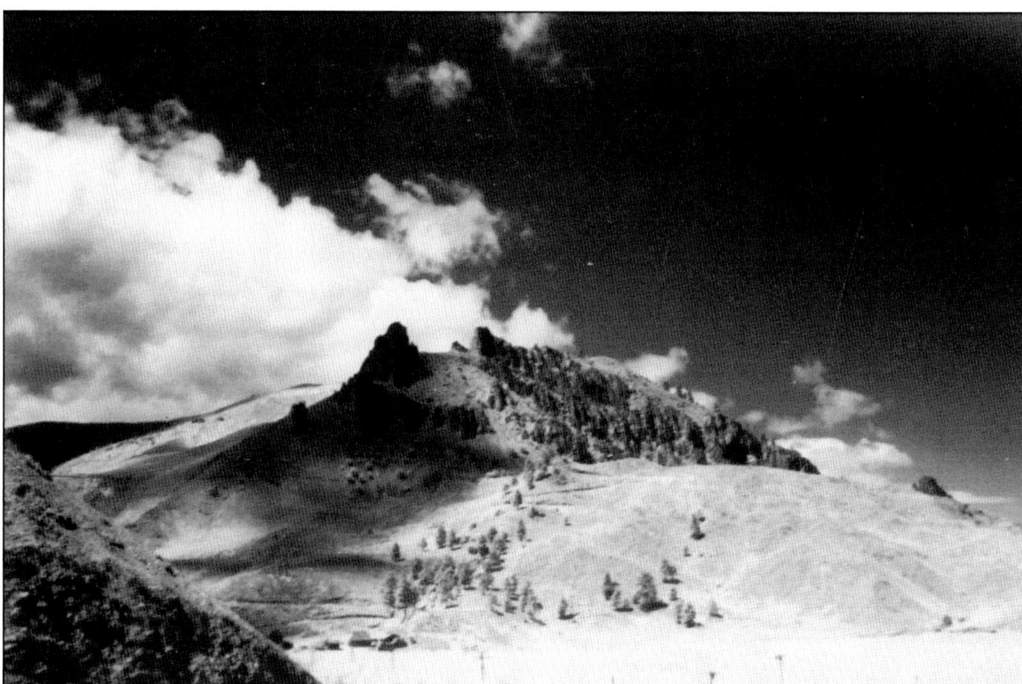

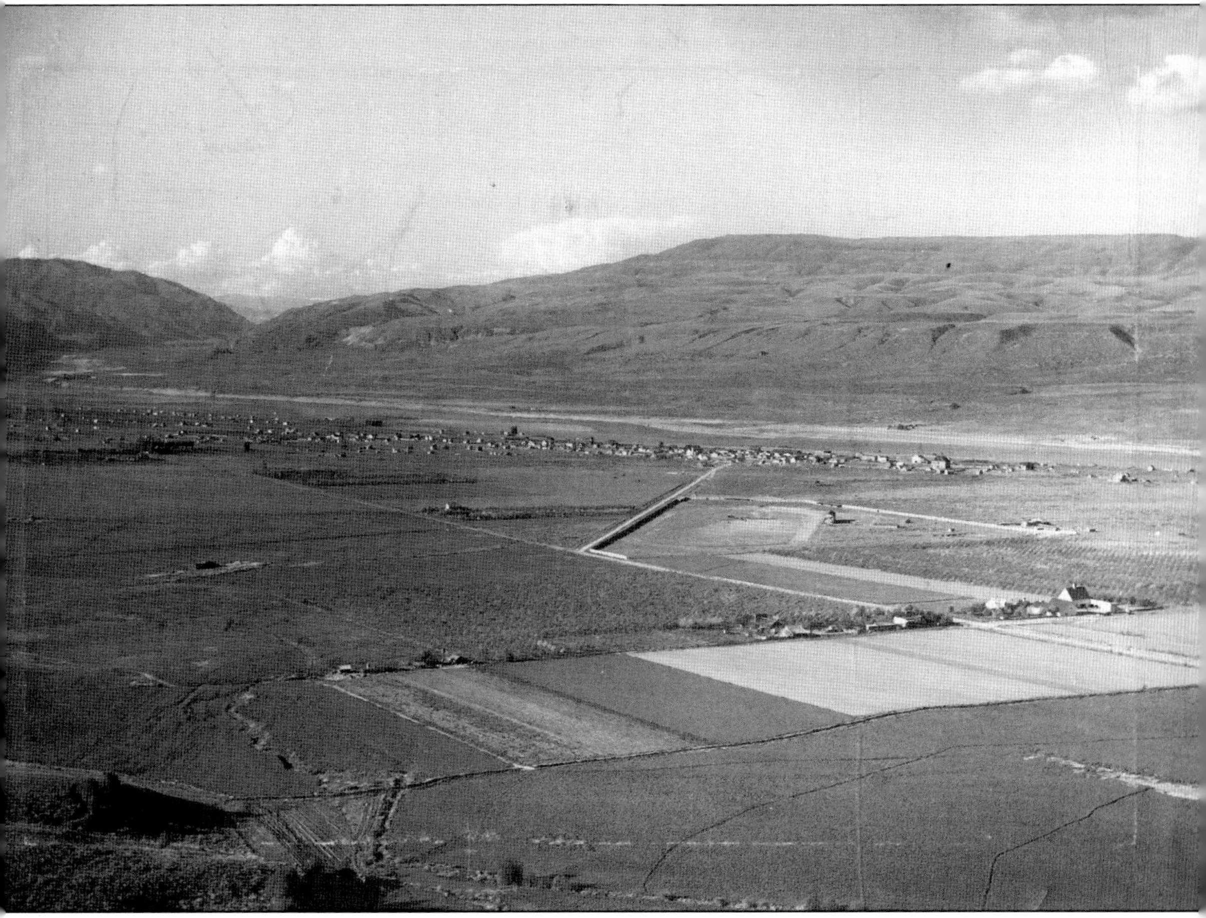

Wenatchee around 1900 was just a string of buildings along the Great Northern Railway line near the banks of the Columbia River. Across the river in Douglas County, only a smattering of homesteads indicates that there would ever be a town called East Wenatchee. This view from Saddle Rock shows some of Philip Miller's orchard and alfalfa land, with Orondo Avenue intersecting north-south Miller Street and leading toward the river. The oval field at the intersection was used for baseball games, rodeos, and fairs (see chapter seven). Miller sold off his vast holdings to developers who platted and resold it in smaller lots. (WVMCC 78-218-12, donated by Mary Anderson.)

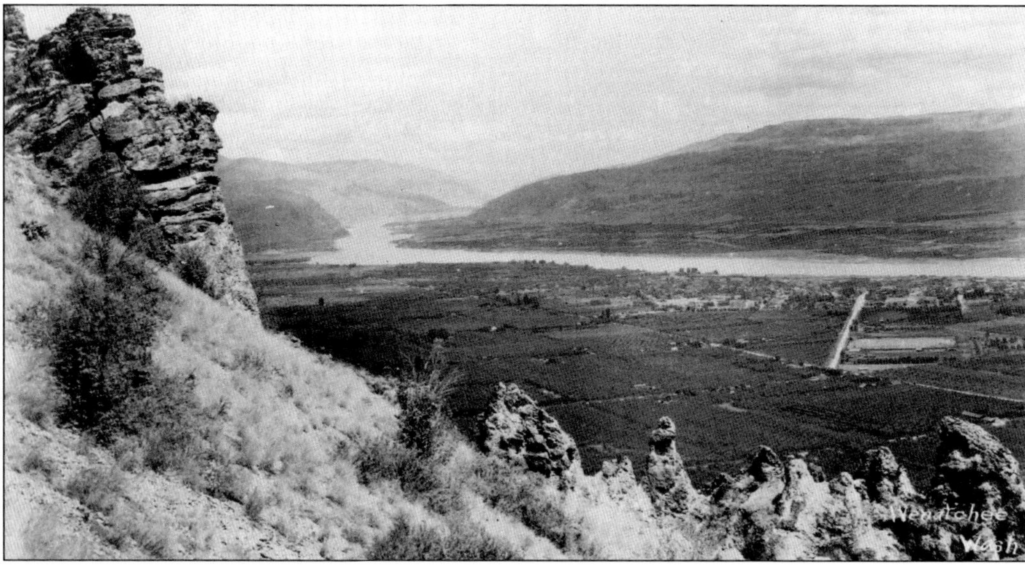

The photograph on this 1930 postcard was taken from Saddle Rock and looks north up the Columbia River, with the Wenatchee coming in from the west (left). Orchards dominate the landscape, from Millerdale below the rock to the Wenatchee River. The wide street at right center is Orondo Avenue. Millerdale took its name from Philip Miller, who arrived in Wenatchee in 1872 and became the largest landowner in North Central Washington before selling off his land. Miller planted some of his acreage in apples, peaches, and other tree fruit. By the time it was subdivided and sold, virtually all of Miller's original 530 acres was orchard land. Rows of small fruit trees can be seen in front of the unidentified house below. (Above, WVMCC 98-26-32, donated by Norm June; below, 86-24-105, donated by Wenatchee Chamber of Commerce.)

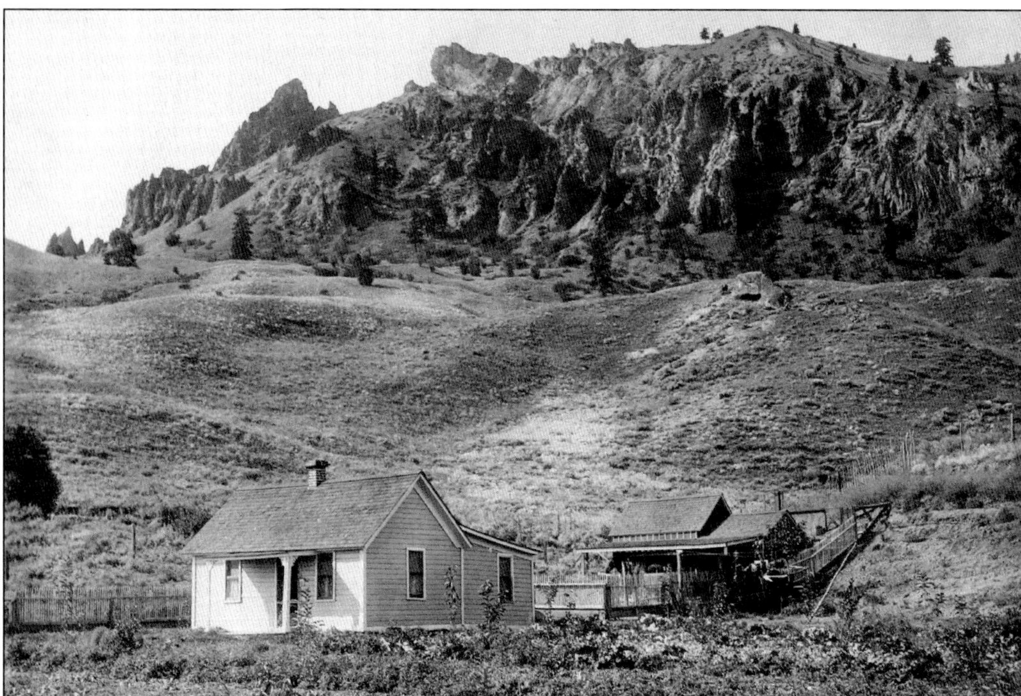

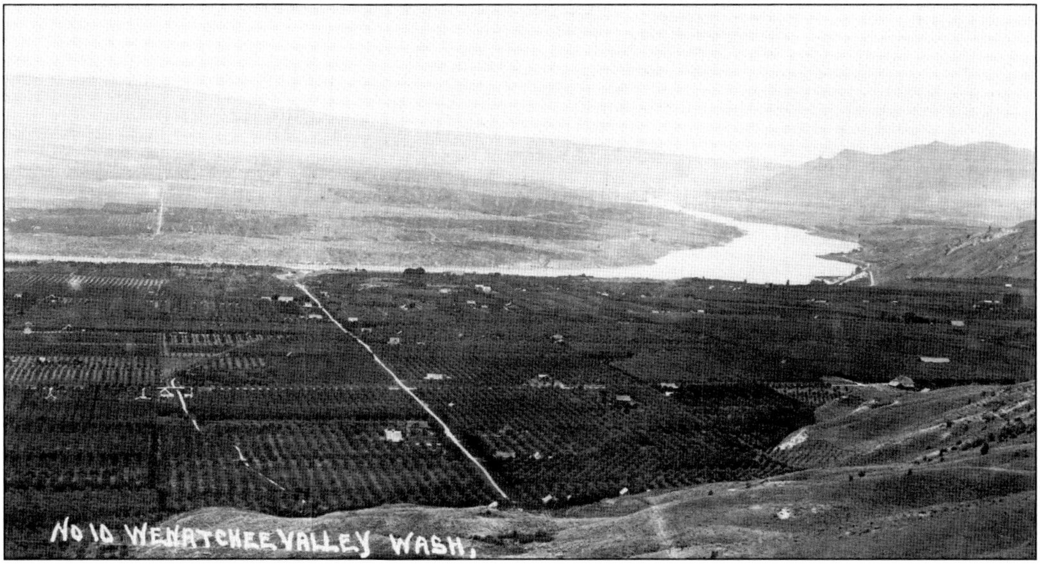

Another panoramic view from Saddle Rock looks south, showing the Columbia River as it winds toward Rock Island. Running between the river and hillside is Crawford Avenue. Across the river in this undated photograph, East Wenatchee has lots of orchards but very few buildings. The orchards of the Millerdale Fruit District dominated the landscape below Wenatchee's western foothills. (WVMCC 87-6-15, donated by Jane Lovejoy.)

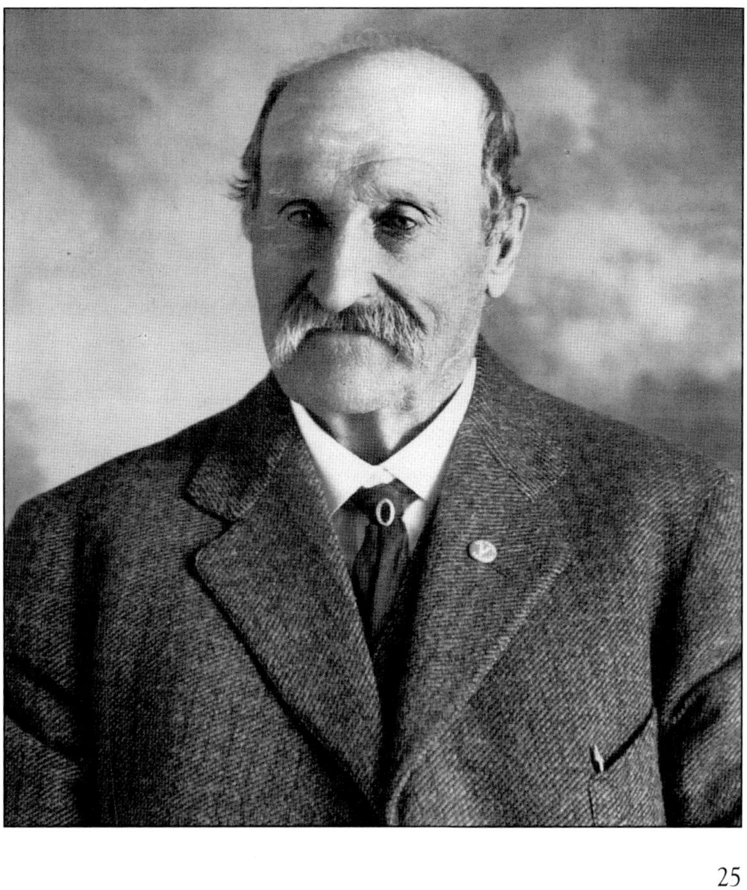

A sturdy and energetic German, Philip Miller (1835–1927) built an irrigation ditch with the help of Indian laborers before taking two mules to Walla Walla to purchase hundreds of fruit tree seedlings—a round-trip of some 350 miles. Reaching the Columbia River near Wenatchee and realizing his mules could not carry both him and the trees, he grasped the reins of both animals and swam with them across the river. When the Great Northern Railway laid its rails through Wenatchee in October 1892, Philip Miller was chosen to drive the silver spike. (WVMCC 75-49-151, donated by Richard Bell.)

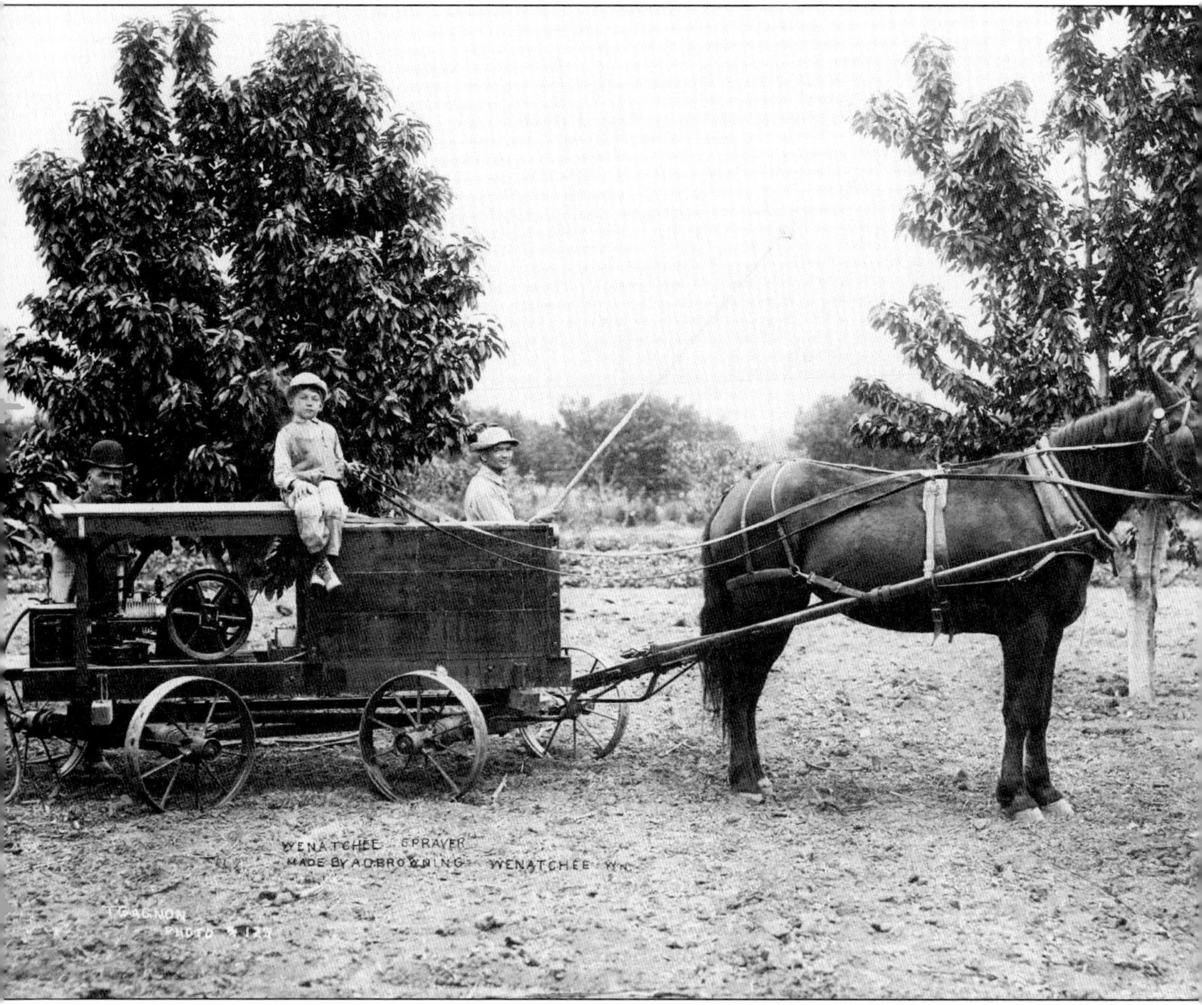

A horse pulls a sprayer in a Wenatchee orchard in 1910. The sprayer, manufactured by A.D. Browning of Wenatchee, was a relatively simple apparatus that used a hose and bamboo spray wand to apply arsenate of lead. This insecticide was used in Washington orchards and farms until 1948 when DDT became available; DDT was banned in 1972. It was not until the second half of the 20th century that orchard workers began to protect their faces with masks while spraying insecticides. (WVMCC 81-98-3, donated by Harold Darlington.)

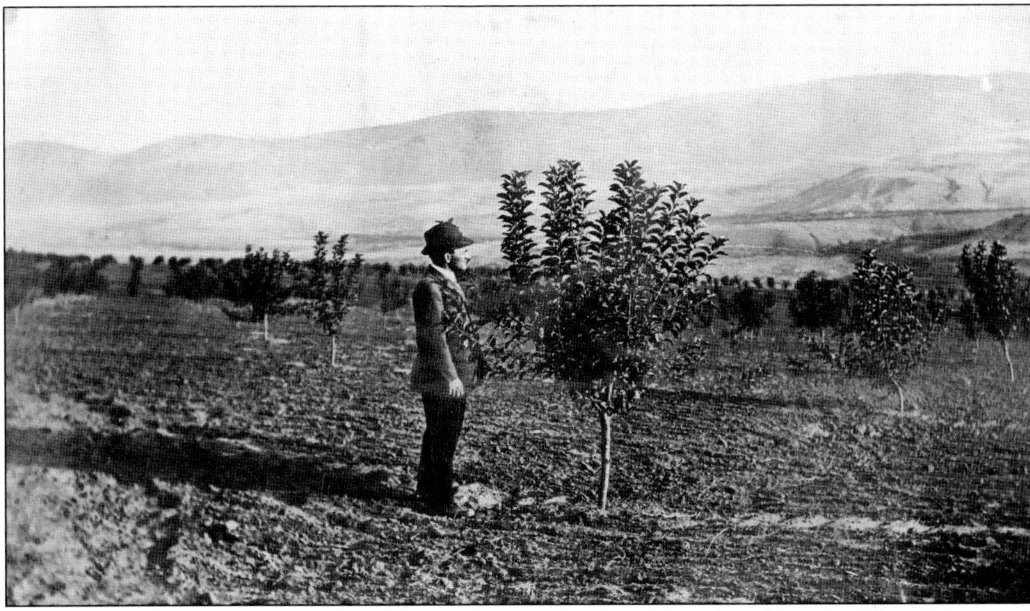

An apple capital of the world starts out with modest plantings of apple trees. This photograph from the early 1900s captures the promise of a young Wenatchee orchard, with small trees as far as the eye can see. Wenatchee's early history and economy were built on the apple industry. Apples are still the largest agricultural crop grown in the state, and Washington leads the nation in apple production. (WVMCC 80-67-123, donated by Madeleine Elliott.)

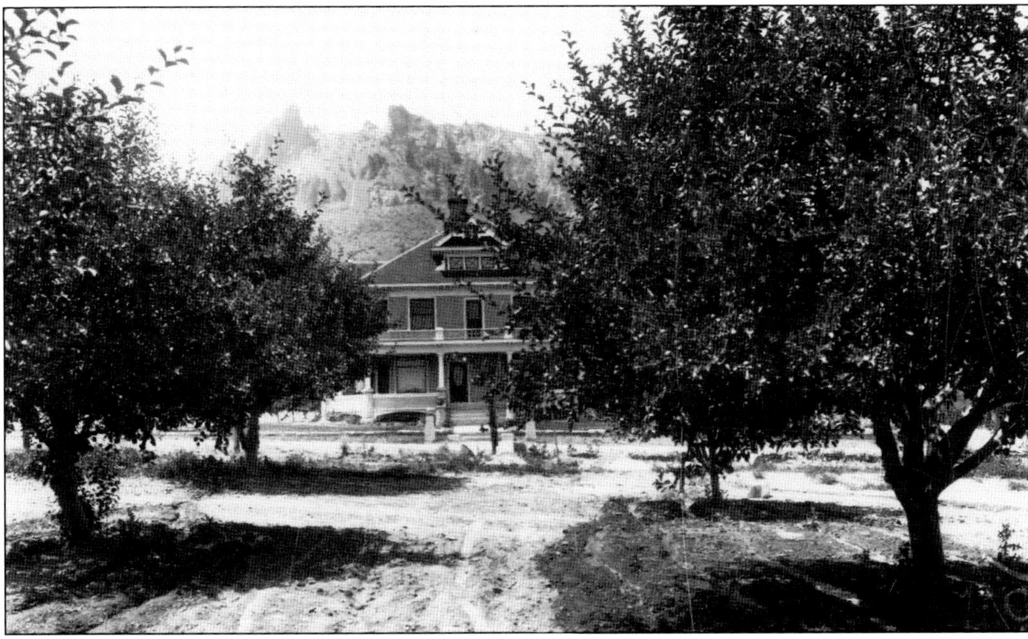

Fruit-grower William Turner built this stately home on a dirt Miller Street below Saddle Rock in the early 1900s; this photograph was taken by Laurence Lindsley in 1910. The Turner family had a lovely view of the Columbia River and town below. In 1920, an auto tour offered to visitors during Wenatchee's first Apple Blossom Festival featured a stop at the Turner Heights lookout point. (WVMCC 99-3-221, donated by Robert Isenhart.)

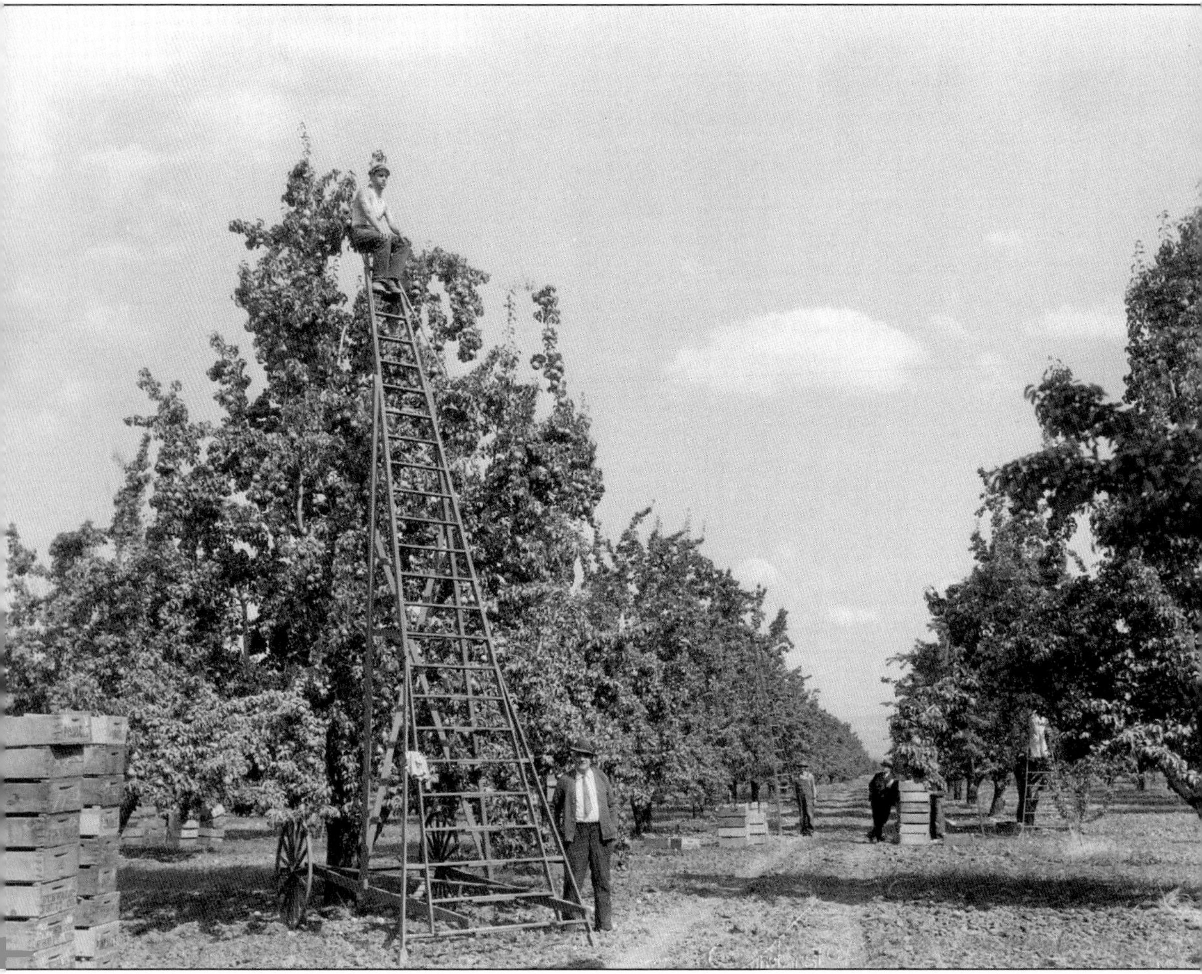

A worker sits at the top of a 24-foot ladder in a Wenatchee orchard, with an unidentified businessman on the ground below. The Wenatchee area's soil, climate, and water resources enabled growers to produce excellent tree fruit crops. Rootstock used in the early 1900s resulted in some enormous trees that required tall ladders to reach the uppermost fruit. The ladder in this photograph has wheels for stability and ease of movement, but it would have been difficult to move without breaking branches. Fruit trees today are usually grown from densely planted dwarf or semidwarf rootstock and remain much shorter. Many newer orchards use a trellis technique where young branches are trained along horizontal cables to simplify pruning, thinning, and picking. (WVMCC 87-42-77.)

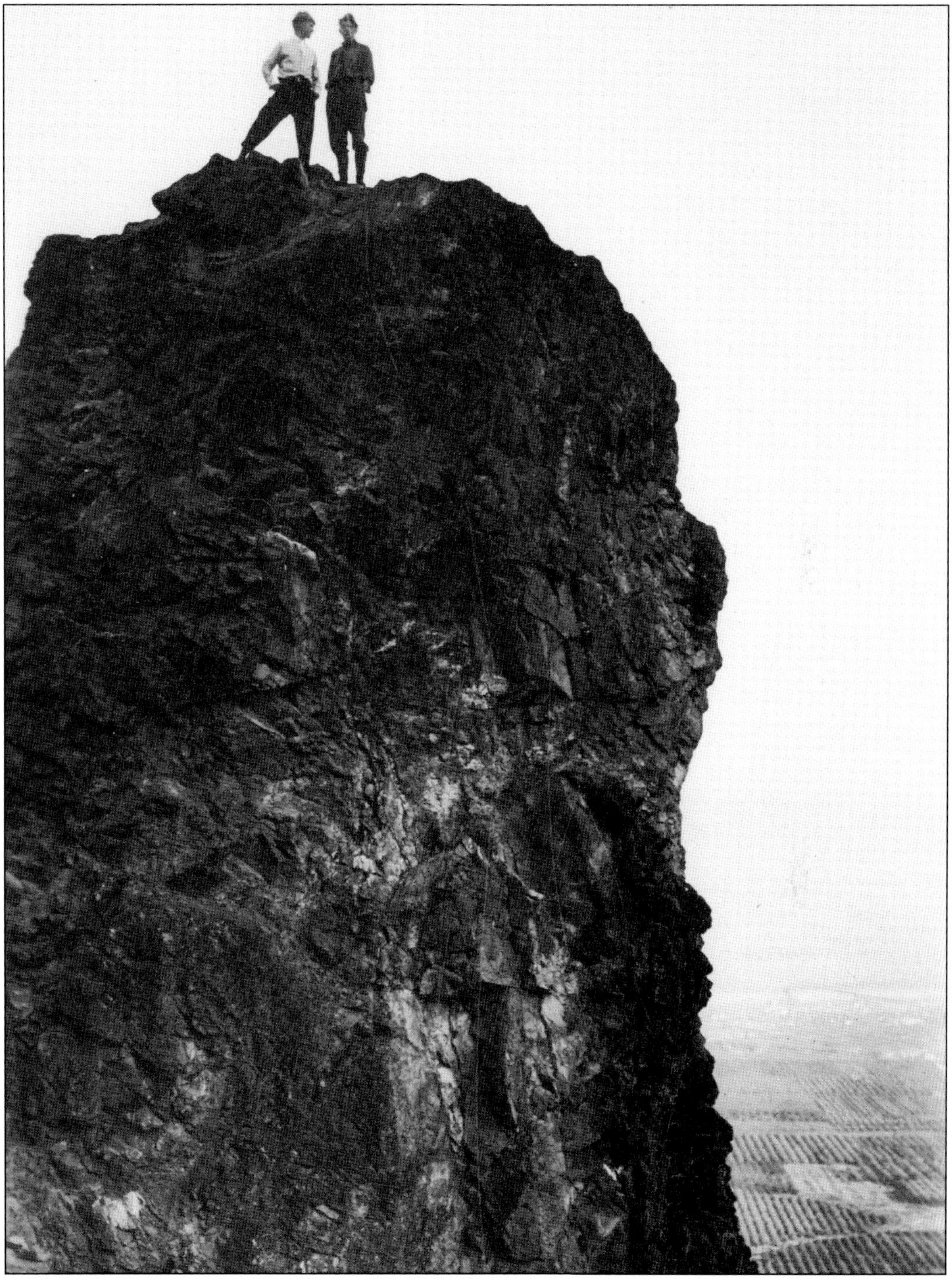

Two men stand at the top of Saddle Rock in 1915. The rock formation has always been a magnet for outdoor enthusiasts. Trails leading to the top may be accessed today from the south, with parking available on Circle Street (just off the south end of Miller Street), and the north, from Skyline Drive (off the south end of Western Avenue). Saddle Rock and the land around it are publicly owned. (WVMCC 93-90-241.1, donated by Richard Bell.)

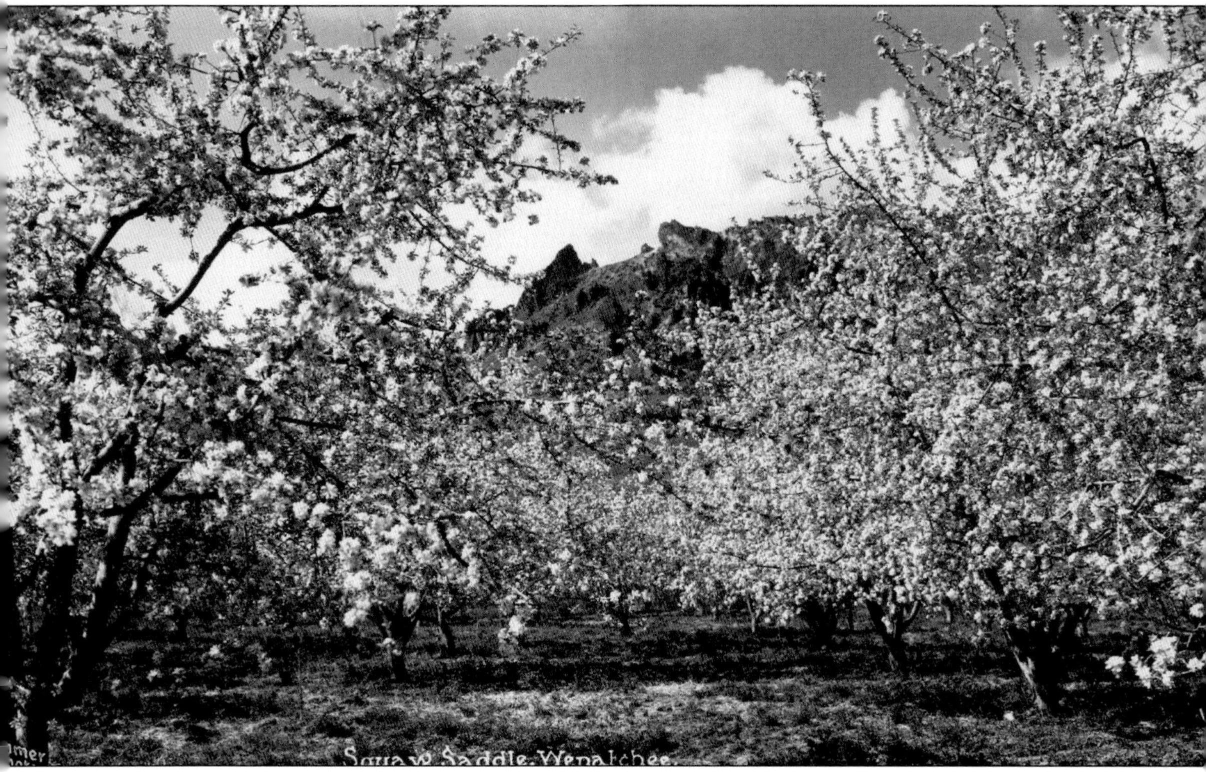

This picture of Saddle Rock was taken by Alfred Simmer, longtime Wenatchee commercial and portrait photographer. The term "Squaw Saddle" was still in widespread use in the 1920s. Apple trees bloom in late April and early May. The annual Washington State Apple Blossom Festival has celebrated this flowering beauty in Wenatchee since 1920. Beginning in 1921, the talented Simmer documented decades of festivals and historic scenes of the Wenatchee Valley's growth. The negatives of most of those pictures were destroyed in a fire in 1939, just after he sold his studio and moved to Olympia to do special photography with the state highway department. (WVMCC 94-65-15, donated by Cathryn Corner.)

Three

Columbia Station

The coming of the Great Northern Railway Company to Wenatchee in 1892 was probably the most significant event in the town's history. James J. Hill's line, the first US transcontinental railroad built without public money, competed successfully with the Northern Pacific, located 100 miles to the south. From St. Paul, Minnesota, across the Rockies to Spokane, the tracks crossed the Columbia River at Rock Island (a few miles south of Wenatchee), paralleled the river through Wenatchee, then veered westward along the Wenatchee River and across Stevens Pass to Seattle. This contact with the "outside world" was a boon to the region's commerce and population growth.

Steamboats were another link to distant communities. From 1888 to 1914, stern-wheelers plied the Columbia River, carrying freight and passengers to and from Wenatchee. The steamboat dock and a railroad spur were located together at the foot of Chehalis Street. This busy area a few blocks south of the downtown business district saw the transfer each day of tons of wheat from upper Chelan, Douglas, and Okanogan Counties onto railcars.

Wenatchee's location along the mighty Columbia River attracted not only productive new citizens but also hobos who built rough shelters on the vacant land between the tracks and the river. "Shacktown," as this area was called, persisted for nearly 50 years until a determined Mayor Jack Rogers ordered the police department to burn it down. The riverbanks south of downtown Wenatchee were also a repository for the community's garbage until the 1960s.

Great Northern's first depot was located at the foot of First Street. A larger depot at the foot of Kittitas Street was dedicated in 1910; this historic brick building was demolished in 1981. Columbia Station, which today serves the Wenatchee Valley's Link Transit and interstate bus systems, was completed in 1997. Amtrak trains stop twice a day very close to Columbia Station. With the Columbia River's water level having been raised by the Rock Island Dam, the old steamboat landing is now underwater, but pedestrians or bicyclists on the Apple Capital Loop Trail can visit the location and imagine the busy transportation hub of a century ago.

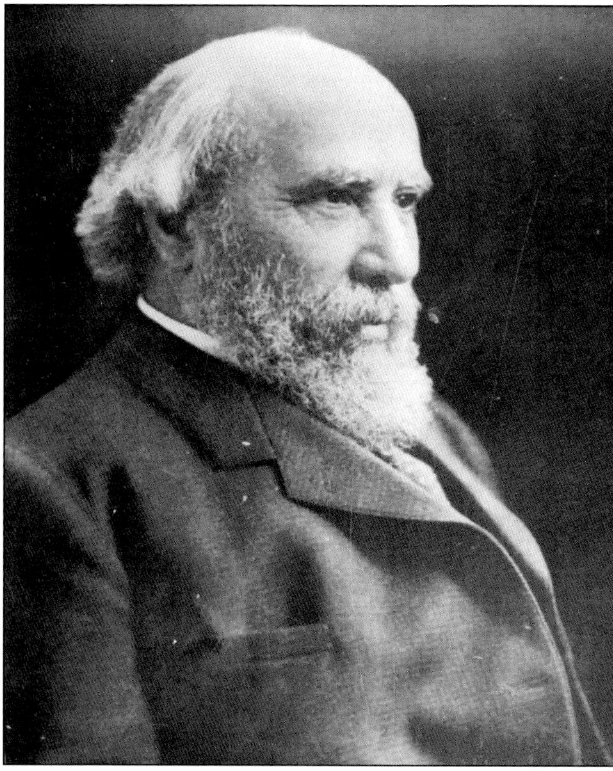

Transportation pioneer James J. Hill (1838–1916) saw potential in the unsettled lands of the Pacific Northwest. His Great Northern Railway Company brought prosperity to the region by encouraging the creation of towns along its route. Hill also heavily promoted the agricultural products his railroad carried from developing communities to the rest of the country. The Great Northern line, completed in January 1893, put Wenatchee on the map. (WVMCC 75-49-155, donated by Richard Bell.)

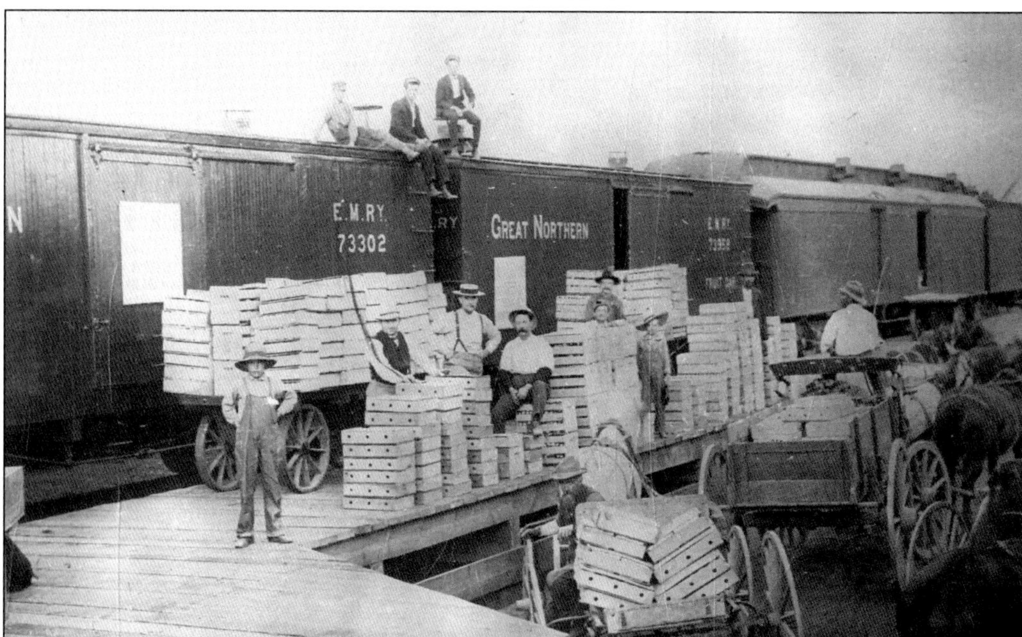

In this 1903 photograph, various wooden box sizes of packed fruit are arriving from surrounding orchards to the Great Northern's freight-loading platform. Second from the left is Conrad Rose, owner of the Wenatchee Produce Company and the first to ship an entire carload of apples from Wenatchee. (WVMCC 76-6-57, donated by R. William Hunter and Salvation Army.)

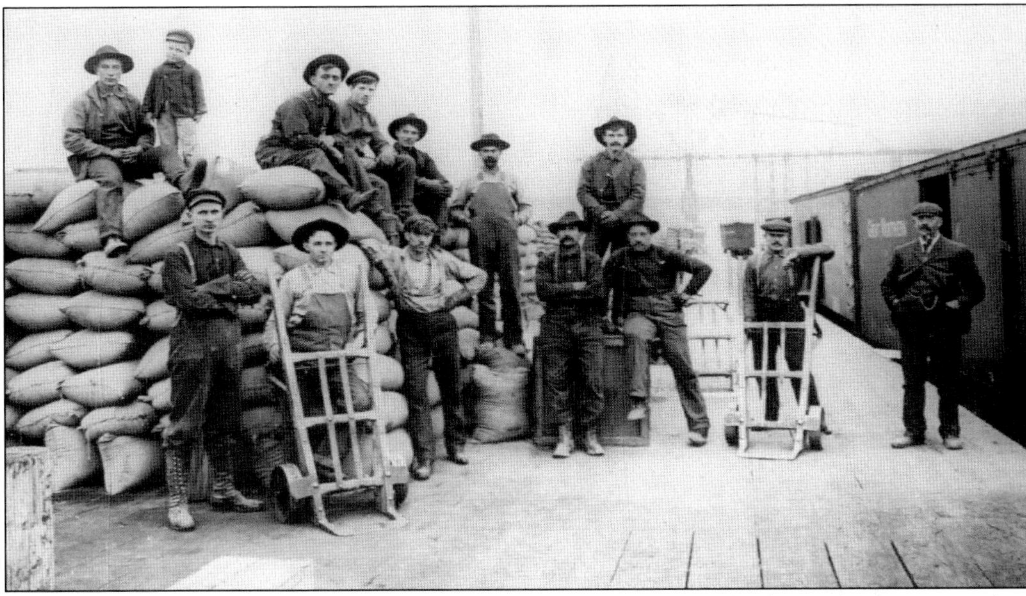

Men pose around 1910 with wheat recently unloaded from a stern-wheeler as they prepare to load the sacks onto a Great Northern railcar. In the background is the faint image of the Columbia River Bridge, completed in 1908. The steamboat landing was a busy place from 1892 until about 1914, when J.J. Hill opened a spur line from Wenatchee north to Okanogan County. Wenatchee's steamboat era ended when farmers recognized that shipping grain by rail was much faster than by stern-wheeler. (WVMCC 76-6-82, donated by R. William Hunter and Salvation Army.)

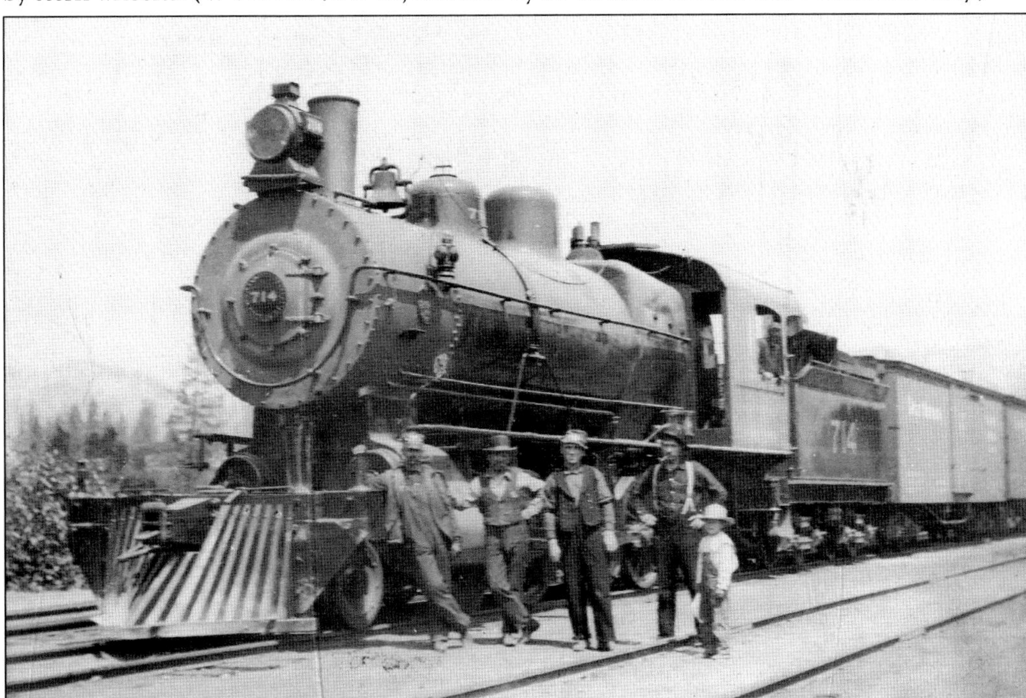

Four unidentified railroad men stand in front of steam engine No. 714 around 1900. (WVMCC 78-218-80, donated by Mary Anderson.)

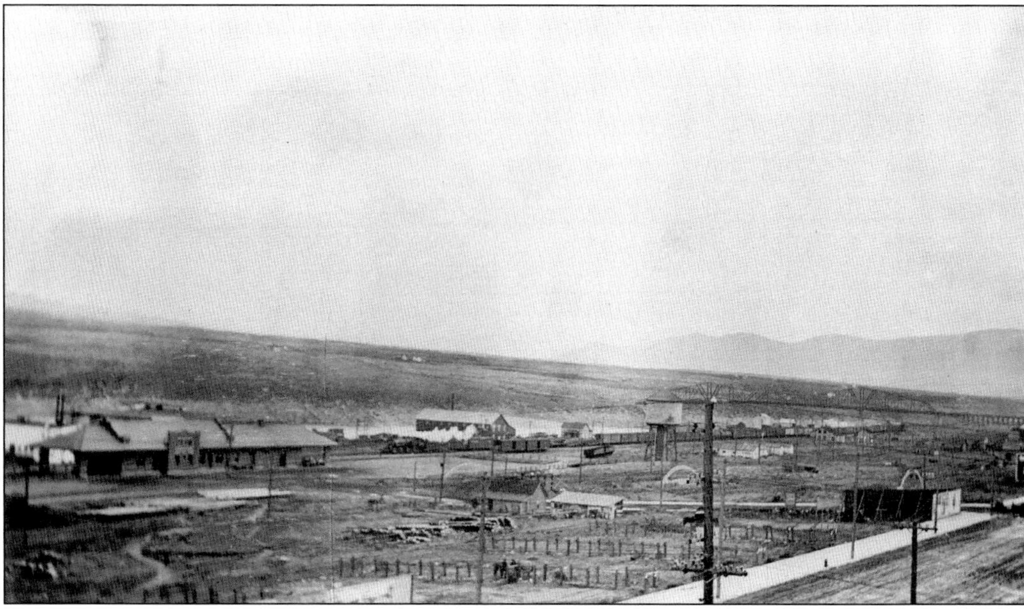

Wenatchee's first Great Northern depot was a small building at the foot of First Street. A larger station at Columbia Avenue and Kittitas Street was dedicated on February 11, 1910. This historic brick building, with its two spacious waiting rooms, went out of use when passenger service to Wenatchee was suspended from 1971 to 1981; the landmark, unfortunately, was demolished in 1981. In the c. 1910 photograph above, much of the land between Columbia and Wenatchee Avenues is vacant. The undated photograph below shows the depot with the Beanery restaurant at right. The long-vacant Beanery still stands on land now owned by the Burlington Northern Santa Fe Railway Company. (Above, WVMCC 80-67-214, donated by Madeleine Elliott; below, 86-24-41, donated by Wenatchee Chamber of Commerce.)

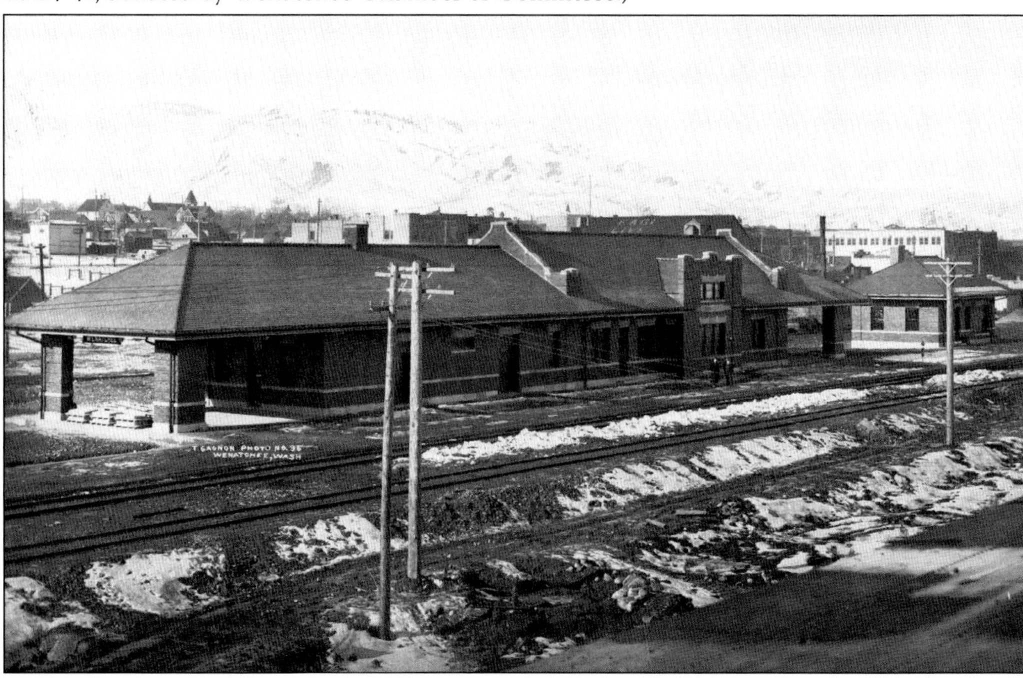

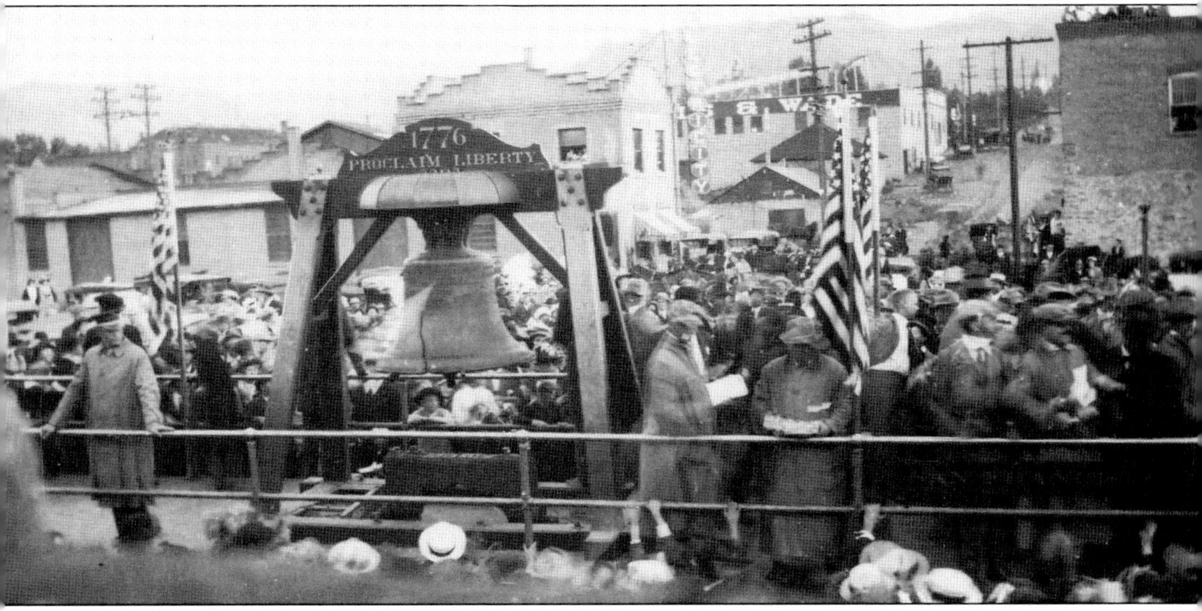

The Liberty Bell stopped at Wenatchee on Tuesday, July 13, 1915, en route to the Panama-Pacific Exposition in San Francisco. It was expected to arrive at 5:30 p.m. but actually pulled in at 7:30 p.m. and stayed one hour. Wednesday's newspaper declared the following: "Full 8,000 Pay Homage - Biggest Crowd That Wenatchee Has Ever Witnessed." One couple with their small blind child traveled 126 miles to see the historic symbol of freedom (now housed in Philadelphia). The child was lifted up and given permission to touch the bell. This scene is at the foot of Yakima Street, a block north of the depot, with Saddle Rock visible in the distance. (WVMCC 85-0-146.)

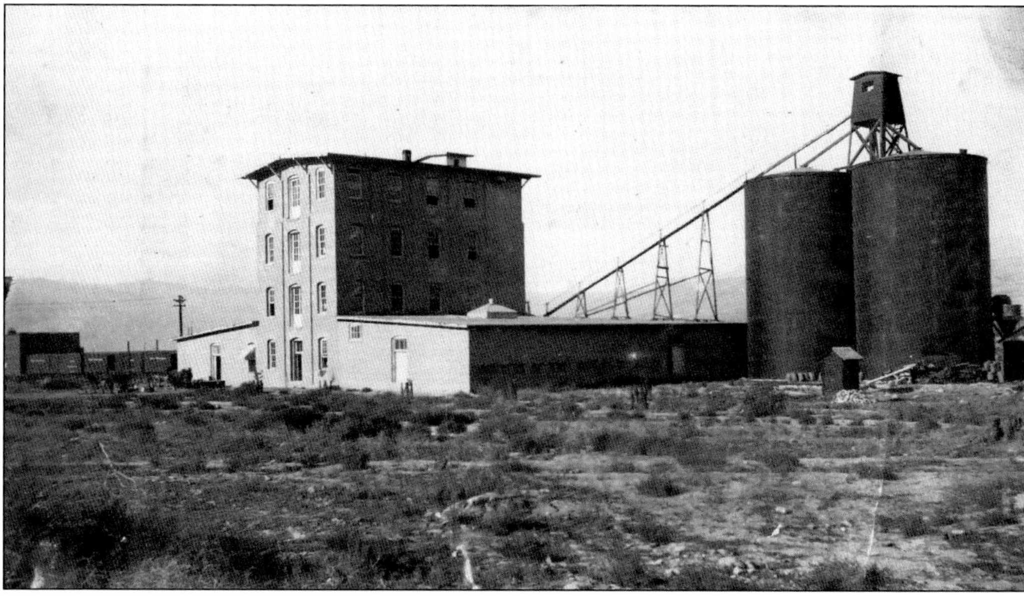

In 1906, D.A. Beal founded Washington Farmer's Grain and Milling Company, a grain-marketing cooperative located just south of the steamboat landing. It lost money, despite an abundance of available wheat from Douglas and Okanogan Counties. In 1909, new owners changed its name to the Centennial Flour (or Flouring) Mill and made improvements that included grain storage silos and a grain elevator. With the change of management, the mill thrived. Under the brand names "Peach Blossom" and "Wenatchee's Best," Centennial sold flour to the US government during World Wars I and II. It ceased operations in 1961, but remnants of the mill are still visible at the foot of Skagit Street. (Above, WVMCC 80-67-15, donated by Madeleine Elliott; below, 88-108-1978, donated by Ileen Taylor.)

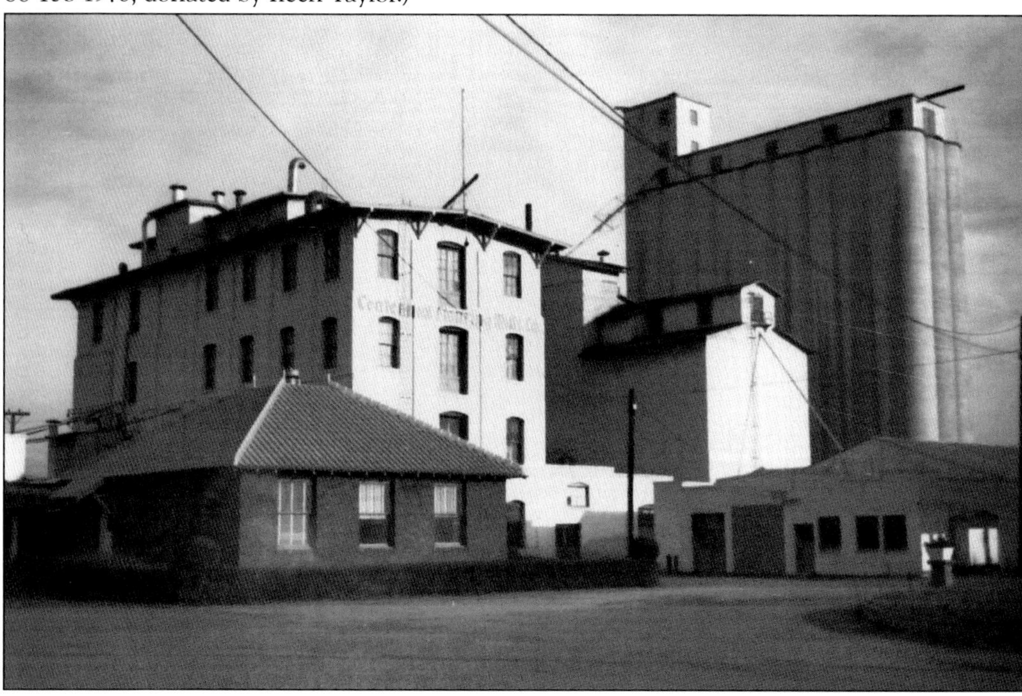

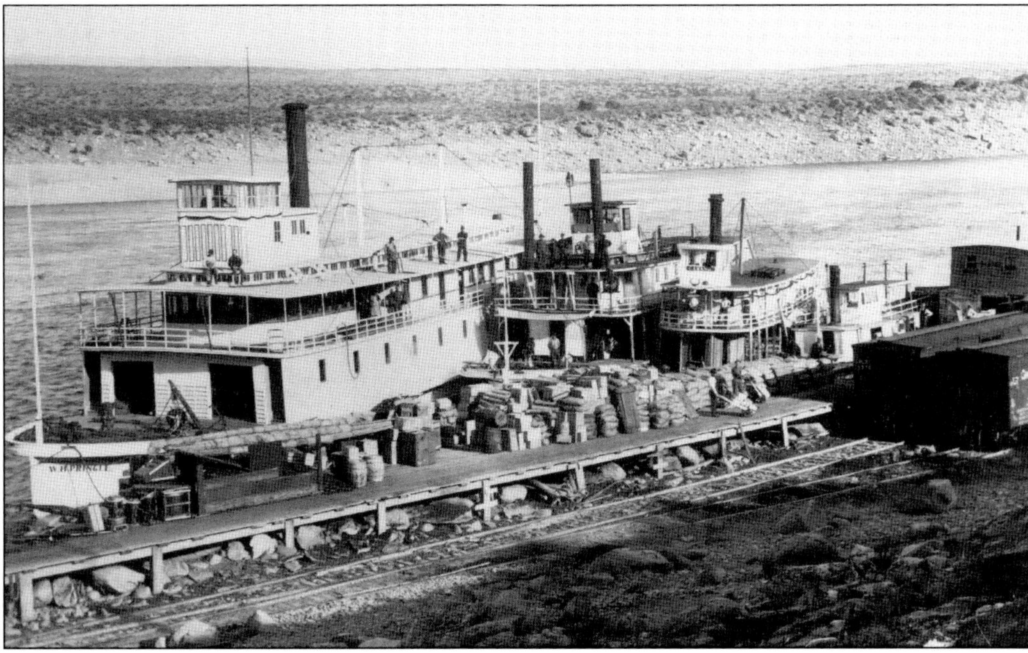

Steamboats *W.H. Pringle, Selkirk, Camano,* and *Echo* are docked at the landing at the foot of Chehalis Street, with sacks of grain and miscellaneous boxes and barrels filling the deck. A railcar awaits loading. The tiny *Echo* carried mail between Wenatchee and upriver communities. (WVMCC 006-42-4, donated by William Whiting.)

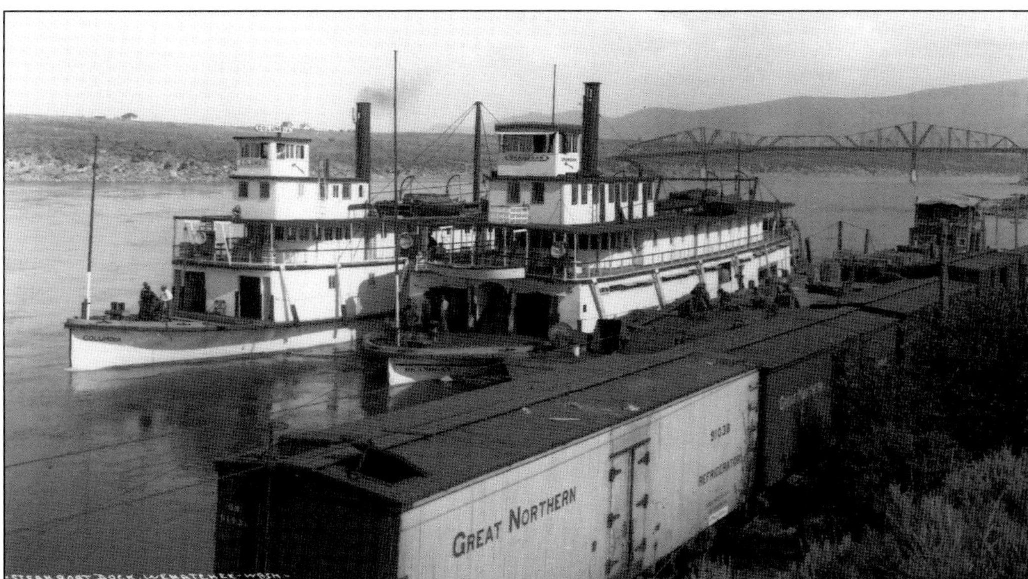

This 1911 photograph shows the *Okanogan* and *Chelan* docked at the stern-wheeler landing, with boxcars waiting to accept their bounty. The Columbia River Bridge is clearly visible in the background. Across the river, Douglas County is still largely undeveloped. (WVMCC 99-3-245, donated by Robert Isenhart.)

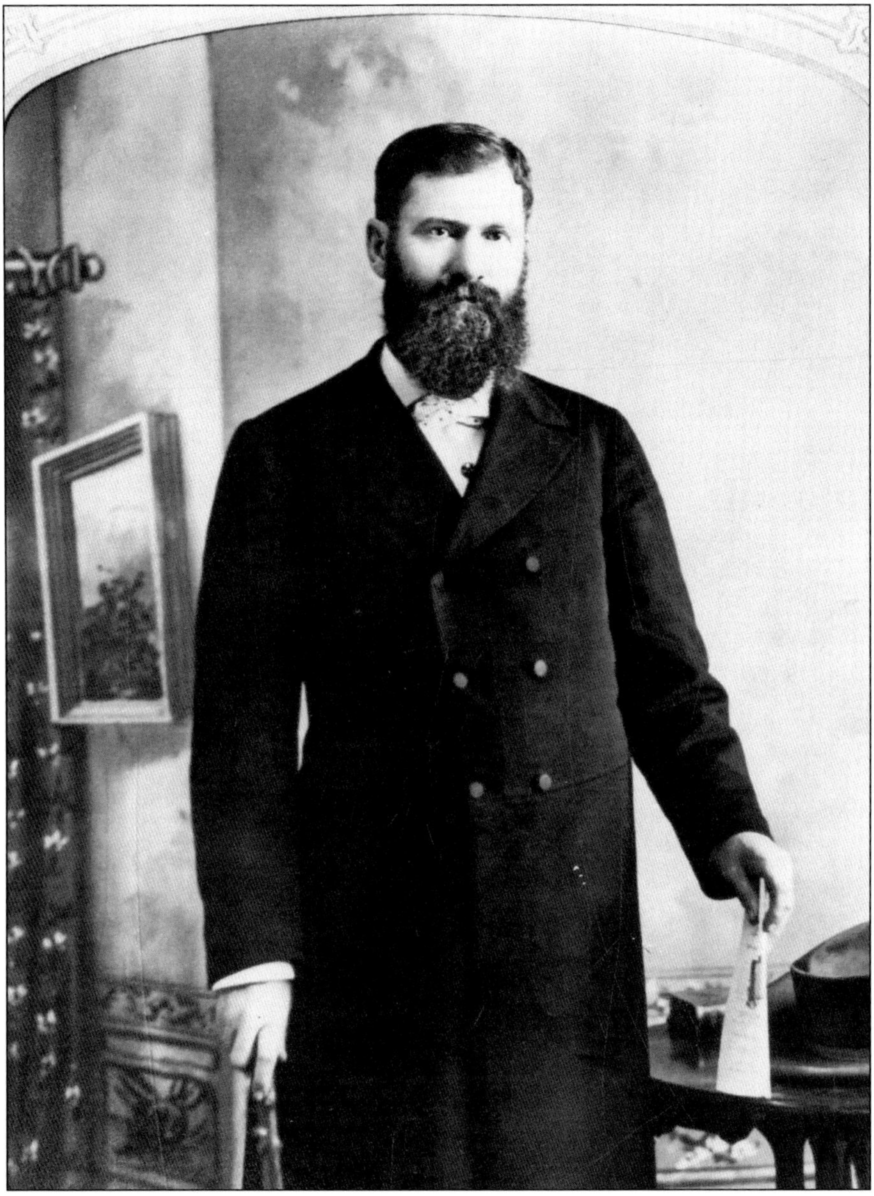

Alexander Griggs (1838–1903) was a Mississippi River steamboat captain and friend of Great Northern founder J.J. Hill. Arriving in Wenatchee around the time of the railroad, he organized the Columbia & Okanogan Steamboat Company in 1893 to navigate the 70-mile stretch of the Columbia River between Wenatchee and the mouth of the Okanogan River. (During high water, the boats could travel another 35 miles to Riverside; Charles Blackwell's general store there would stock up with a year's worth of supplies till the next spring's high water.) Five of the stern-wheelers plying the river belonged to Griggs: the *W.H. Pringle*, *Chelan*, *Selkirk*, *Gerome*, and *Alexander Griggs*. All but the *Pringle* were built at the Wenatchee shipyard at the foot of Fifth Street (see chapter four), and Griggs financed the construction of most of the others built there. Griggs had four sons who carried on the business after his death. Capt. Bruce Griggs became president and general manager, aided by captains Ansel, Clifford, and Jay Griggs. (WVMCC 006-42-33, donated by William Whiting.)

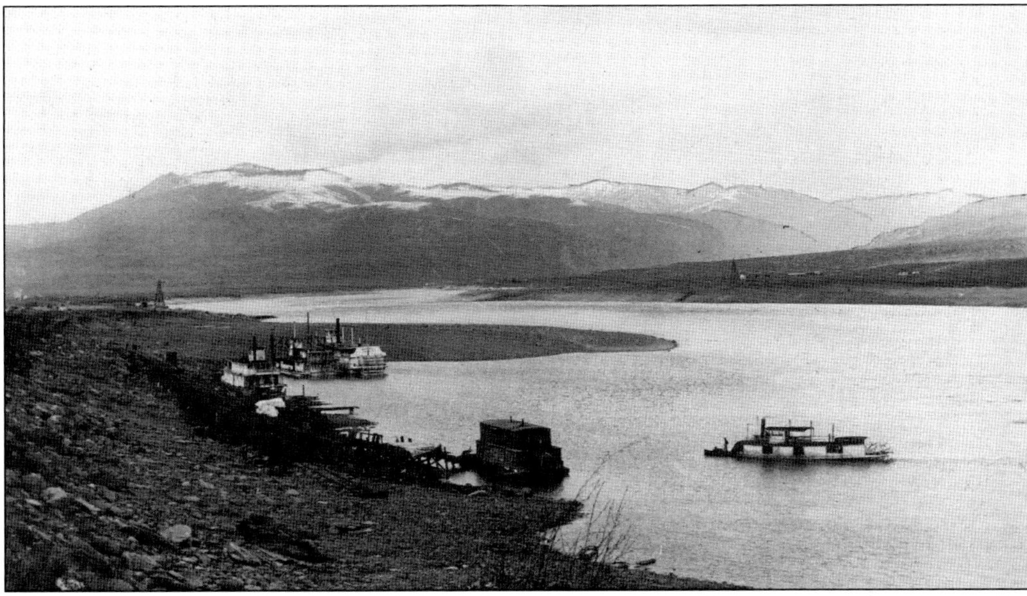

Three stern-wheelers idle onshore as another approaches the Wenatchee landing in 1897. At left is the Great Northern spur track; the floating wharf served as a makeshift office before a true office was constructed (below). As highways north from Wenatchee were nonexistent, stern-wheelers were the lifeline to upriver communities—providing two-way passage, delivering supplies from needles to threshing machines, and hauling agricultural cargo to market. (WVMCC 86-24-241, donated by Wenatchee Chamber of Commerce.)

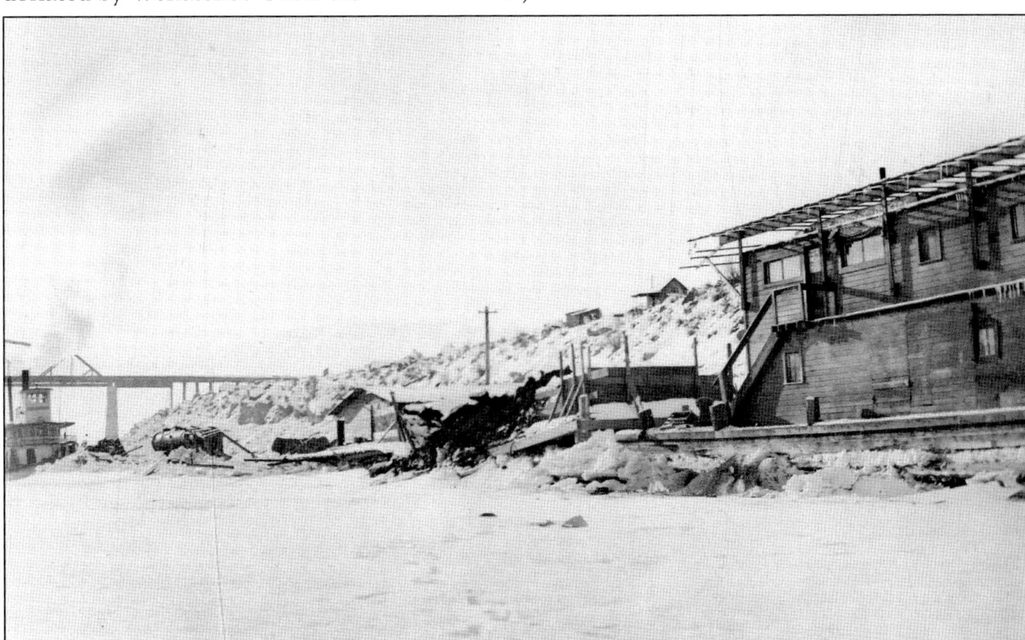

The C&O Steamboat Company's office, located at the boat landing, is shown in this snowy photograph from January 1910. During extremely cold spells, workers sometimes used dynamite to crack thick ice on the Columbia River so the stern-wheeler could navigate. The vessels were grounded by ice an average of eight days a year. (WVMCC 88-108-7, donated by Ileen Taylor.)

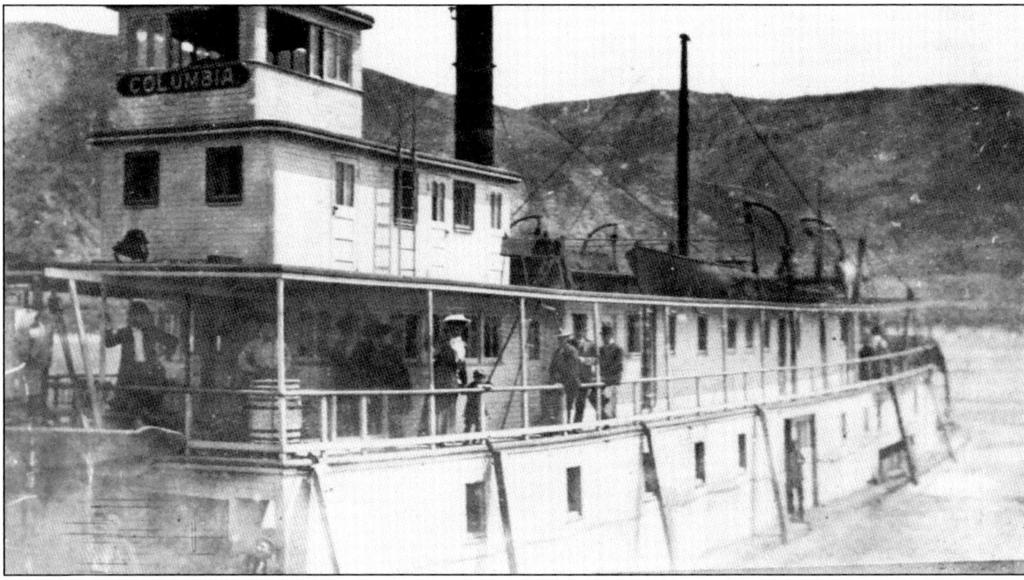

Passengers look out from the second deck of the *Columbia*, a 131-foot stern-wheeler built in Wenatchee in 1904. Cargo was carried on the main deck. On the passenger deck were ladies' and gentlemen's cabins, a dining room, and saloon. The third deck was reserved for the steering mechanism and lifeboats. An excursion from Wenatchee to Brewster took about 12 hours; the downstream return trip took about eight hours. (WVMCC 006-42-10, donated by William Whiting.)

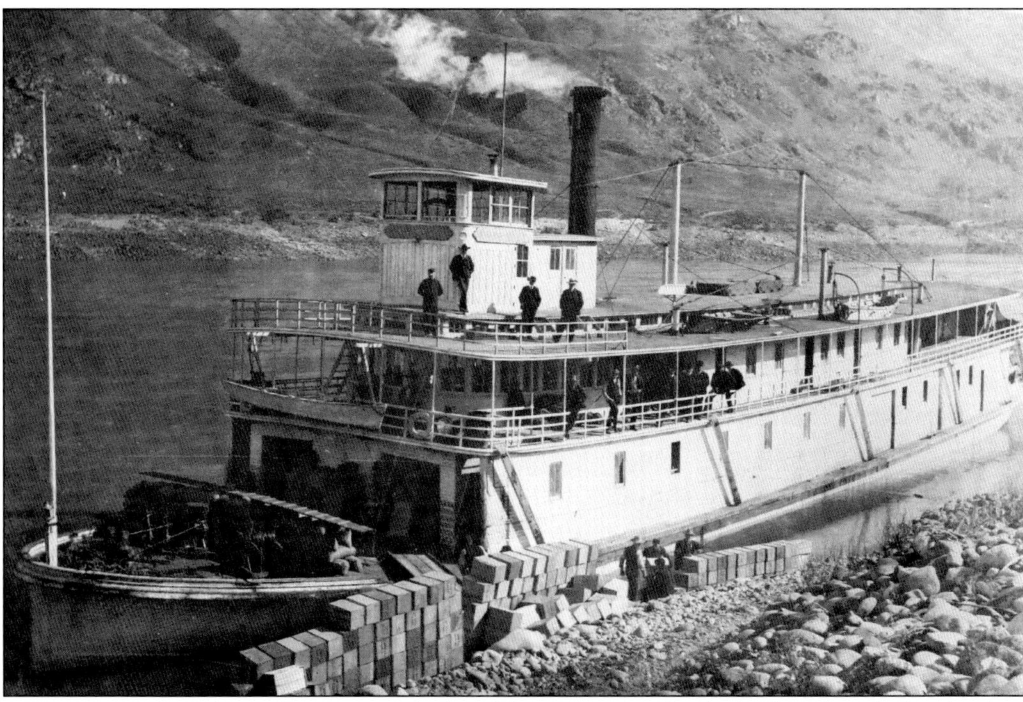
Men pose on the pilot and passenger decks of the *W.H. Pringle,* docked at the Chelan landing. The stern-wheeler was to be loaded with boxes of apples destined for Great Northern railcars in Wenatchee. From this dock, a bumpy three-mile stagecoach ride took passengers up the hill to Lake Chelan. (WVMCC 006-42-24, donated by William Whiting.)

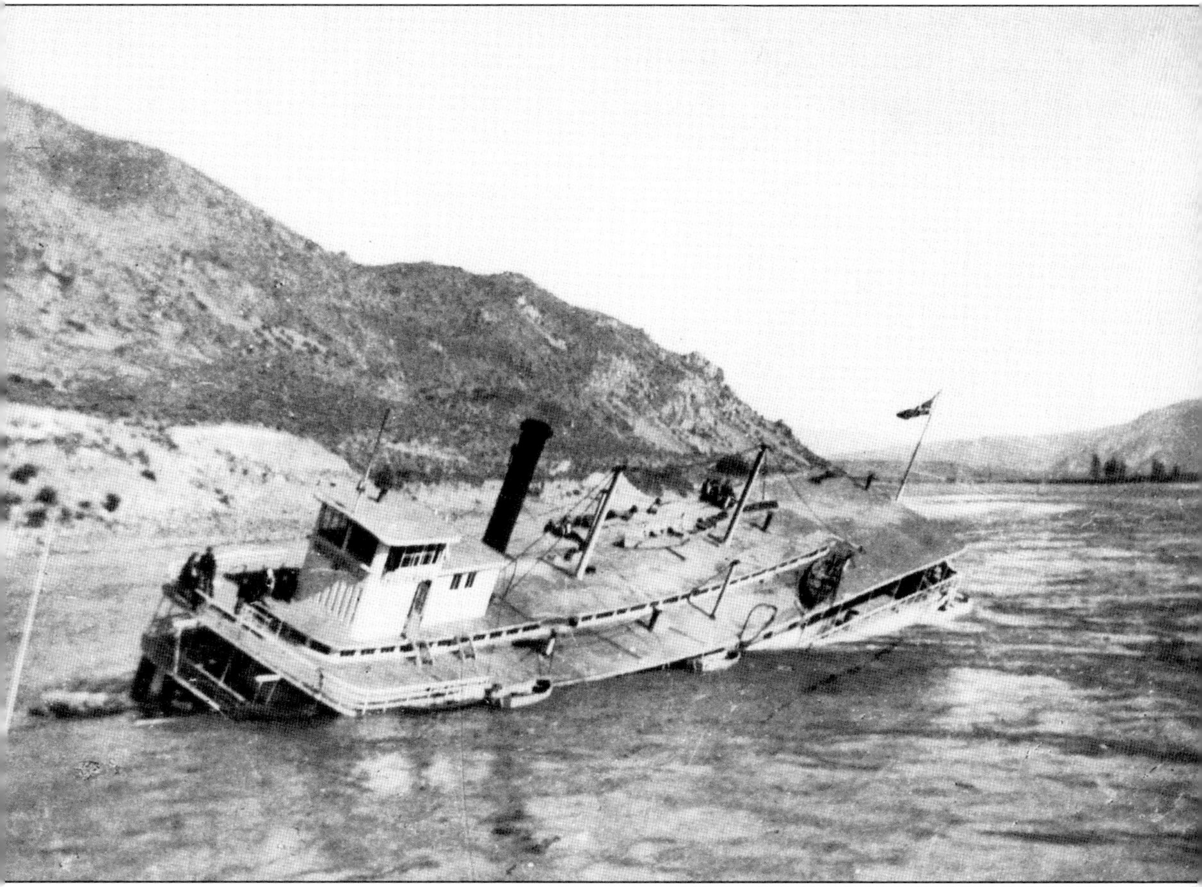

The *W.H. Pringle* came to ruin in the Entiat Rapids on October 10, 1906, when a paddle wheel shaft broke and the steamer smashed into a boulder, breaking a hole in her side. The cargo of 4,300 sacks of wheat and a carload of apples was lost. Fortunately, the *Columbia* was nearby and rescued the crew of 20. There were no passengers. Also wrecked in the Entiat Rapids were the *Camano* in 1902 and the *Alexander Griggs* in 1905. The mighty *Selkirk* met her end at the Rock Island Rapids in 1906. The *Gerome* went to its watery grave between Pasco and The Dalles in 1905, and the *Enterprise*, which had wrecked in the Entiat Rapids and been salvaged and rebuilt, was destroyed at the Brewster Ferry in 1915. (WVMCC 006-42-19, donated by William Whiting.)

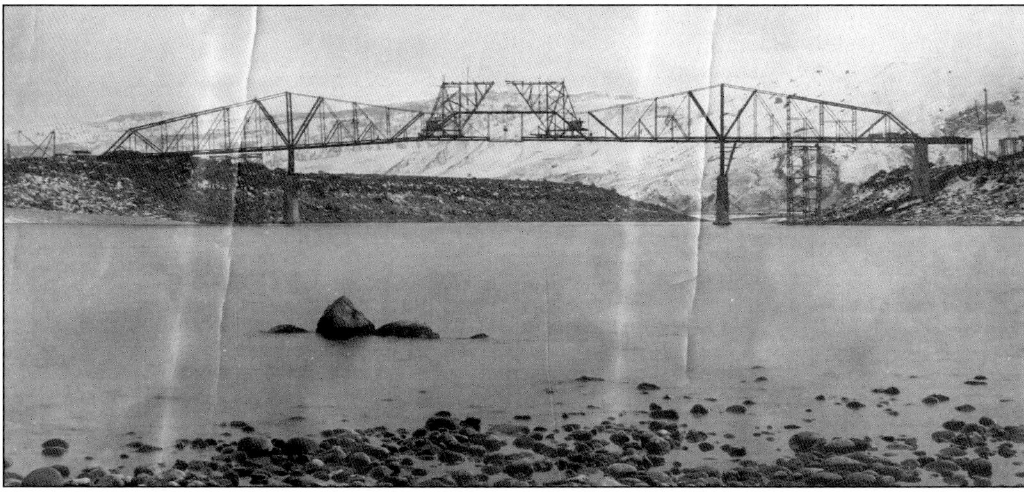

Developer William T. Clark obtained the financing for and directed construction of the first vehicular bridge across the Columbia River at Wenatchee. The bridge's main purpose was to extend Clark's Highline Canal to irrigate the arid lands of Douglas County through two large pipelines, making this land more attractive to potential settlers. Construction crews worked from both sides of the river. The two spans were connected on December 23, 1907. (WVMCC 93-46-9, donated by Richard Bell.)

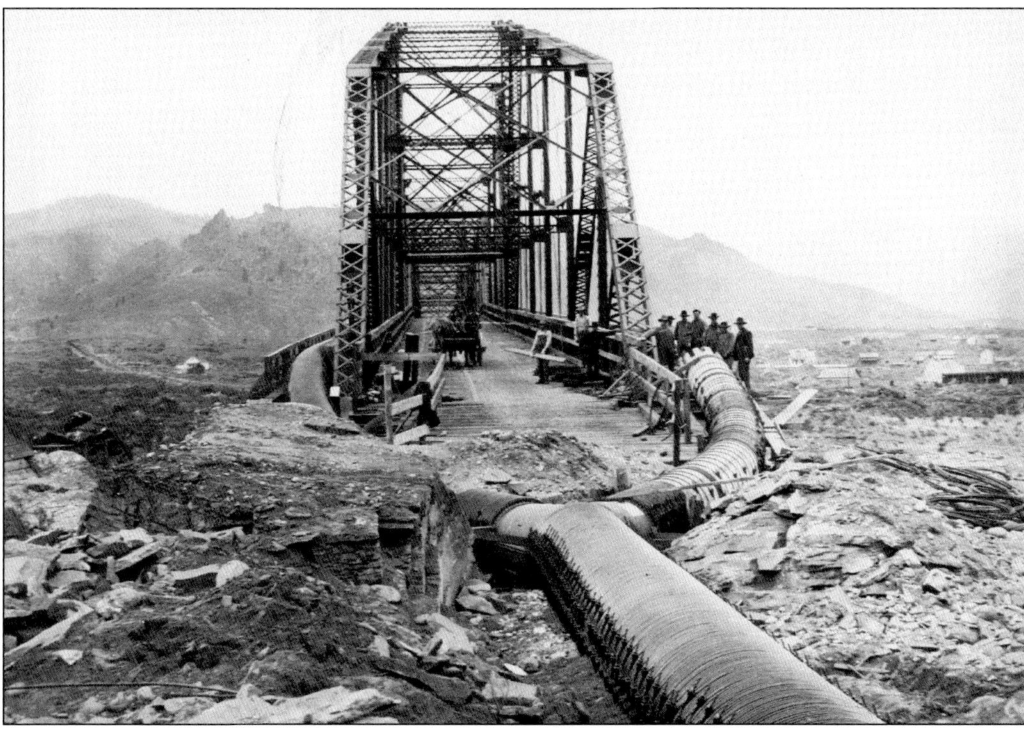

Men pose in January 1908 by a pipeline designed to carry irrigation water across the Columbia River Bridge to open some 4,000 acres in Douglas County to agricultural development. A side benefit of the bridge was easy travel across the river by horse, wagon, or automobile without having to use a ferry. It became part of the state highway system, facilitating wagon and auto traffic between Seattle and Spokane. (WVMCC 85-103-1, donated by Larry Deal.)

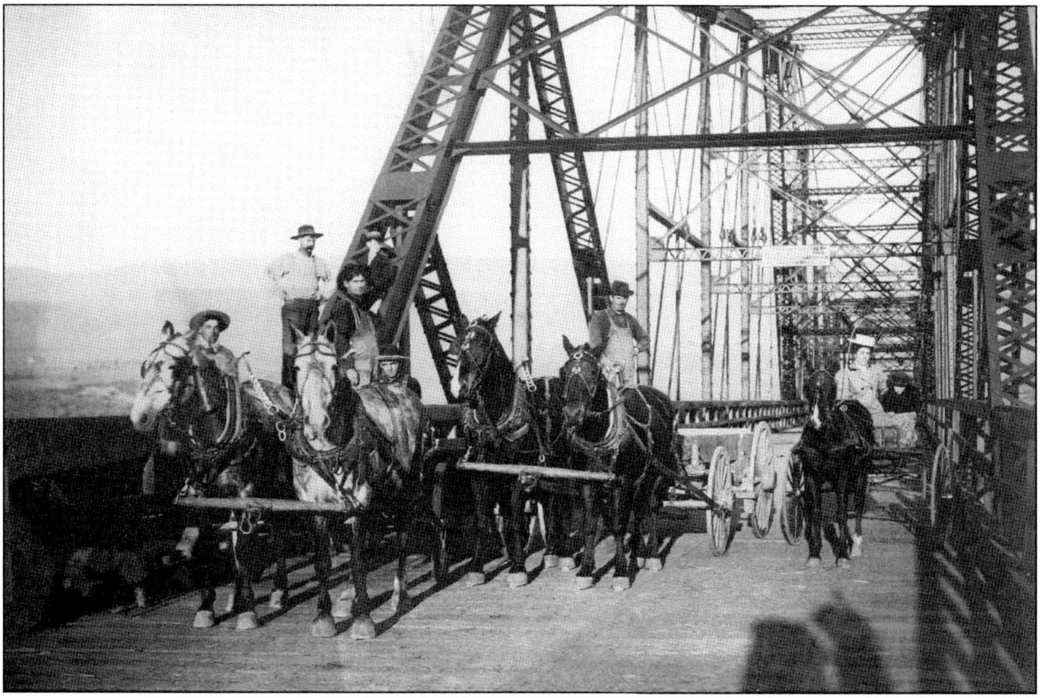

After two years of planning and two years of construction, the bridge opened on January 20, 1908. In the above photograph, two teams of horses pulling wagons and one horse-drawn buggy pose on the bridge coming from the Chelan County side of the river. A sign on a crossbeam reads, "$25.00 fine for riding or driving across the bridge faster than a walk. Washington Bridge Co." Below, wagons approach the bridge from the east side. The George Sellar Bridge, completed in 1950 at the south end of town, and the Odabashian Bridge, completed in 1976 just north of town, are now Wenatchee's vehicular bridges. The 1908 pipeline bridge, which still carries irrigation water, is part of the Apple Capital Loop Trail and open only to pedestrians and bicyclists. (Above, WVMCC 83-12-3, donated by Marcelene King; below, 99-88-13, donated by Marjorie Stevenson.)

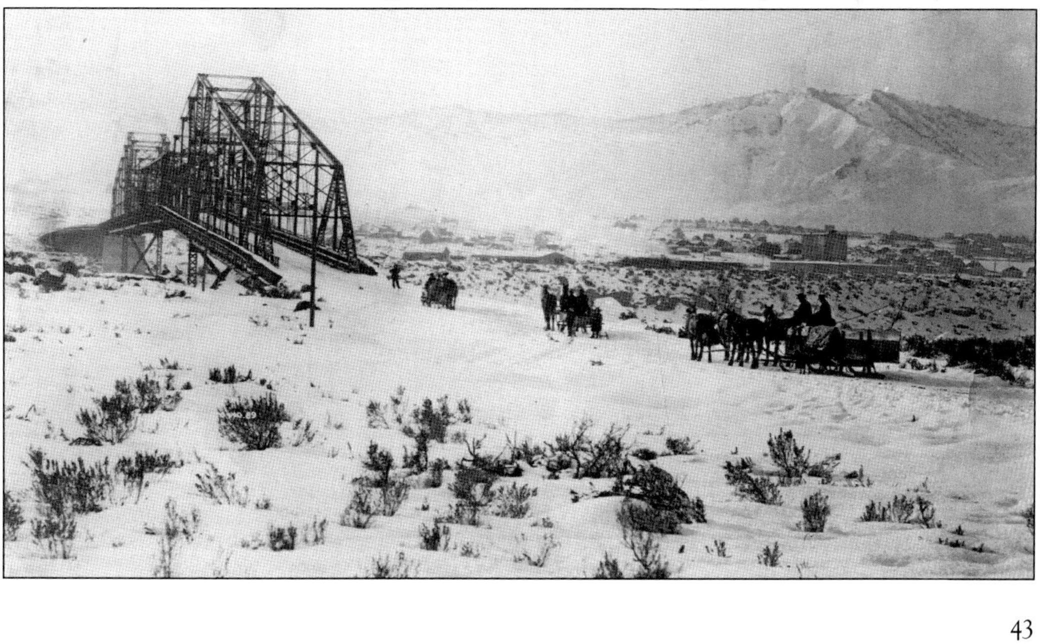

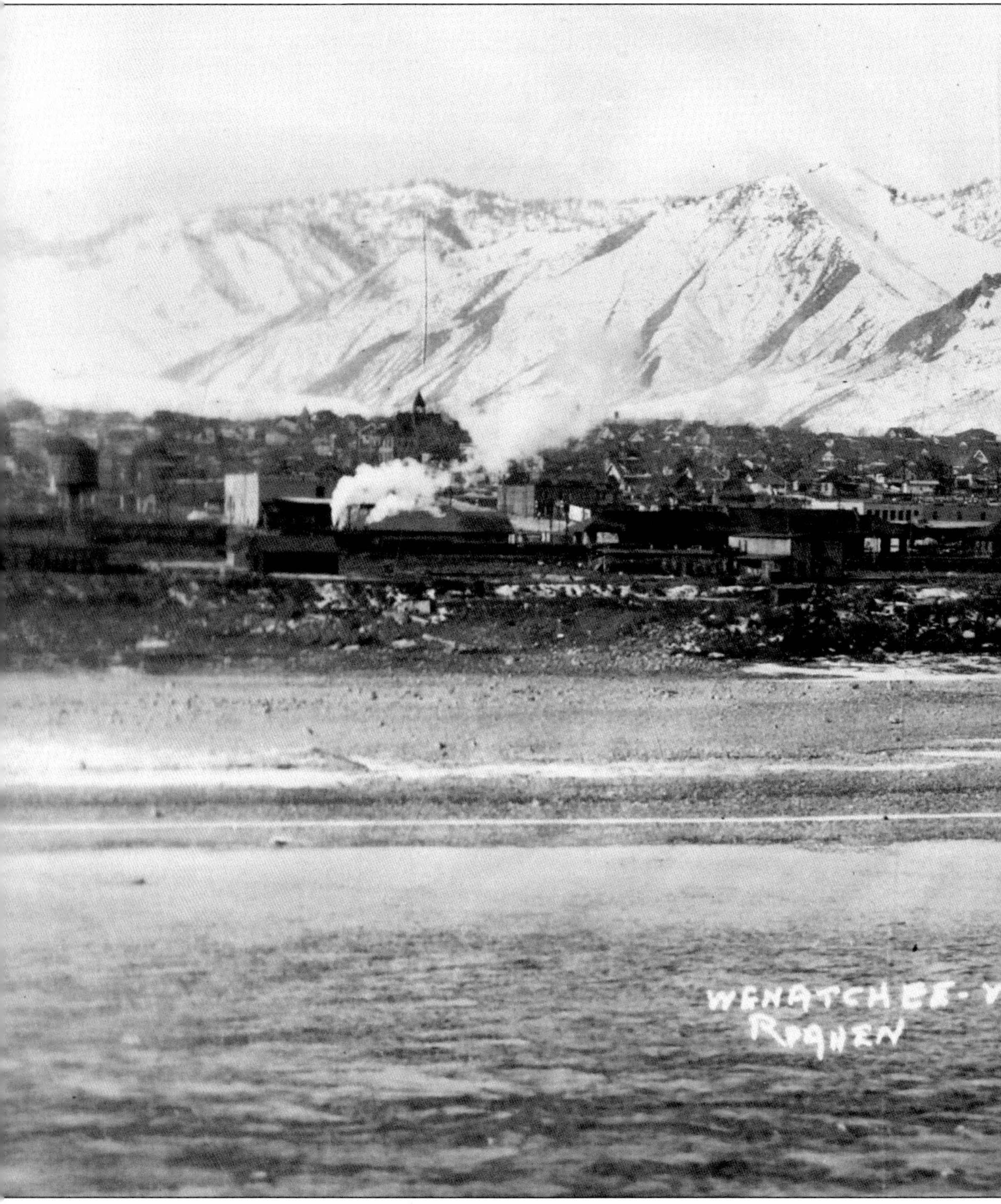

This panorama of Wenatchee, taken around 1925 from the Douglas County side of the Columbia, shows steam rising from Great Northern engines waiting at the freight station; the slant-roofed depot is just to the right and at the foot of Kittitas Street. The railroad was crucial to the development of Wenatchee's tree fruit industry and population growth. Downtown is just a few blocks north of

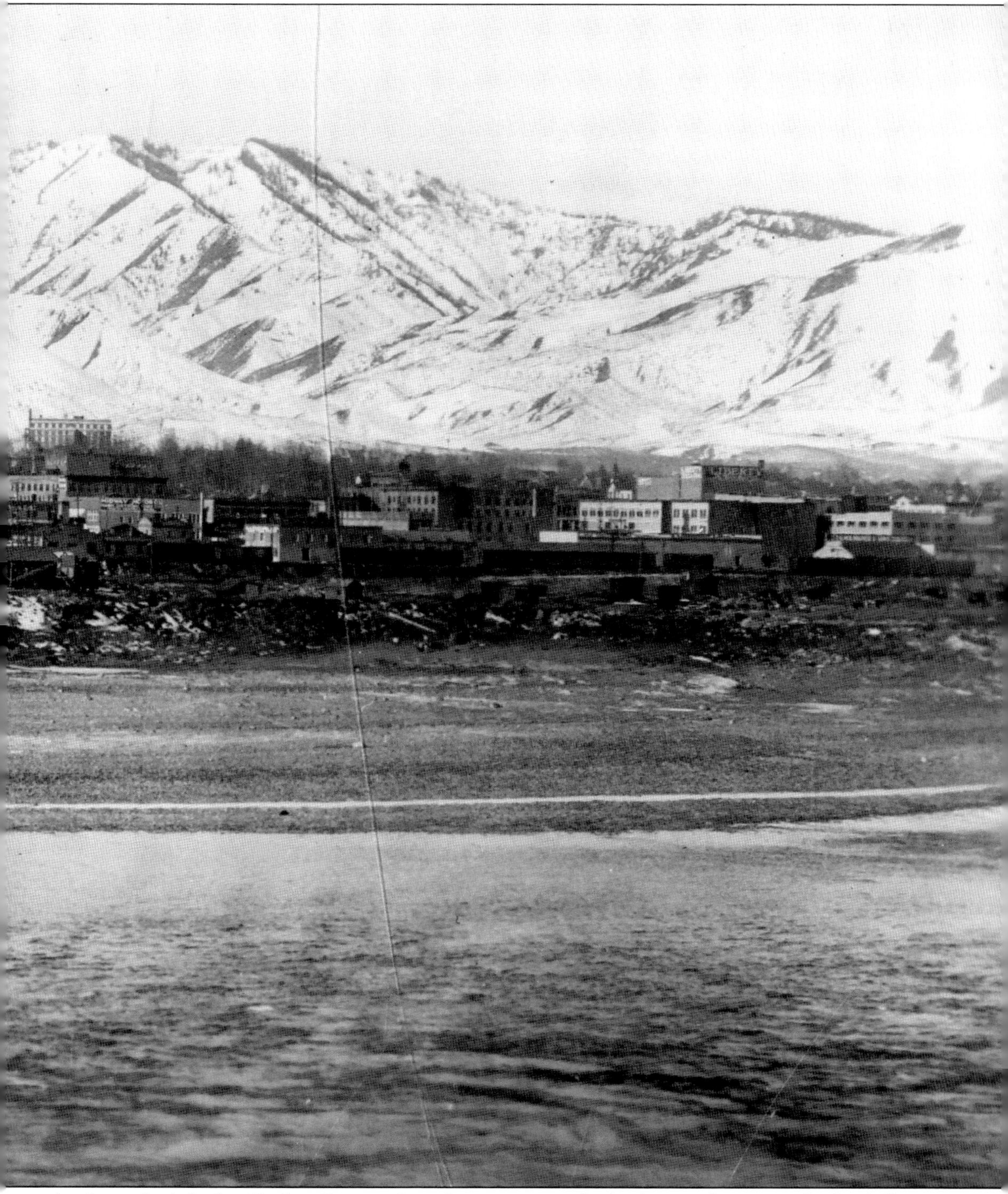

the depot (right); the Chelan County Courthouse rises in the background, against the foothills; and just left of the engine steam appears the cupola of the Stevens School, now the site of the US post office. At far right, the white Olympia Hotel building and Liberty Theatre sign can be seen. (WVMCC 98-26-28, donated by Norm June.)

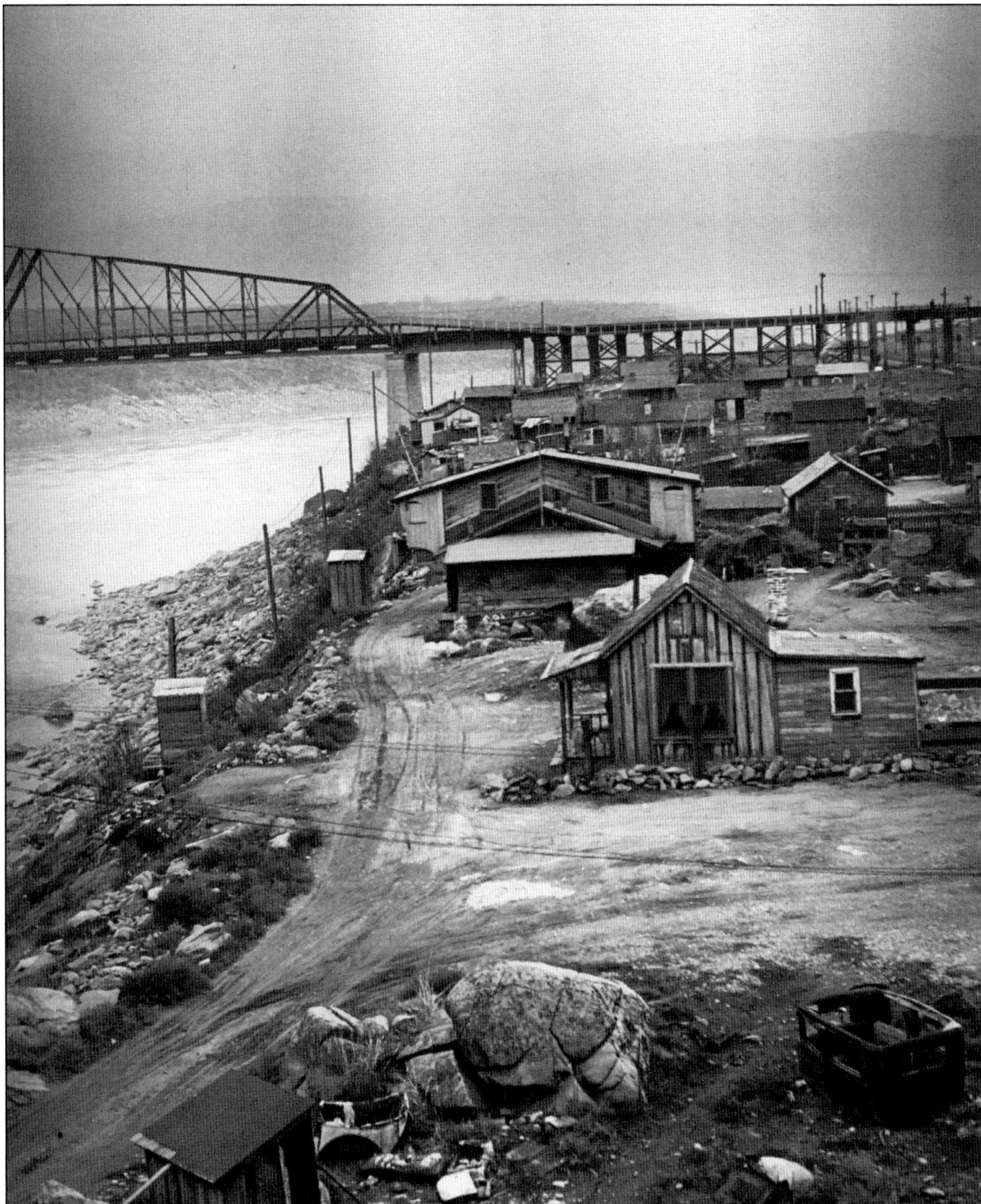

In 1898, a hobo got off the train at Wenatchee and, liking what he saw, built himself a shack on vacant land on the Columbia River shoreline. This squatting grew to an unsightly 60-acre settlement known as Shacktown, consisting of tar paper–roofed cardboard hovels, rag tepees, wooden buildings, piles of bottles and cans, wrecked carriages and cars, cast-off tires, and clothes fluttering from clotheslines. According to Wenatchee mayor Jack Rogers, residents of the neighborhood were "the scum of the community, bums and renegades" that included bootleggers, prostitutes, junk dealers, and alcoholics. This view of Wharf Street in 1933 shows some of the structures that persisted until Rogers directed the police and fire departments to demolish Shacktown. They burned down 137 homes and outbuildings on June 14, 1945. (WVMCC 82-105-123.)

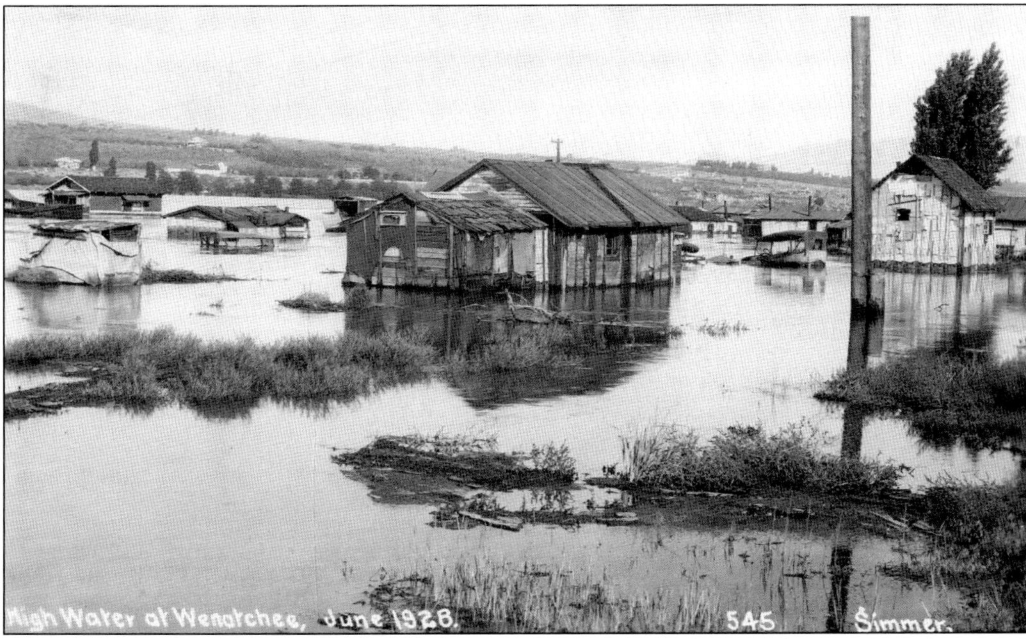

Shacktown did not fare well when the Columbia River flooded, as in this Simmer photograph from June 1928. The City of Wenatchee tried several times to rid itself of the community, even tearing down most of its structures in May 1924, but people soon moved back to the site and built new dwellings. The high water of 1928 temporarily forced residents to flee, but they soon returned. (WVMCC 97-105-1.)

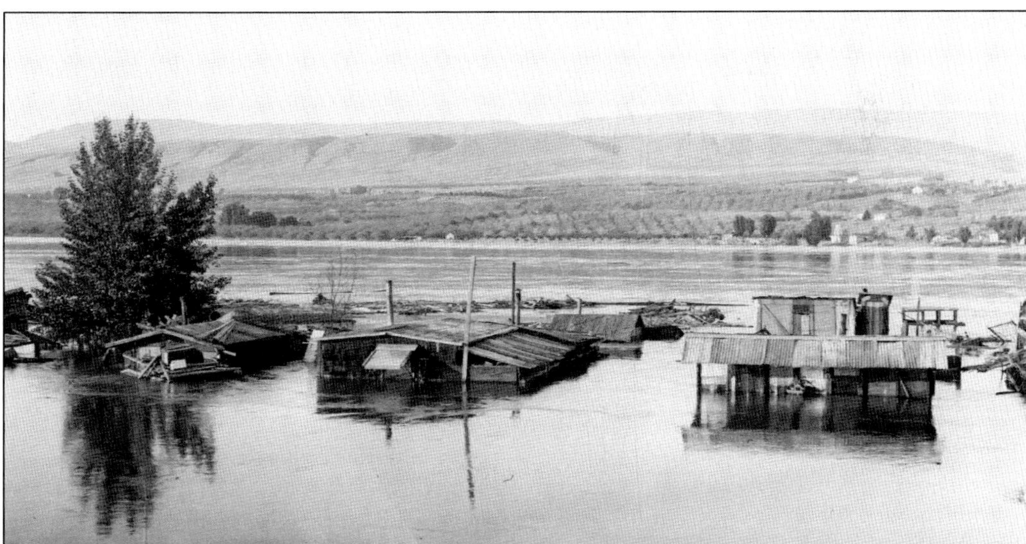
High water flooded Shacktown again in 1933. This was the year the Rock Island Hydroelectric Project, the first dam to span the Columbia River, was completed. The dam, 12 miles south of Wenatchee, formed a pond that permanently raised the river's level. Shacktown residents close to the water's edge simply moved higher on the bank, undeterred. Shacktown was permanently demolished in 1945. (WVMCC 006-38-1, donated by William Martin Padoshek.)

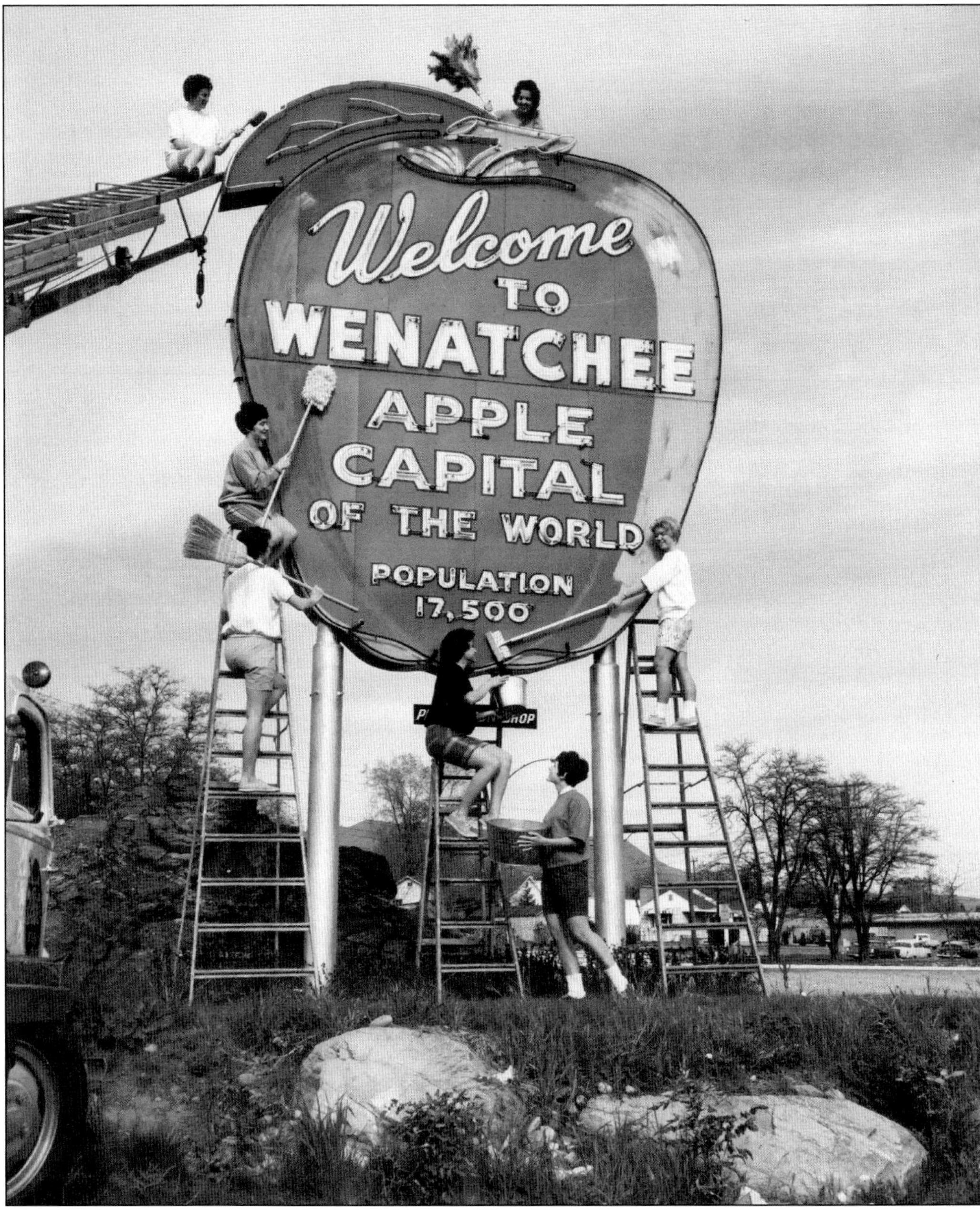

Seven of the top 10 royalty candidates for the 1962 Washington State Apple Blossom Festival clean the apple-shaped sign that stood in Locomotive Park in south Wenatchee. The sign, erected in the 1950s, greeted motorists crossing the Columbia River on State Highway 2 via the George Sellar Bridge. Today, a modernized version of this sign welcomes travelers entering Wenatchee from the north, located just before they cross the Wenatchee River Bridge. The royalty candidates are, counterclockwise around the apple beginning at the top, Beryl Brownlow, Lynda Robbe, Sharon Harris, Karen Pulsipher (climbing ladder), Carol Michel (on ground), Pamela Kirby, and Carole Niemela. (WVMCC 86-24-262, donated by Wenatchee Chamber of Commerce.)

Four

STERNWHEELER PARK

Brisk steamboat traffic between Wenatchee and the mouth of the Okanogan River in the late 1800s and early 1900s led to a demand for new boat construction and repair facilities. The steamboat yard at the foot of Fifth Street in Wenatchee was built in 1896, providing employment for scores of men and turning out 15 stern-wheelers by the end of the upper Columbia River steamboat era in 1917. Today, this part of the Apple Capital Loop Trail is called Sternwheeler Park. Visitors can admire a life-size bronze statue of steamboat captain Alexander Griggs near the parking lot.

In Wenatchee's early days, drinking water came straight from the Columbia River. Horse-drawn wagons delivered water to homes and businesses for 25¢ a barrel. The city's earliest pumping plant and reservoir were built at the foot of Fifth Street in 1907, just south of the steamboat yard. In the early 1920s, the city built a few more reservoirs, added water mains, and enlarged the pumping plant. A filtration system was installed in 1926.

In 1916, Abram Piper built a swimming pool just west of the boatyard on Wenatchee Avenue. Troubled by reports of children drowning in the Columbia, he wanted to provide a safer alternative for the community and for his own young sons. The Piper Natatorium closed in 1936, when the City of Wenatchee purchased a tract of land at the foot of Fifth Street and crews began building a public pool.

The new outdoor pool was located near the Cedergreen Brothers' Columbia Ice and Cold Storage manufacturing plant. This plant turned out 40 tons of ice each day for use on Great Northern railcars. Vast quantities of warm water went to waste during the ice-making process, so the Cedergreens agreed to pipe it to the Hughes Memorial Pool, named for Wenatchee mayor C.B. Hughes, who died in office shortly before its completion. The pool boasted a continuous filter system, something Piper's Natatorium had lacked.

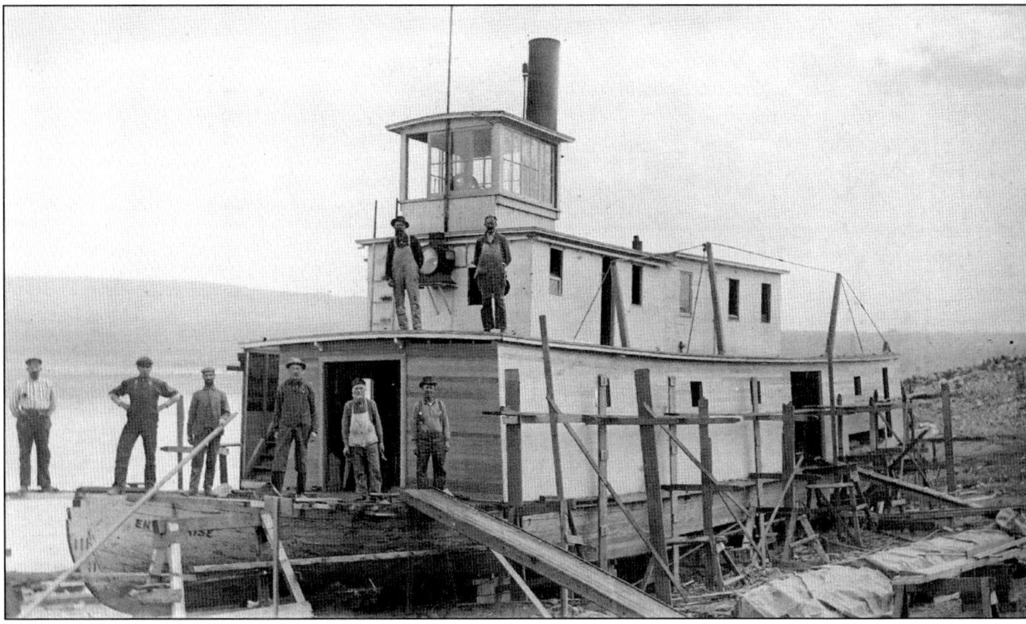

Workers at the Wenatchee steamboat yard at the foot of Fifth Street make repairs to the *Enterprise* in 1910. The stern-wheeler sits on the drydock, which consisted of several log skidways extended from the shore into the water and allowing men and horses to pull the boats by means of ropes and capstans (drums rotating on shafts). A Great Northern spur line brought materials to the drydock, where boats were repaired or new ones put into service. The busy boatyard extended to Piere Street and had a blacksmith shop, sail and paint shop, lumber storage building, watchman's house, and office. The *Enterprise* was built at the Wenatchee boatyard in 1903 and wrecked at Brewster in 1915. Below, boatyard workers pose by an unidentified stern-wheeler in drydock. (Both, WVMCC 85-110-1 and 85-110-7, donated by Richard Bell.)

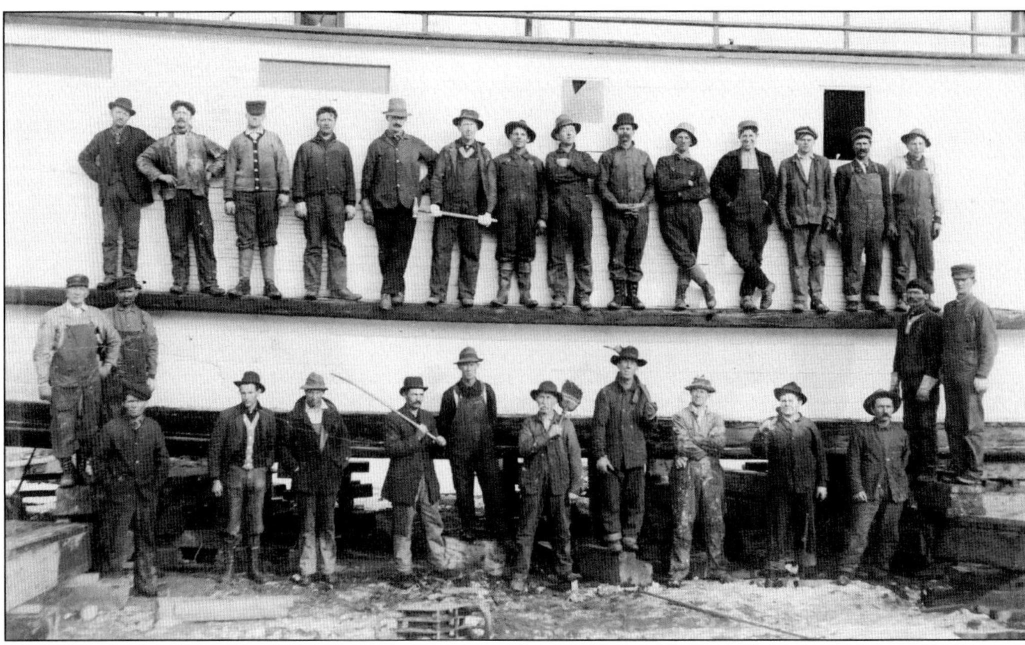

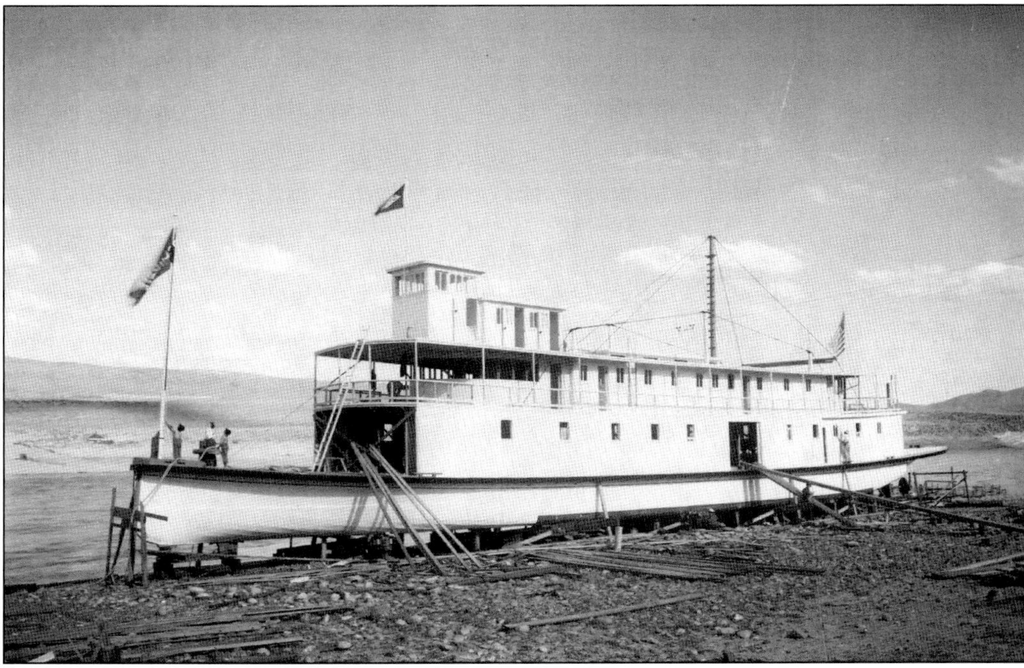

Workers raise a flag on the brand-new steamer *Chelan* at the Wenatchee boatyard in 1900. The *Chelan* was the fastest of the upper Columbia River stern-wheelers. At 125 feet in length, she had accommodations for 110 passengers. Wenatchee residents thought it great fun to come down to the boatyard to watch the launching of a new stern-wheeler, which occurred about once a year. (WVMCC 86-24-223, donated by Wenatchee Chamber of Commerce.)

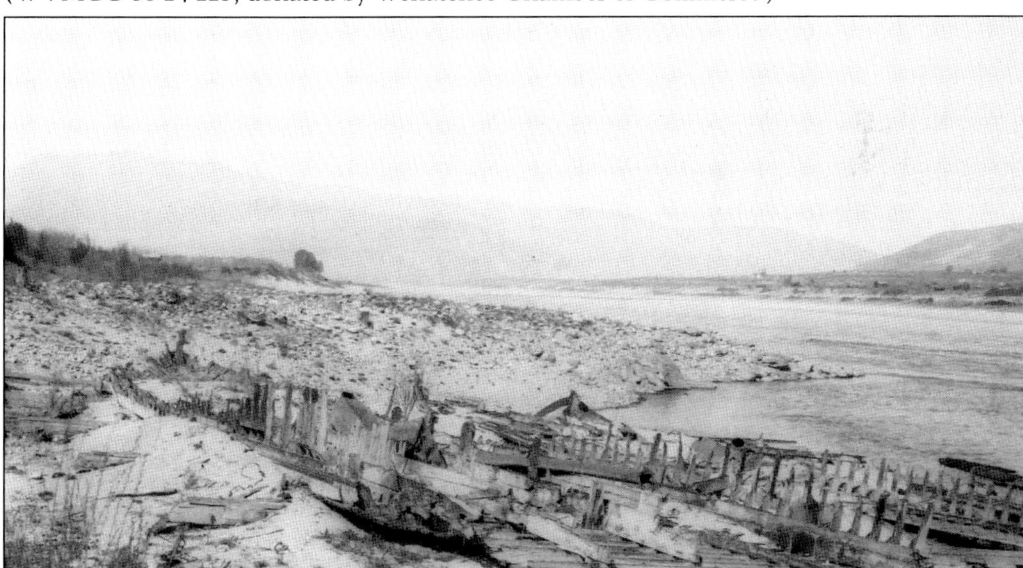

Charred carcasses are all that is left after an early-morning fire destroyed four stern-wheelers at the Wenatchee boatyard on July 8, 1915. The fire spread rapidly, and firemen devoted their attention to saving the boatyard's buildings. The fire may have been caused by boys, wishing to warm up after a midnight swim in the Columbia, sneaking onto one of the boats and lighting a small fire on the deck. (WVMCC 88-108-9, donated by Ileen Taylor.)

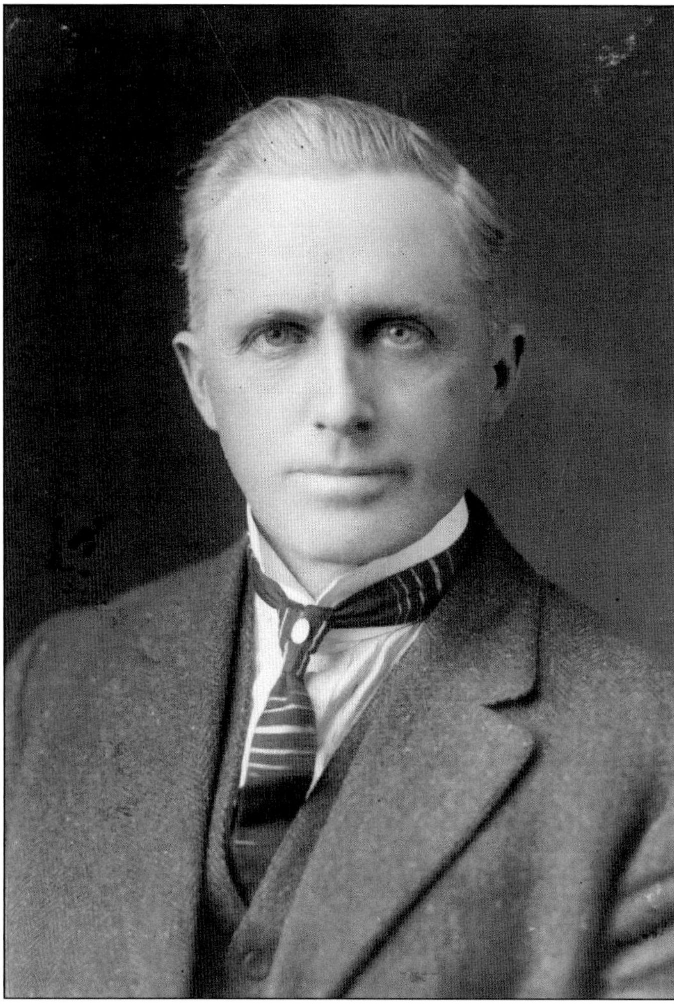

Abram A. Piper (1868–1948) was the Great Northern Railway Company's freight and passenger agent at Wenatchee. A popular man and community leader, he is shown here in his 1922 Elks Club membership photograph. Piper invested his own money in 1916 to build a public auditorium and swimming pool near the boatyard on Wenatchee Avenue and Fifth Street. (WVMCC 005-74-74, donated by Dewey Stedman.)

The Piper Natatorium was a favored place on warm summer days. This photograph shows "Girls' Day" in August 1931. Piper built the pool to give local children, including his two sons, an alternative to swimming and possibly drowning in the Columbia River. (WVMCC 77-73-2.)

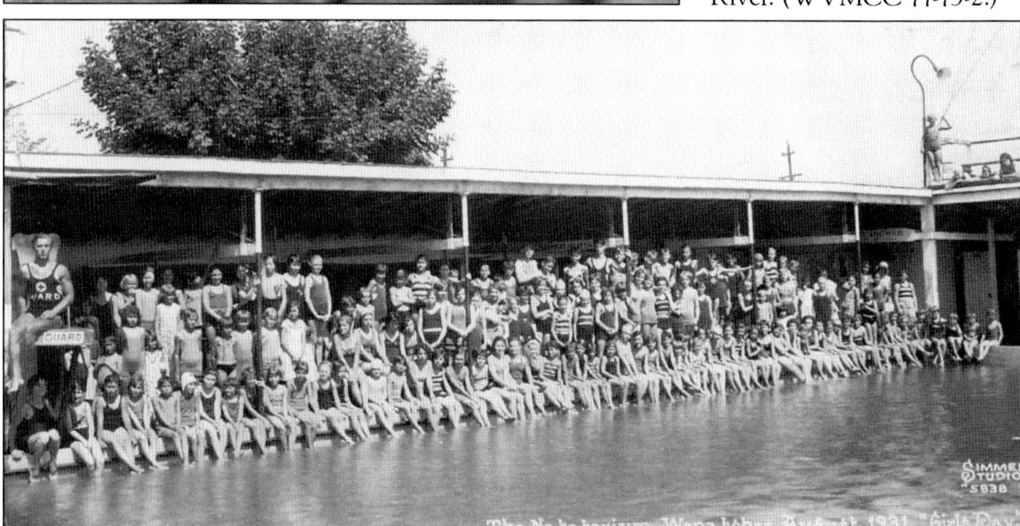

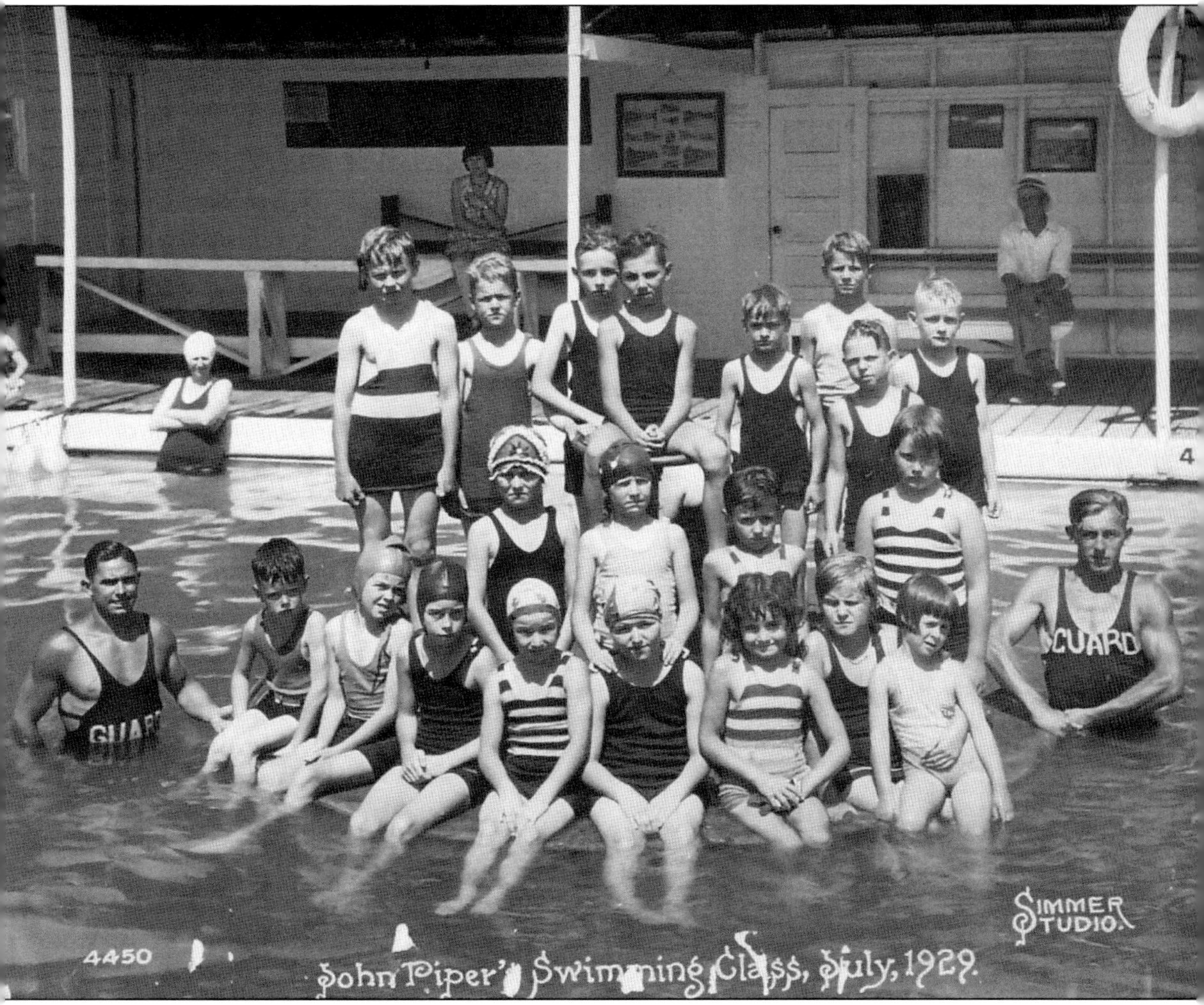

Abram Piper's son John was one of the swimming instructors at the Natatorium. It is unknown which of the young men in this 1929 photograph, labeled "John Piper's Swimming Class," is John. The Piper Natatorium closed in 1936; the Chelan County Public Utilities District headquarters now occupies its location. (WVMCC 77-73-1.)

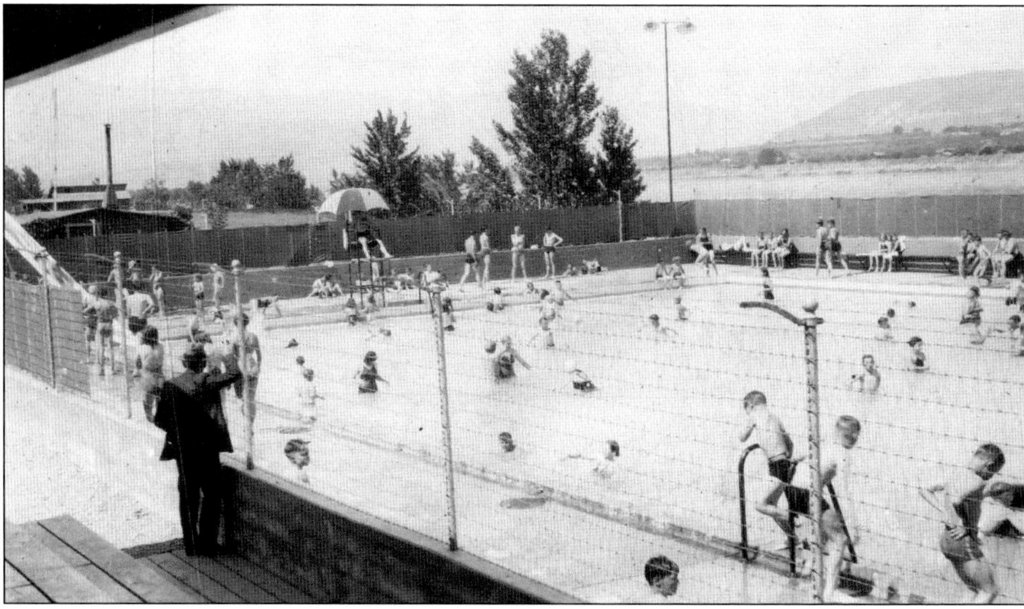

The Hughes Memorial Swimming Pool was closer to the Columbia River than the Natatorium, which closed when the new city pool was completed in 1936. The outskirts of East Wenatchee can be seen across the river in this northward-looking photograph from the 1940s. (WVMCC 97-48-260, donated by Wenatchee Public Works.)

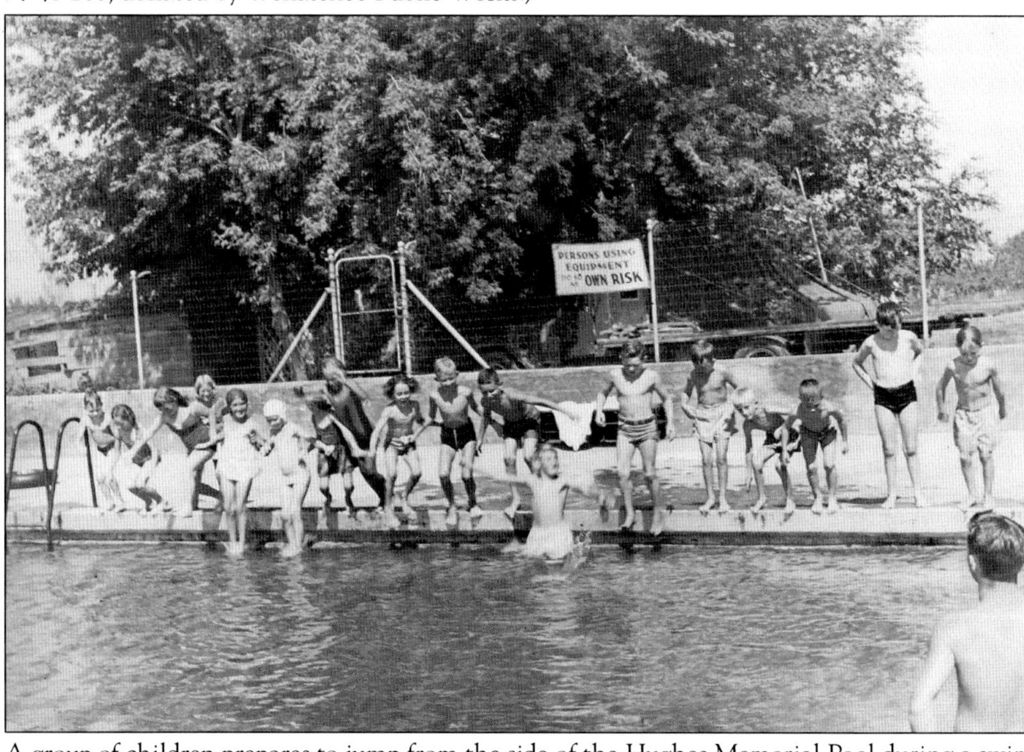

A group of children prepares to jump from the side of the Hughes Memorial Pool during a swim class about 1948. The sign behind them says, "Persons using equipment do so at own risk." (WVMCC 007-37-240, donated by Robert Loffelbein.)

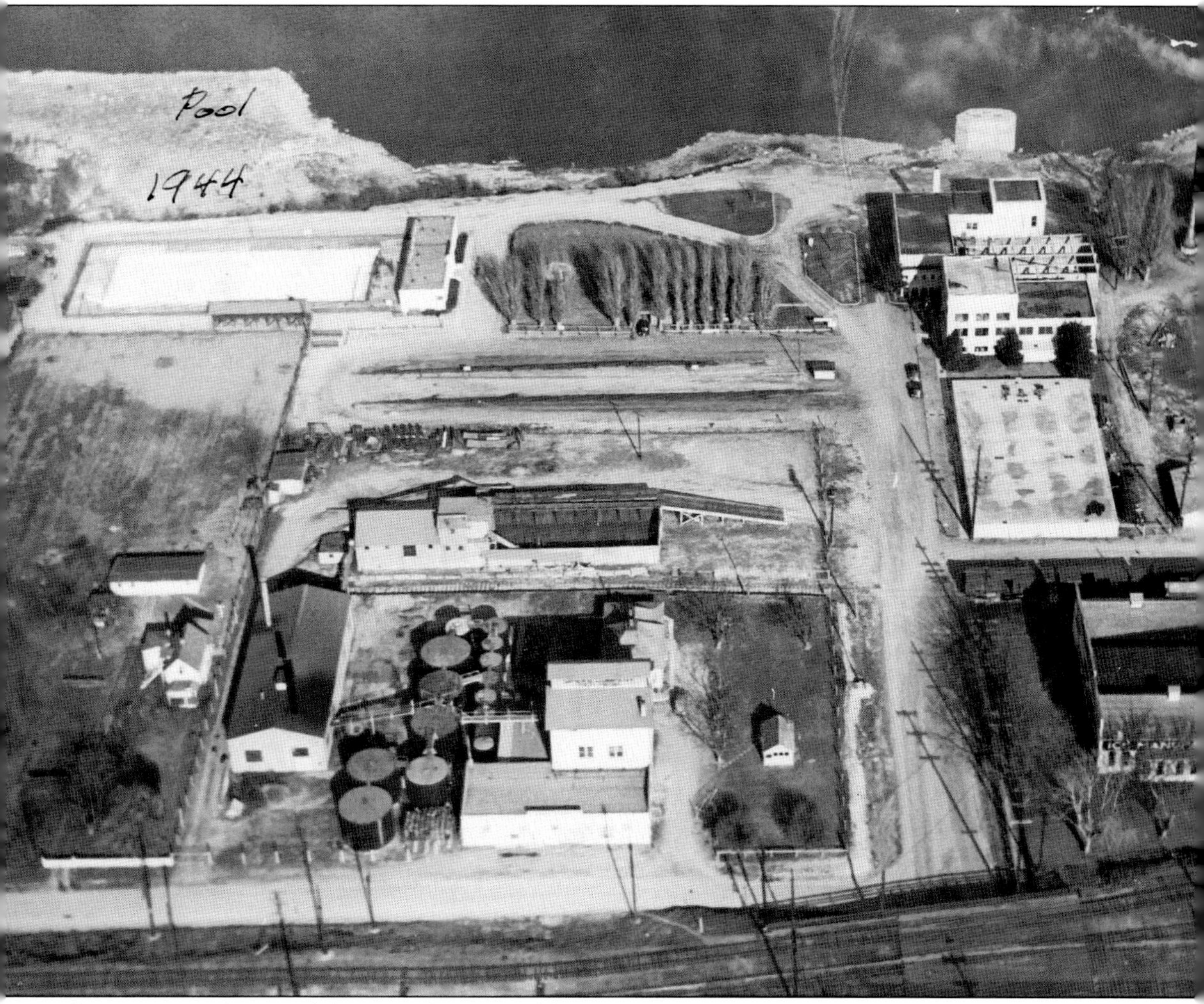

This 1944 aerial view of the waterfront at Fifth Street shows, clockwise from upper left, the city pool, a small park, the city water filtration and pumping plant, Columbia Ice and Cold Storage, and the Speas Vinegar Company processing plant at center. The vinegar plant was established in 1925 on the site of a building previously used for lumber storage at the boatyard. It capitalized on the huge tonnage of cull apples produced in the Wenatchee Valley, grinding and pressing them into cider that was then converted to vinegar. After several months of aging, the vinegar was sterilized and shipped in barrels and tank cars to wholesale markets. Thousands of tons of culls were pressed each year, yielding up to a million gallons of vinegar that were mostly sold in the Midwest. The plant ceased operations in 1976. (WVMCC 97-48-397, donated by Wenatchee Public Works.)

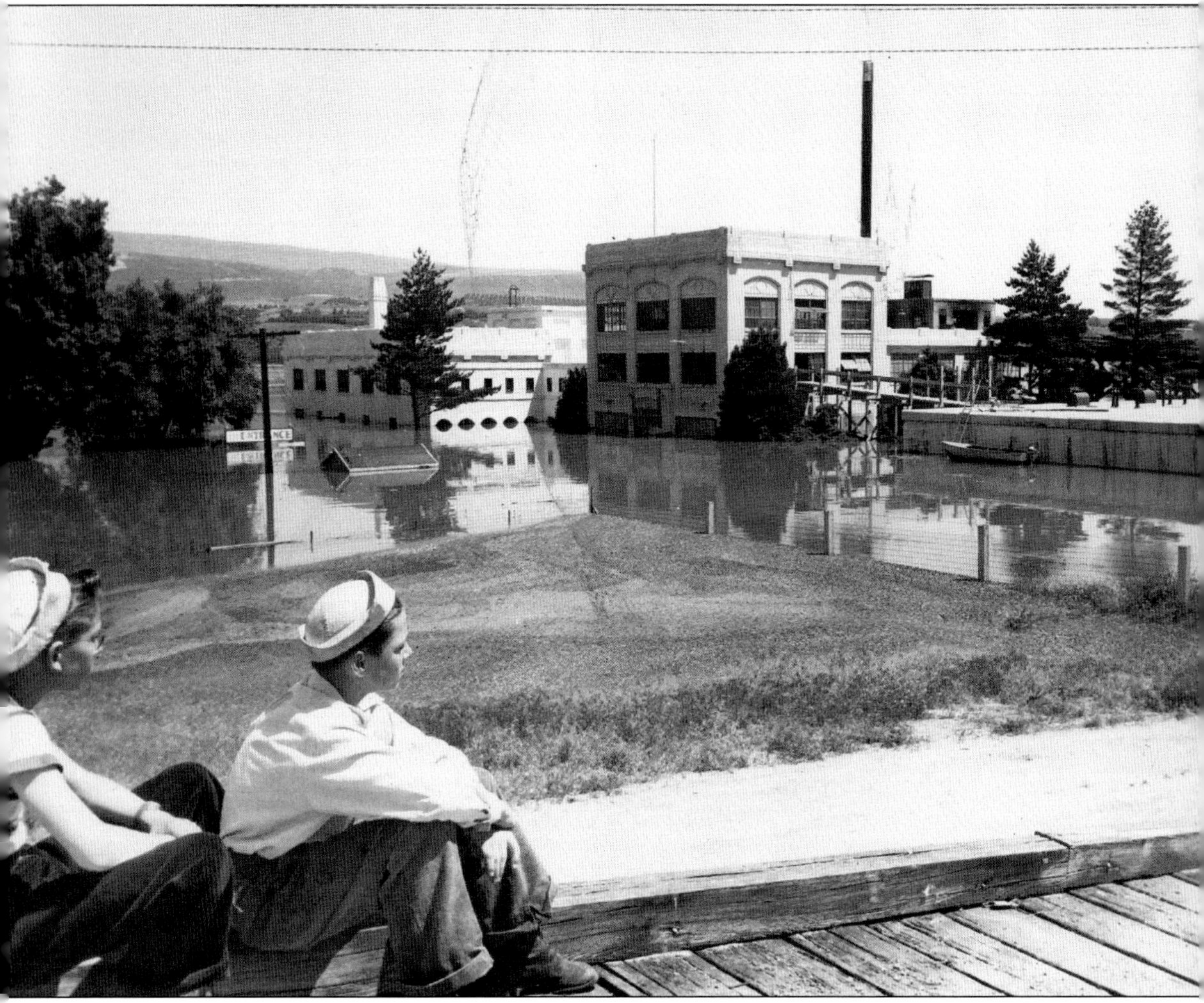

The flood of 1948 was one of the worst catastrophes ever to hit North Central Washington. A winter of heavy snow was followed by an April with four times the normal precipitation, resulting in sodden watersheds. Up and down the Columbia River, these drainages were unable to absorb the sudden discharge of water as a long, hard, warm rain in late May melted snow in the high country. Rivers overflowed their banks on their way toward the Columbia. At Wenatchee, the Columbia River rose more than 29 feet; high water pushed the river right up to the Great Northern tracks. Buildings and orchards were flooded, transportation and telephone service were cut off, and the city's pumping plant failed. Open barrels of untreated river water were placed along city streets for commercial and sanitary use. Drinking water was distributed in tank trucks throughout the residential area until the water plant was restored to service. (WVMCC 97-48-406, donated by Wenatchee Public Works.)

Four young men pose while cleaning the Hughes Memorial Pool after the flood of 1948. Bob Thomas holds a fish that was evidently trapped when floodwaters receded. The others are Gary Staples, Bob Loffelbein, and John Piper, grandson of Natatorium owner Abram Piper. (WVMCC 007-37-340, donated by Robert Loffelbein.)

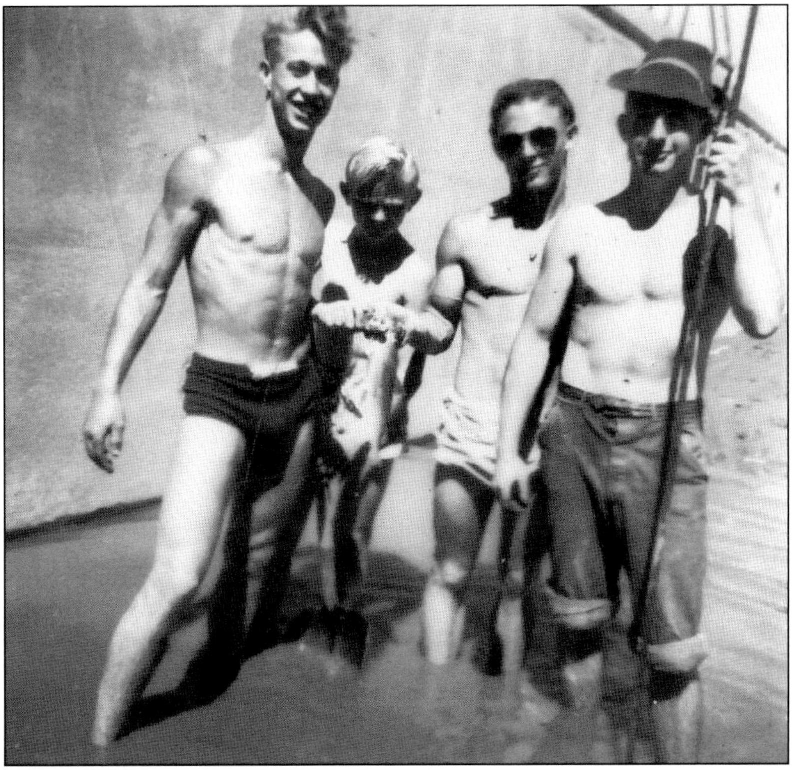

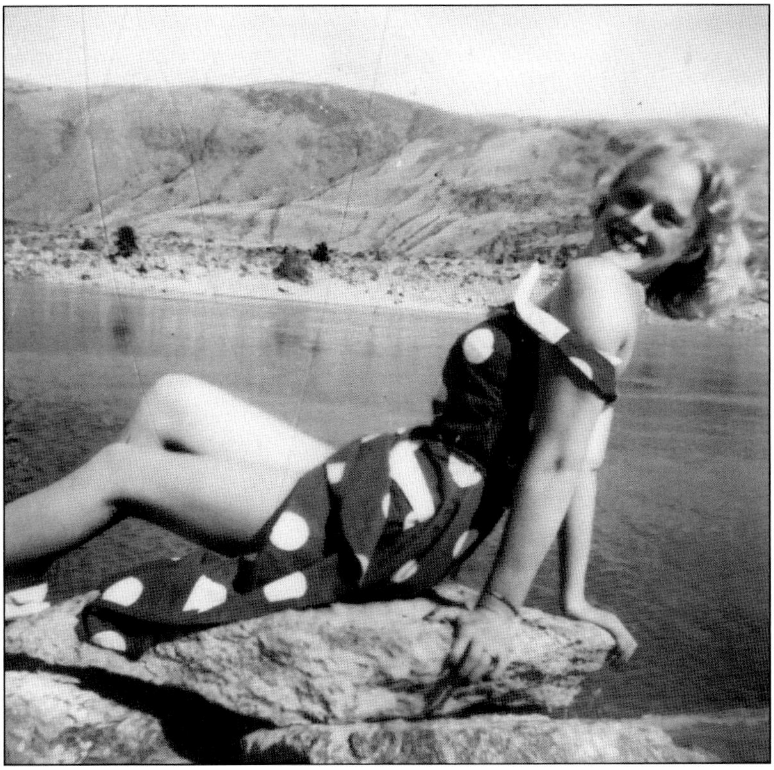

The waterfront has always been a magnet for sunbathers. Here, Berdina Schille poses in a polka-dot sundress along the Columbia River near the Wenatchee city pool in 1949. (WVMCC 007-37-6, donated by Robert Loffelbein.)

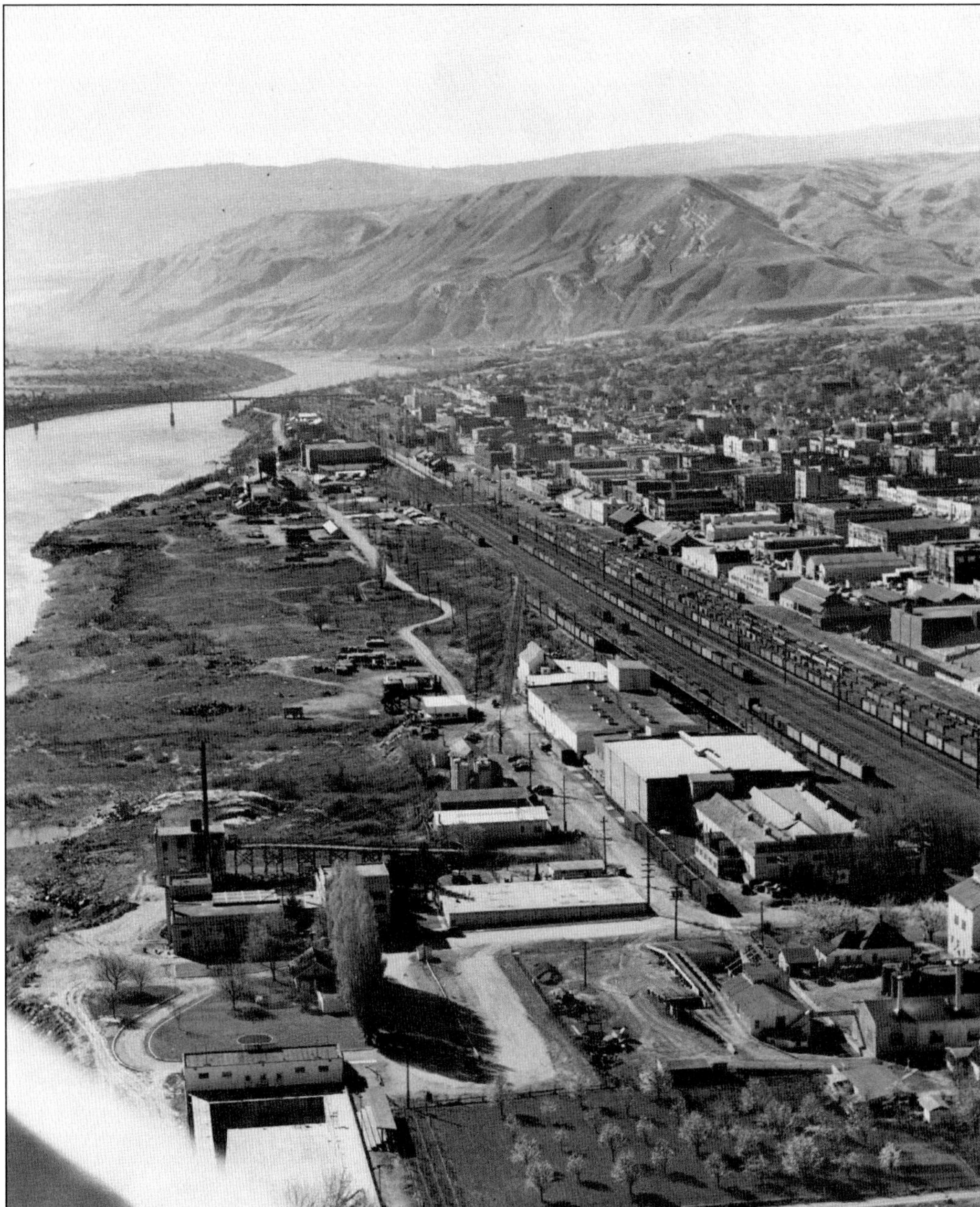

In the foreground of this aerial photograph of the Wenatchee waterfront in 1948 are the city pool, pumping plant, and Speas vinegar plant. Left of the railroad tracks on Worthen Street are the city garbage incinerator, the dog pound building, and Shell Oil Company; across the street are the Cedergreen Frozen Pack plant buildings. At the far south end of Worthen are the E.T. Pybus steel plant and Cascadian Fruit Shipper building, with the train depot and Beanery to the right. Shacktown was gone by this time, but its debris remained. Note the 1908 pipeline bridge crossing the Columbia River. The George Sellar Bridge in south Wenatchee was built two years later and replaced the old bridge as part of the state highway system. (WVMCC 97-48-366, donated by Wenatchee Public Works.)

Five

Downtown Wenatchee

Wenatchee's first commercial district, before the coming of the railroad, was a handful of buildings on the dusty flats about a half-mile from the waterfront, around today's Miller Street and Springwater Avenue. Great Northern Railway Company paid to move the buildings next to its tracks and depot on First Street in 1892–1893. Downtown Wenatchee spread out from there. Hotels, banks, blacksmith shops, hardware stores, dress shops, attorneys and insurance company offices, and other businesses multiplied along with the town's population, which grew from 451 in 1900 to 4,050 in 1910 and 6,324 in 1920.

Wenatchee Avenue was (and is) the main thoroughfare, running north and south. Businesses also thrived on Mission Street, one block west of and parallel to "The Ave." The parallel street to the east, between Wenatchee Avenue and the railroad tracks, was Columbia Street; it housed fruit and merchandise warehouses. Downtown stretched from east-west Fifth to Kittitas Streets, a little less than a mile along Wenatchee Avenue and Mission Street. Many buildings in the National and Wenatchee Registers of Historic Places can be seen in this area today. They reflect a variety of architectural styles, including Classical, Federal, Mission, Georgian Revival, Art Deco, Beaux Arts, and Art Moderne.

The 1920s were big years for downtown growth. By this time, Wenatchee had four large banks; major department stores, including Ellis Forde, J.C. Penney, Montgomery Ward, and Sears, Roebuck and Co.; and national dime store chains, such as Woolworth's and Ben Franklin. Movie theaters included the Gem, the Alcazar, the Rialto, the Vitaphone, and the Liberty. Hotels multiplied from 13 in 1914 to 25 in 1928. There continued to be an increase in businesses related to community growth, such as lumber companies, real estate sales, restaurants, auto dealers, attorneys, doctors, retail shops, and, of course, equipment and supplies for the ever-growing tree fruit industry. From coffee shops to pool halls, downtown Wenatchee was a vibrant place.

In 2003, Wenatchee received the Great American Main Street Award, the highest honor in a community-driven national program for revitalizing older, traditional business districts. The Main Street program encourages economic development within the context of historic preservation. Wenatchee's downtown also has the distinction of being designated a National Register historic district.

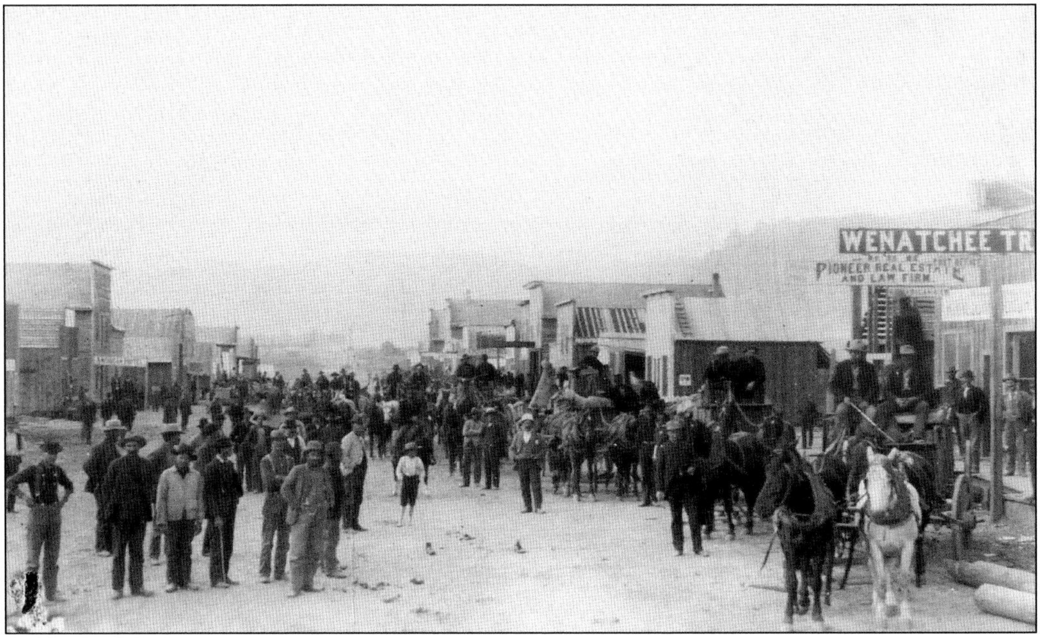

The original townsite of Wenatchee was on Miller Street, between today's Fifth Street and Springwater Avenue. W.E. Stevens's general store and hotel, Columbia Valley Bank, Horan's butcher shop, a blacksmith shop, real estate and law firm, public hall, and at least one saloon served the small population of settlers and transient railroad men. Above, the Great Northern grading crew poses in 1892 before teams of horses and mules moved buildings to the new site. Below, the new townsite takes shape in this 1892 photograph, taken from the tower of the Columbia River ferry at the foot of Orondo Avenue. Railroad tracks have not yet been laid. The eight-windowed building at upper right is a furniture store at Mission Street and Orondo Avenue. Saddle Rock is visible in both photographs. (Above, WVMCC 83-12-7, donated by Marcelene King; below, 94-31-2, donated by Eleanor Spangler.)

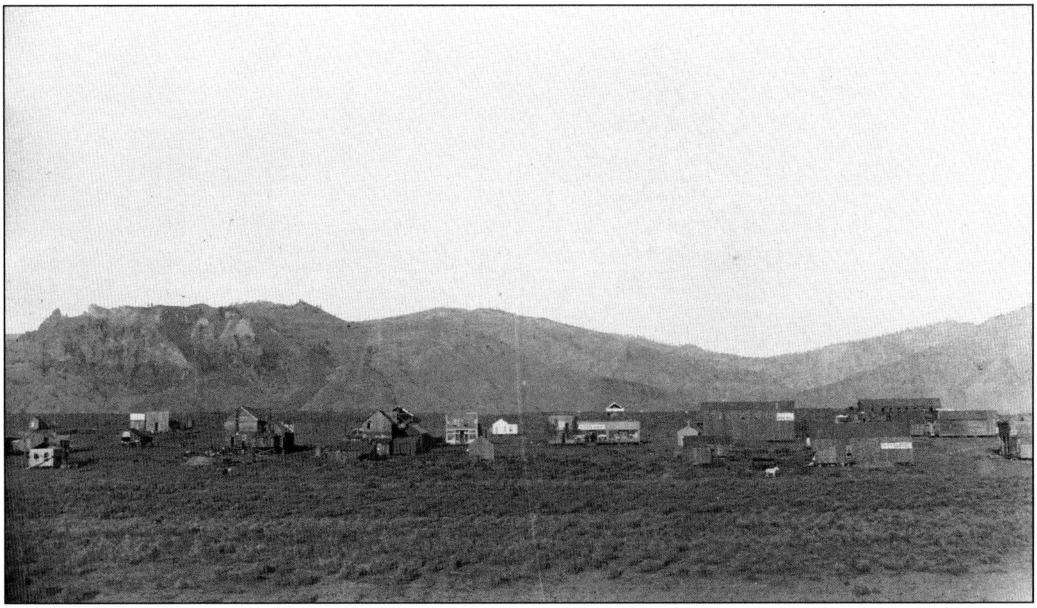

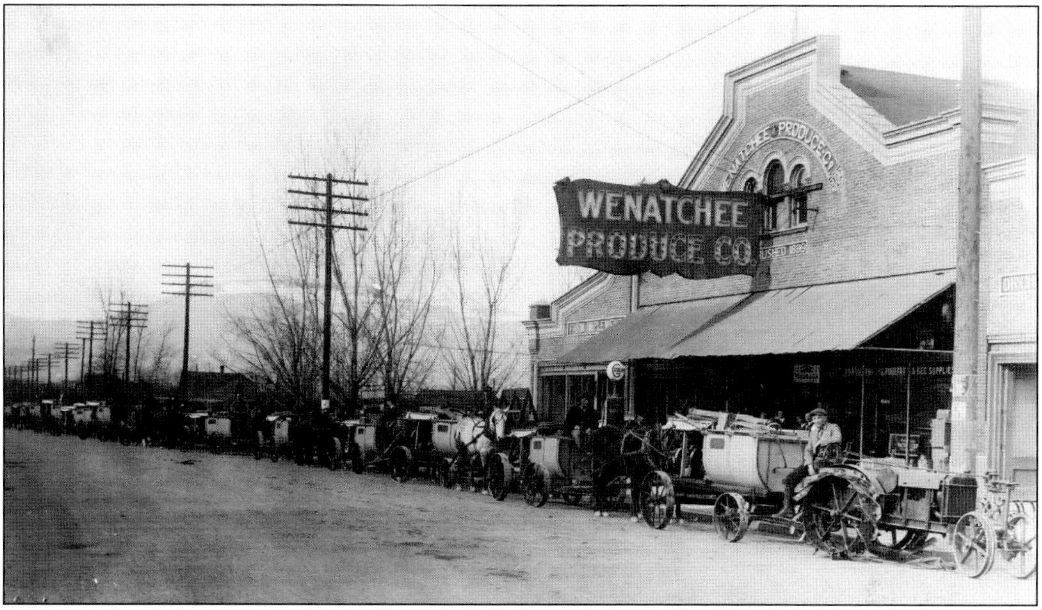

Missouri transplant Conrad Rose established the Wenatchee Produce Company in 1899. Five years later, he built a large warehouse, stretching 400 feet along North Wenatchee Avenue and the railroad tracks. The company started by shipping tree fruit but expanded into sales of orchard supplies, feed, machinery, and Studebaker automobiles. In this 1908 photograph, a long line of horse-drawn sprayers and tractors is seen outside the building. (WVMCC 90-24-1, donated by Margaret Weed.)

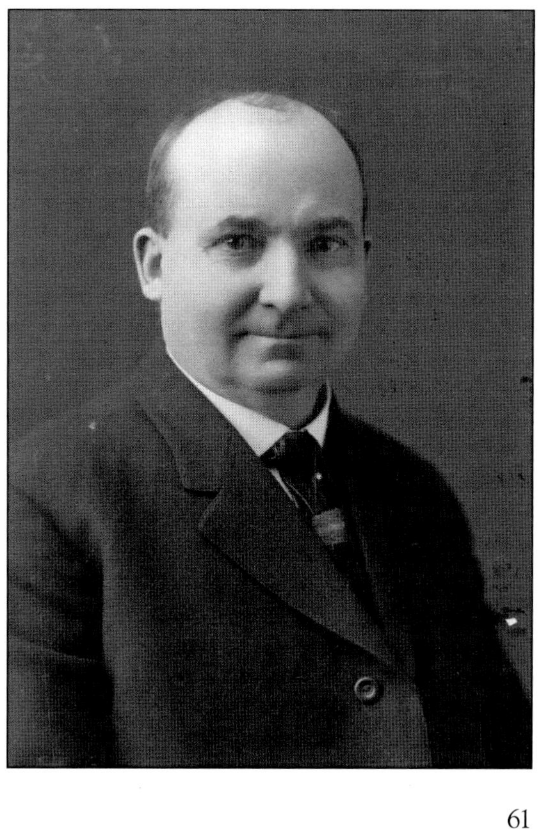

Conrad Rose (1862–1938) and his family arrived in Wenatchee in 1887. They bought a 160-acre farm and planted peach trees and other crops. Judicious selling of some of his land financed the very successful produce company. Trusted as a safe and reliable man to deal with, Rose was generous with his customers. During the Great Depression, he forgave many debts rather than see community members go hungry or lose their orchards. (WVMCC 005-74-106, donated by Dewey Stedman.)

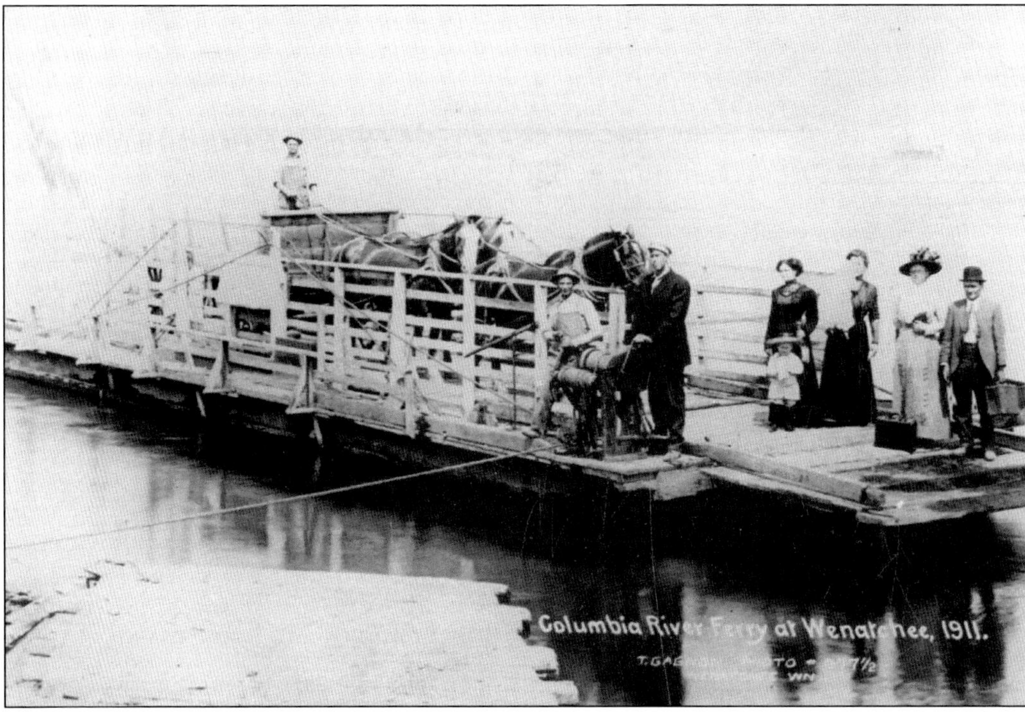

Before bridges were built across the Columbia, travelers relied on ferries. By the 1880s, Indians were taking passengers across the river in dugout canoes. After the Burch family ceased ferry operations above the Wenatchee confluence in 1889, three men began running a cable ferry at the foot of Orondo Avenue downtown. Towers on each bank of the river supported sturdy steel cables; smaller cables on pulleys were attached to each end of the vessel, and the ferry pictured above used the current to propel itself across the river. It was discontinued a few years after the wagon-pipeline bridge was completed in 1908. The photograph below, taken around 1900 from the top of the cable tower, shows Columbia Avenue between Orondo Avenue and Palouse Street. The Presbyterian church and Olympia Hotel are at right. (Above, WVMCC 86-24-281, donated by Wenatchee Chamber of Commerce; below, 78-218-2, donated by Mary Anderson.)

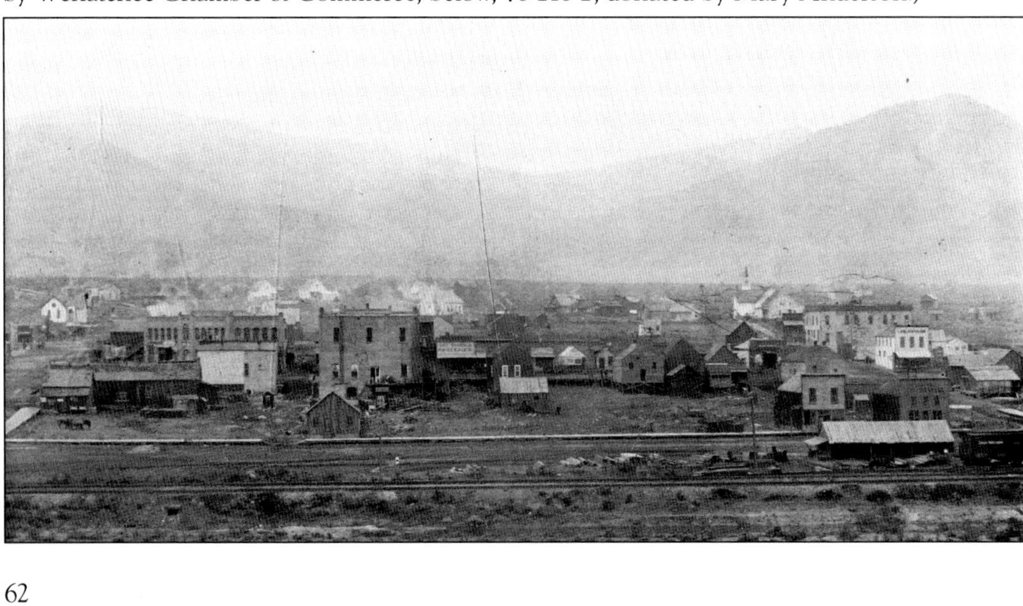

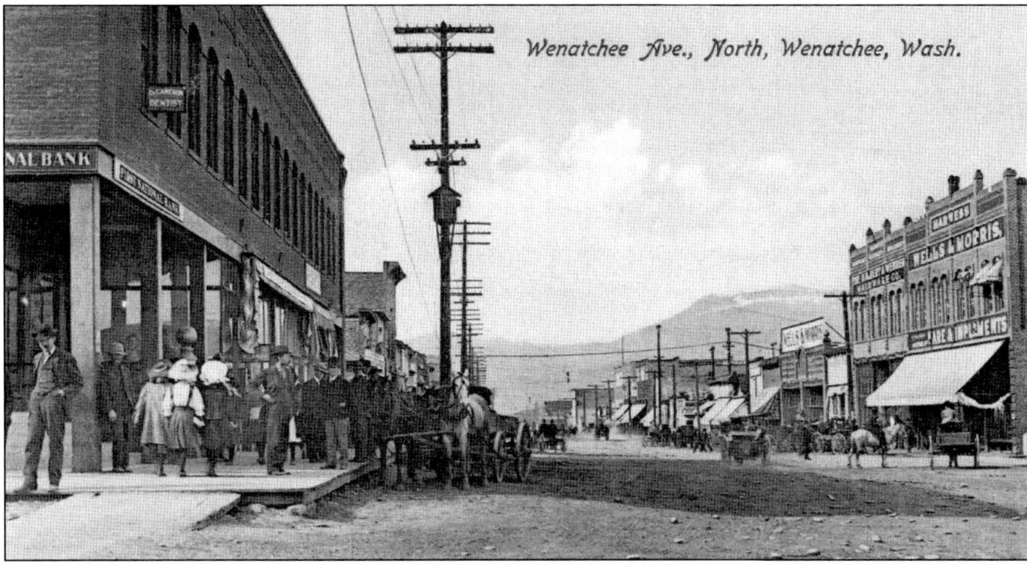

No cars are shown in this undated postcard photograph of Wenatchee Avenue looking north from Orondo Avenue, but there is plenty of foot and horse traffic. The First National Bank, at left, was founded in 1906. Across the street, the Wells & Morris store sold hardware, agricultural implements, harnesses, guns, ammunition, sporting goods, irrigation pipes, pumps, and plumbing and heating supplies. Below, from left to right, A.Z. Wells, Bard Stewart, Otto "Mike" Anderson, and Alfred Morris stand inside the store in 1908. Wells and his nephew, Morris, dissolved the partnership amicably in 1914. Morris kept the building and hardware business; the Morris Building still stands, though it has been altered and a third story added. Wells joined J.M. Wade in operating a fruit warehouse and, later, a large hardware store. (Both, WVMCC 85-0-91 and 85-0-213.)

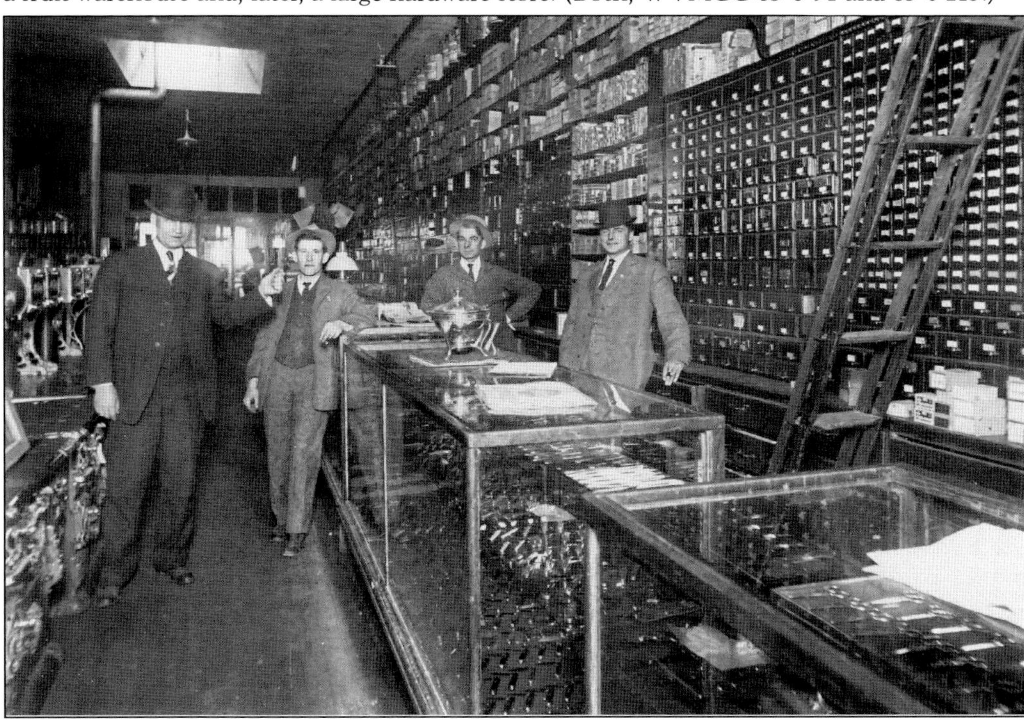

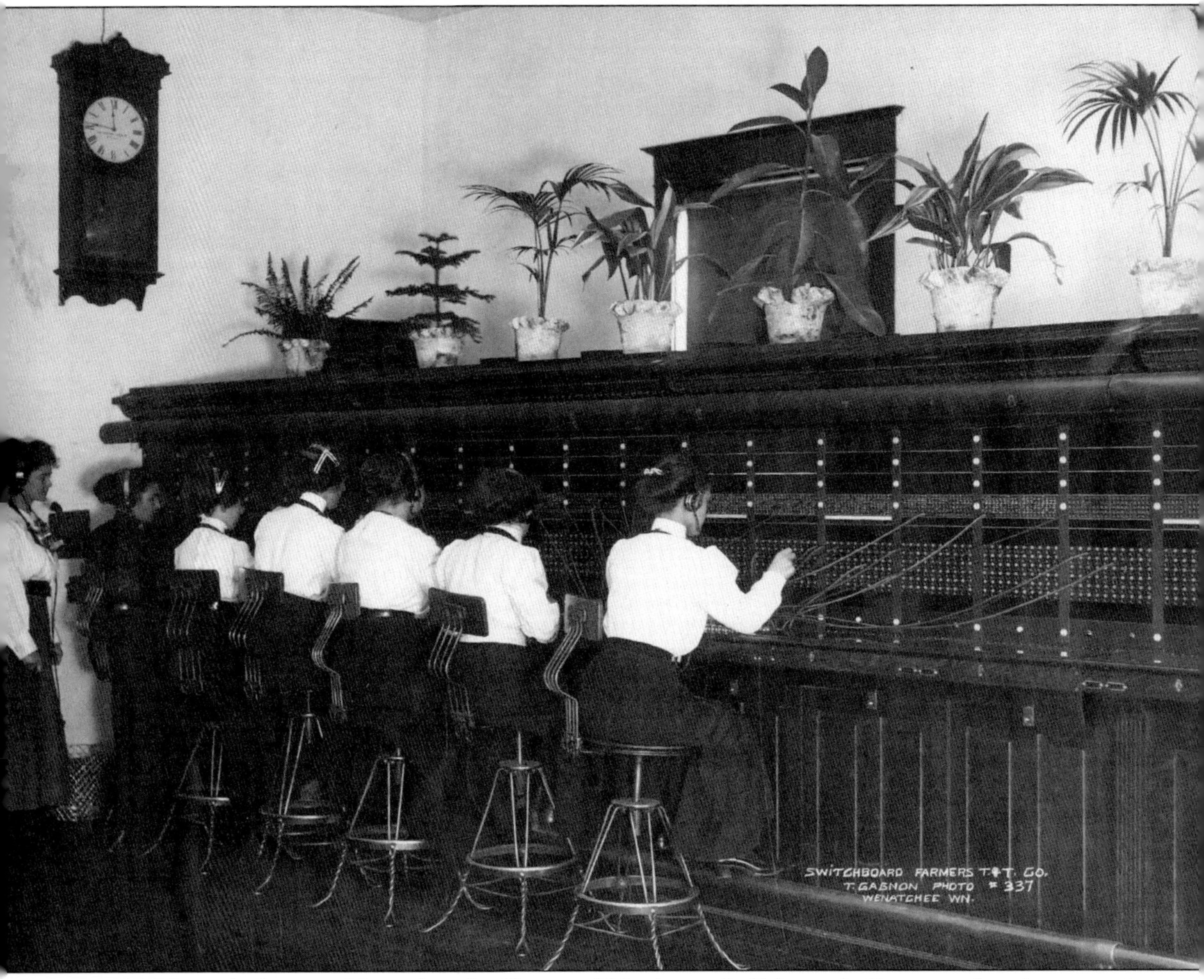

Ladies work the switchboard in the Farmers Telephone & Telegraph Company headquarters in 1910. The Pacific States Telephone Company had connected Wenatchee with Waterville by means of a single iron wire in 1893 but set high rates for additional service in Wenatchee. A group of men led by Z.A. Lanham created the independent Farmers T&T in 1904. A formidable competitor, it built phone lines throughout Wenatchee Flats and up several canyons to serve far-flung orchards. In 1907, Pacific agreed to abandon all local service if it could conduct its long-distance operations in the Farmers Building at 115 South Chelan Street (next to today's city hall). This arrangement worked well. Pacific States, later General Telephone, moved to its own office across the street in 1925; Farmers became part of the Interstate Telephone & Telegraph Company in 1929. (WVMCC 86-24-62, donated by Wenatchee Chamber of Commerce.)

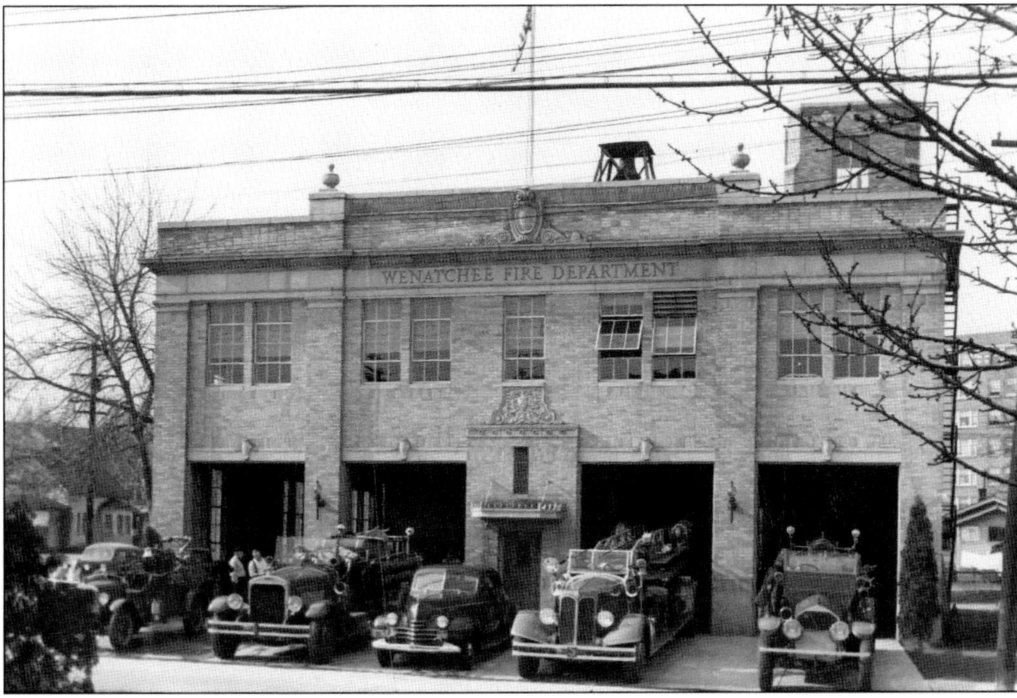

Firefighting in Wenatchee started with bucket brigades before a volunteer fire department was organized and the town bought a manually drawn hose cart and hose in 1901. The city later bought a horse-drawn hook-and-ladder outfit and began to pay firefighters. In the 1910s, it acquired gas-powered fire engines, storing them in a brick building owned by the chamber of commerce until this fire station was completed in 1929. (WVMCC 001-6-10, donated by Nancy Meyer.)

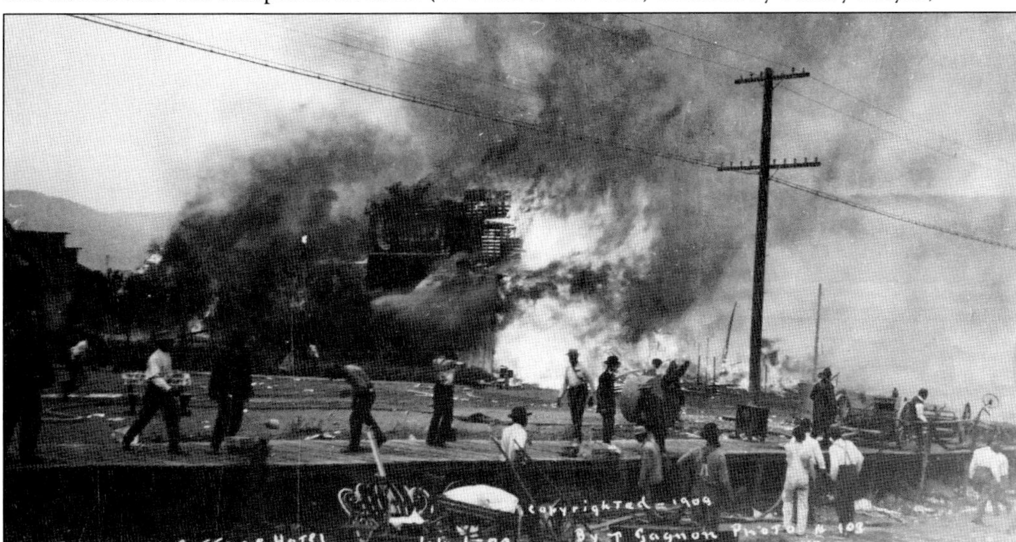

Firefighting equipment was inadequate to douse a large fire that broke out in Emil Frank's Central Market on July 6, 1909, and spread to other wooden buildings on Mission Street and Orondo Avenue. The fire took out the temporary power to the pumping station, so firemen diverted water from the Highline Canal to fill their hoses. More than a dozen businesses were damaged or destroyed, including the Cottage Hotel at 206 Orondo Avenue. (WVMCC 85-0-21.)

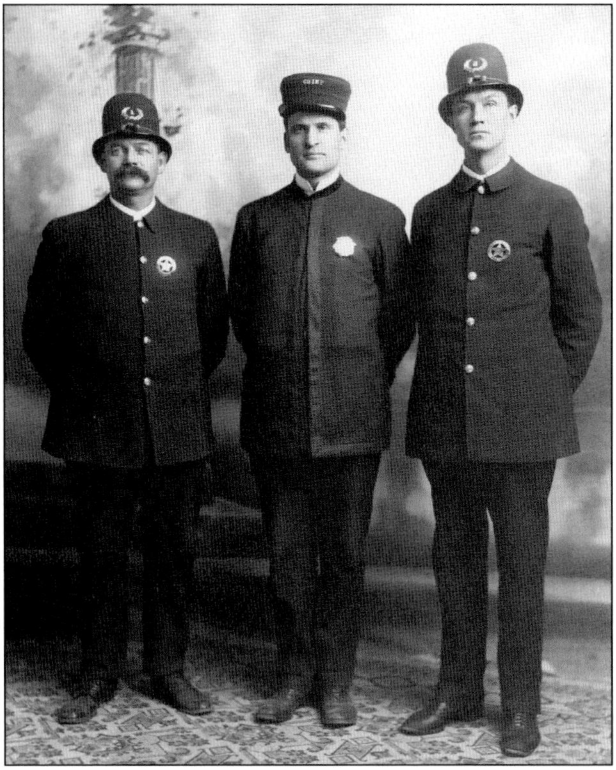

The three-person Wenatchee Police Department was issued its first uniforms in 1908. From left to right, Nate Inscho, Chief Ed Ferguson, and Bob Nelson had their hands full keeping order, with roughnecks from railroad and construction crews frequently causing trouble. Burglaries, knifings, fights, and looting of boxcars were common. Chief Ferguson, whose father had served as town marshal in the 1890s, was elected Chelan County sheriff in 1908, holding two top law enforcement jobs at the same time. He also owned and managed the Wenatchee Theater, often acted in community theater, and took small roles in traveling stock company productions. Ferguson is at far right of the front row in the photograph below. (Both, WVMCC 90-56-56 and 76-6-62, donated by J. Edward Ferguson.)

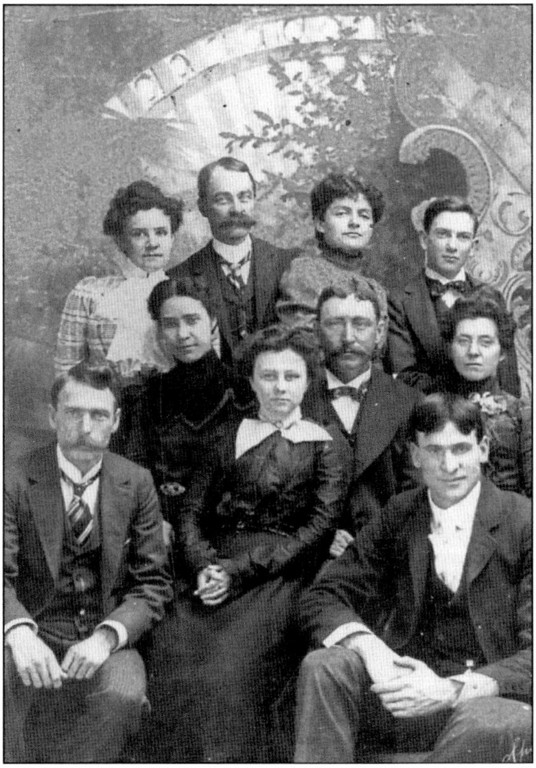

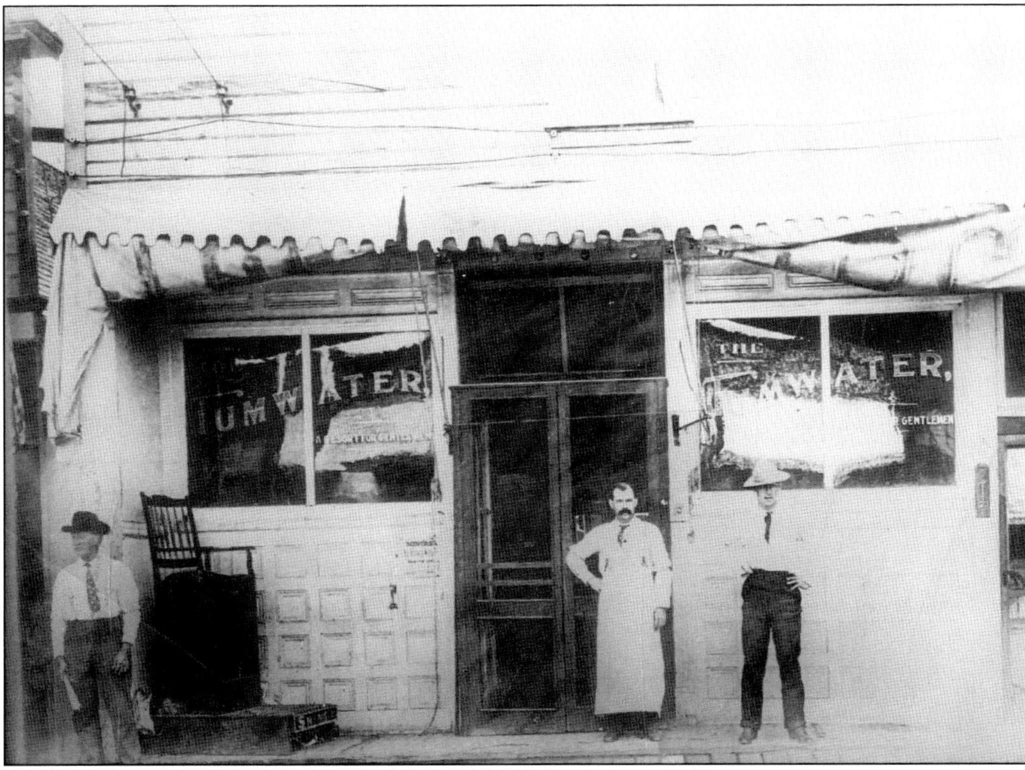

Bartender Dave Evans stands in the doorway of the Tumwater Saloon at 13 South Wenatchee Avenue around 1905. The saloon had a ladies' entrance (at right), but few ladies ever entered the premises. The Tumwater served Olympia Beer. (WVMCC 76-6-100, donated by Salvation Army.)

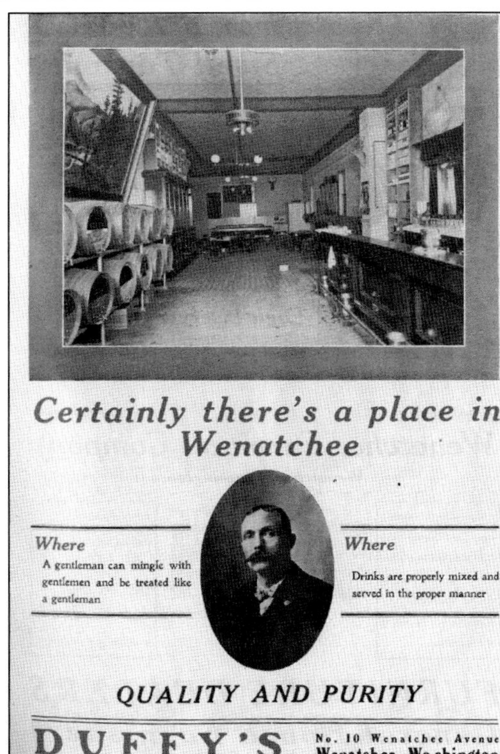

This ad appears in the 1906 Christmas edition of the *Wenatchee Republic*, a hardcover book distributed far and wide to promote the Wenatchee Valley as a fine place to live. The book raves about Wenatchee's orchards and business opportunities, with photographs and glowing descriptions of some of the nicer homes and leading citizens. Evidently, Duffy's Saloon qualified as an establishment of which Wenatchee could be proud. (WVMCC 74-43, donated by Pat Scott.)

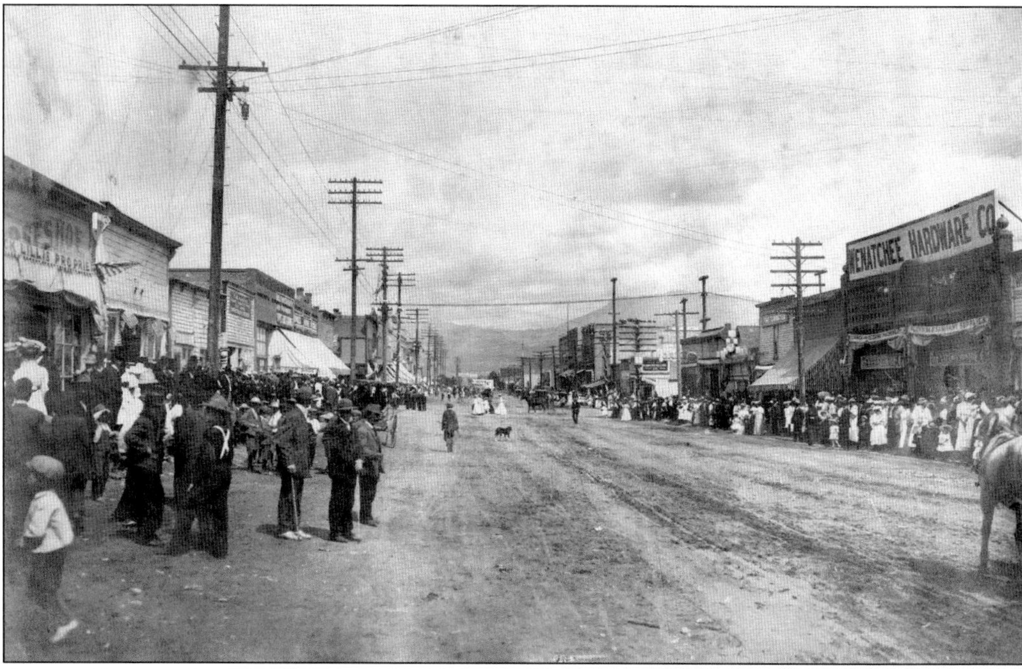

A crowd lines a then dirt Wenatchee Avenue in 1905, probably waiting for the Independence Day parade. Looking north, the photograph shows Rick Lillis's horseshoe shop at left. Across the street are the Wenatchee Hardware Company, Tumwater Saloon, the office of Hammond Milling Company, and other businesses. (WVMCC 99-12-41, donated by Kirby Billingsley.)

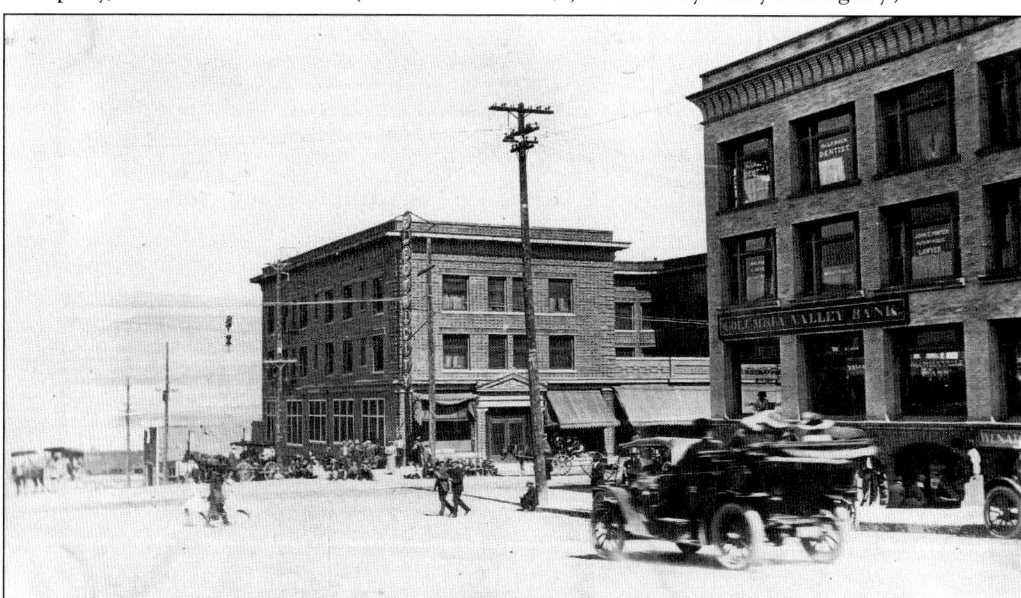

A touring car with three ladies in the rumble seat passes the Columbia Valley Bank at the corner of Orondo and Wenatchee Avenues. Across the avenue is the Wenatchee Hotel, the city's finest in 1910 when this photograph was likely taken. Its dining room seated 200 guests. The building still stands, but its two upper floors were removed in 1960 in an effort to modernize it. (WVMCC 80-67-223, donated by Madeleine Elliott.)

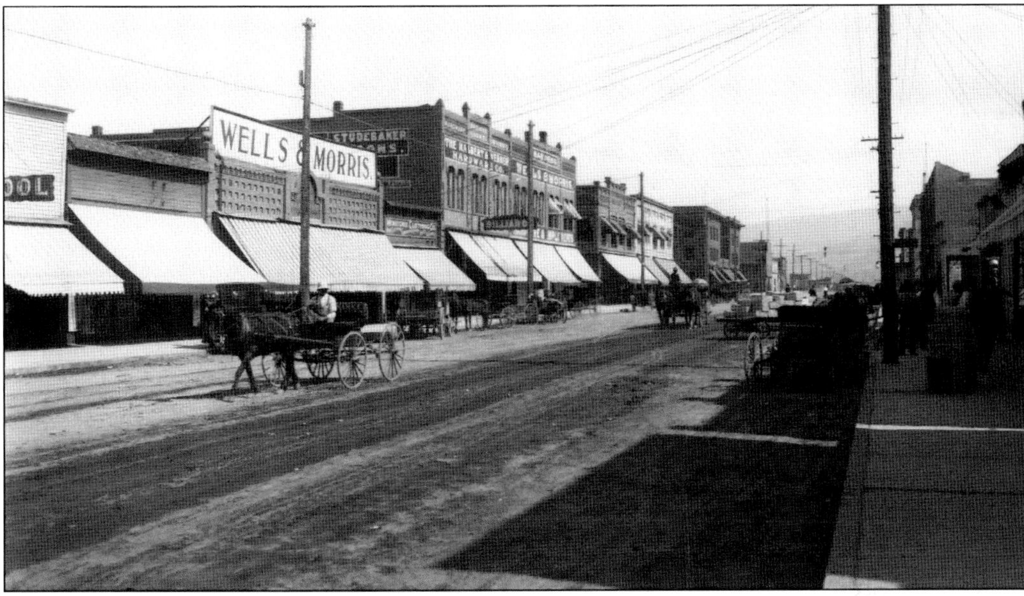

Horses pull wagons past the Wells & Morris hardware store on Wenatchee Avenue in 1911. A pool hall at left and the Wenatchee Clothing Store and a billiard hall at right flanked the store. No cars are visible, but by 1911, there were 84 automobiles in Wenatchee, 41 in Cashmere, and two in Leavenworth. (WVMCC 99-3-235, donated by Robert Isenhart.)

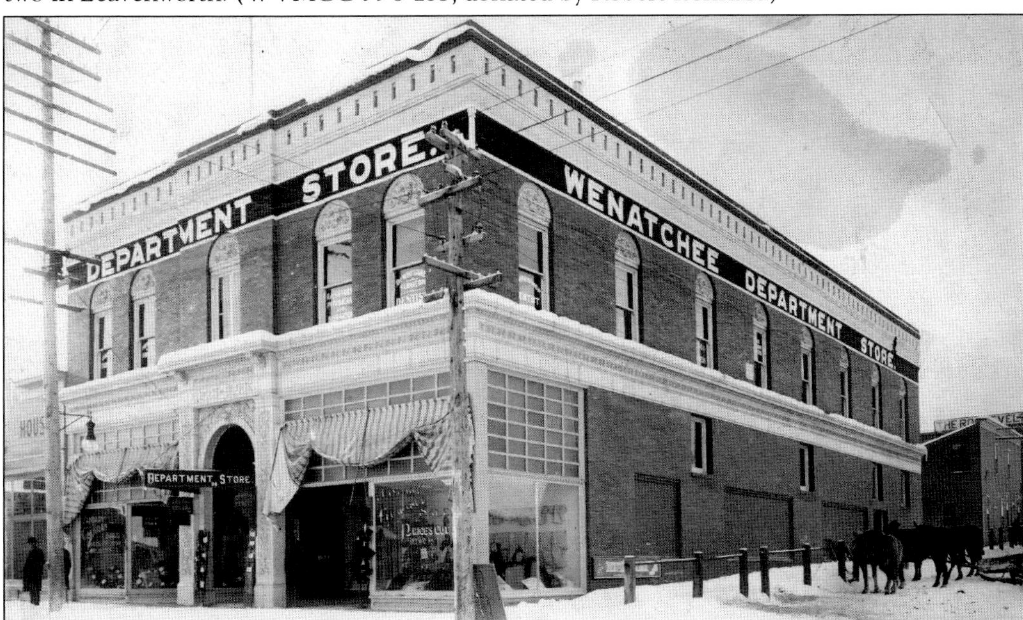

Steamboat captain Alexander Griggs constructed this two-story brick building in 1903 at First Street and North Wenatchee Avenue. Nathan Neubauer, who had come to Wenatchee the year before and purchased a dry goods business, moved his store into the Griggs Building in 1905. The Miller Department Store occupied the structure for many years, followed by the Hirsch Value Center in 1972. The building has survived three fires. (WVMCC 90-56-71, donated by J. Edward Ferguson.)

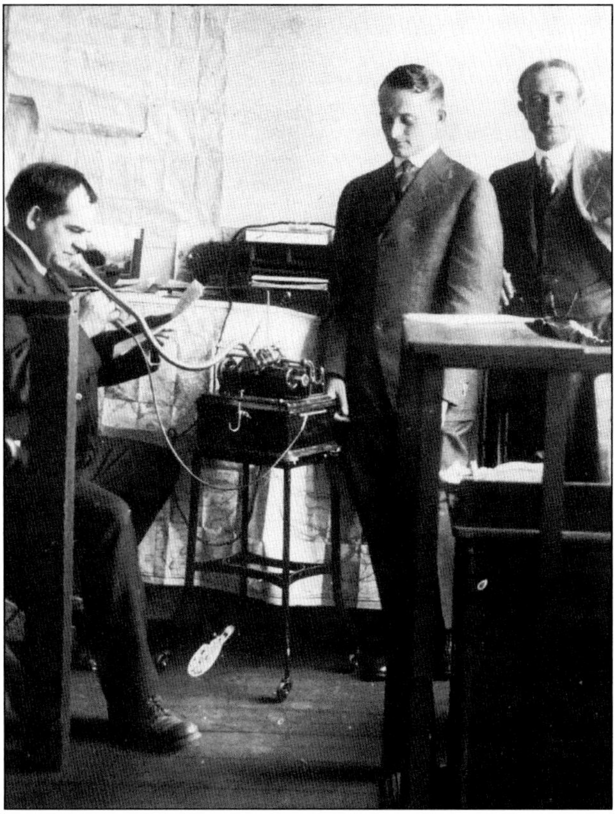

Rufus Woods, owner and publisher of the World-Advance Publishing Company, speaks into Wenatchee's first Dictaphone in 1916. With him are W. Homer Barnhart, center, owner of Barnhart's Music House, and Charles Stohl, advertising manager of the *Republic* newspaper. The *Republic* and *Advance* were weekly papers, the former tending toward a conservative and the latter a more liberal viewpoint; both closed by 1914. Woods worked for both weeklies, then took over the struggling *Wenatchee Daily World* in February 1907 to turn it into a successful and enduring mouthpiece for North Central Washington. Woods, shown below later in life, was an influential community leader who championed the building of Grand Coulee Dam and other hydropower and irrigation projects. (Left, WVMCC 007-18-4, donated by Phyllis Gill; below, 83-84-40, donated by John A. Brown.)

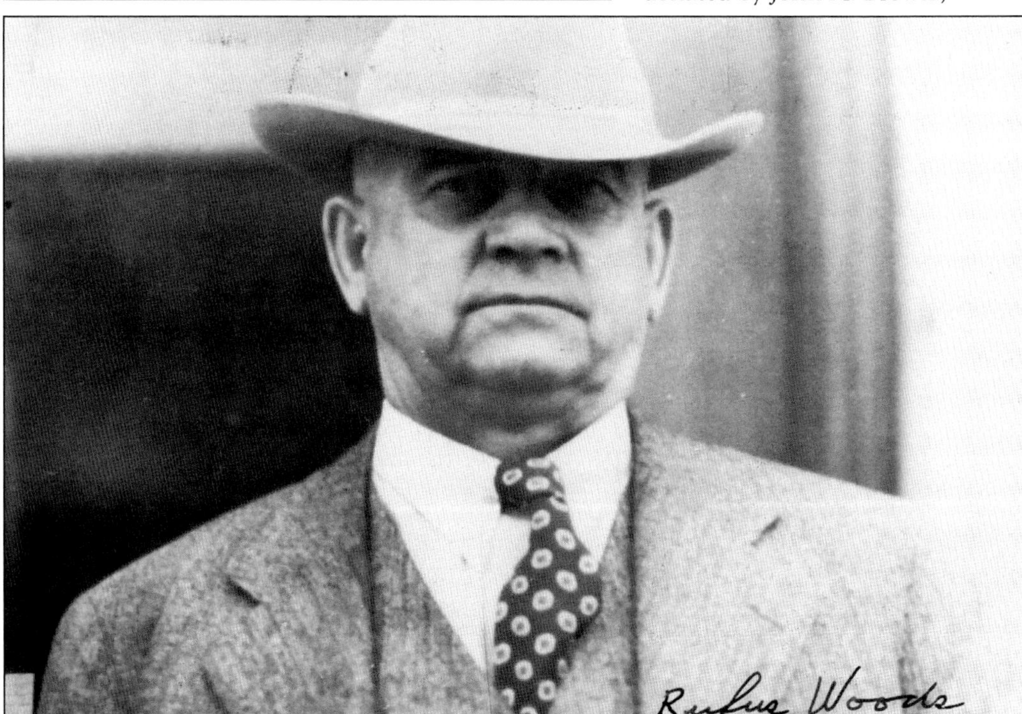

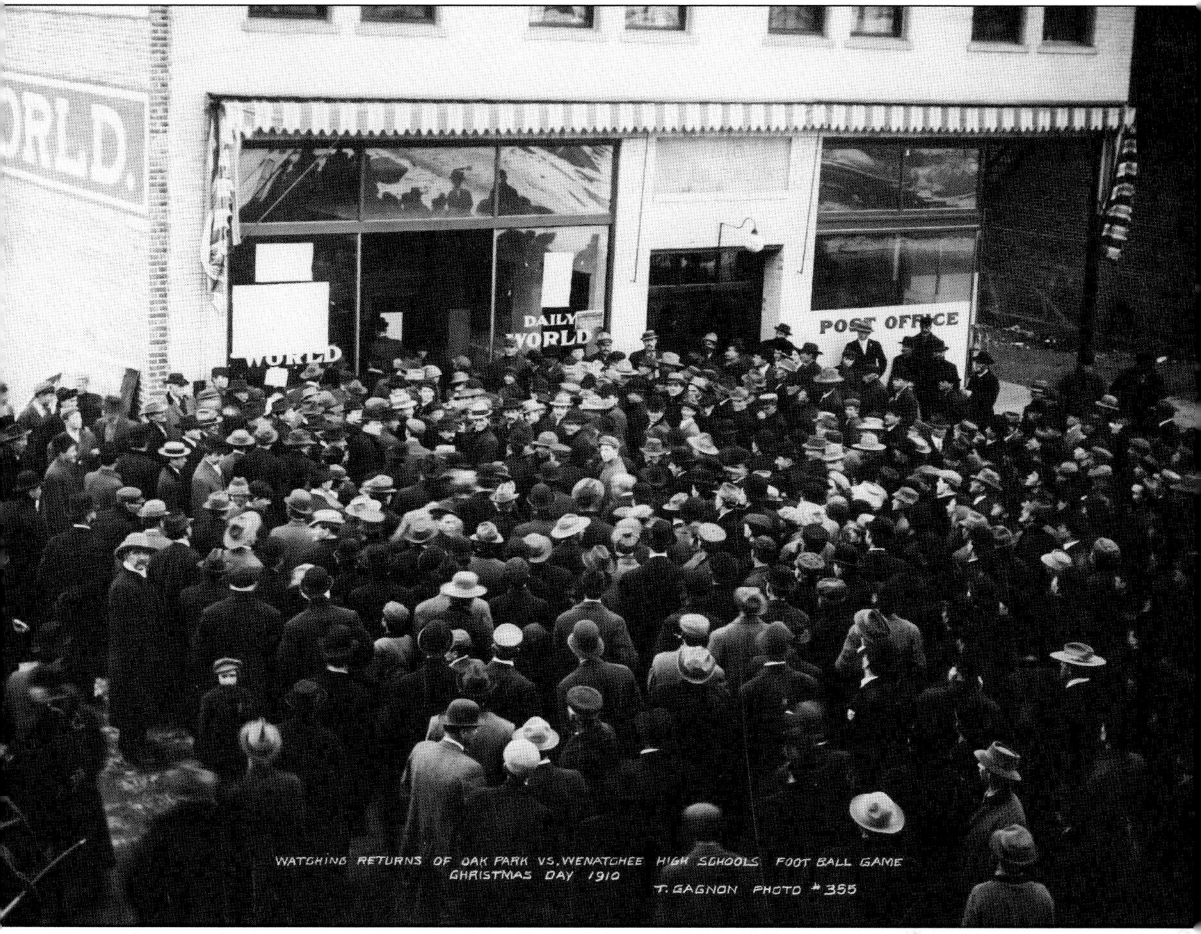

Wenatchee residents converge outside the office of the World Publishing Company on December 25, 1910, to learn the teletyped results of the state championship football game between Oak Park and Wenatchee High School. The *Wenatchee Daily World* (now called the *Wenatchee World*) has been a crucial link to the outside world for residents of North Central Washington for more than a century. After Rufus Woods's death in 1950, the publishing firm was headed by his son Wilfred, who, in 1997, turned over the reins to his son Rufus G. Woods. Wenatchee's first radio station, KPQ, made its debut in 1929 and is still going strong. The World Building at 23–27 South Mission Street stands today. (WVMCC 86-24-51, donated by Wenatchee Chamber of Commerce.)

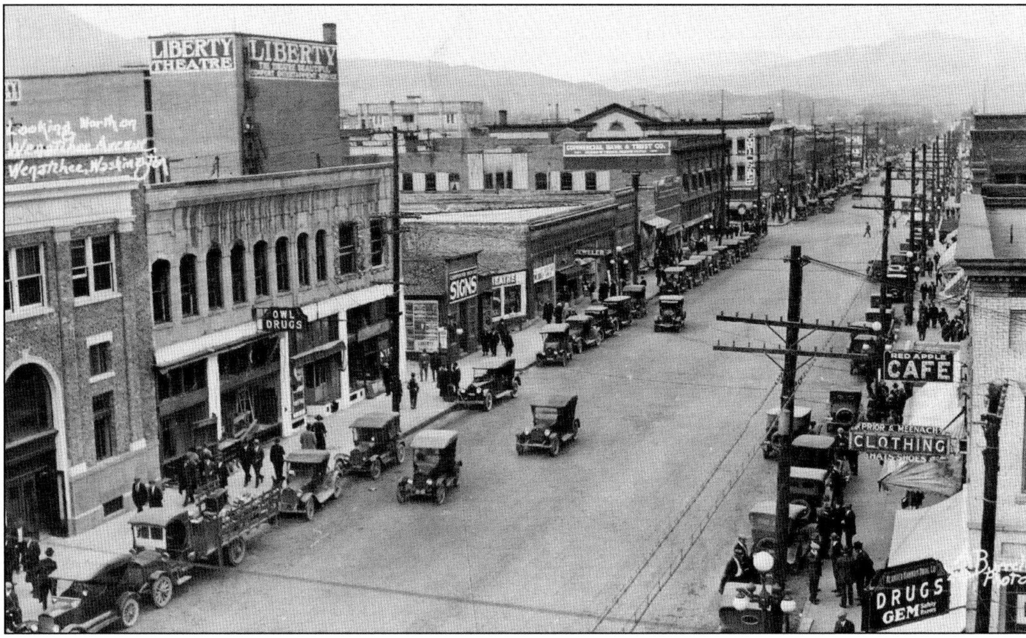

Looking north on Wenatchee Avenue in 1922, one can see part of the First National Bank, Owl Drug, Carpenter Sign Company, a jeweler, and Commercial Bank & Trust. On the next block at the corner of Wenatchee Avenue and Palouse Street is the Olympia Hotel, built in 1908. Businesses on the east side of Wenatchee Avenue (to right) included the Prior and Meenach Clothing Company, Red Apple Café, and Polison's Café. (WVMCC 86-24-286, donated by Wenatchee Chamber of Commerce.)

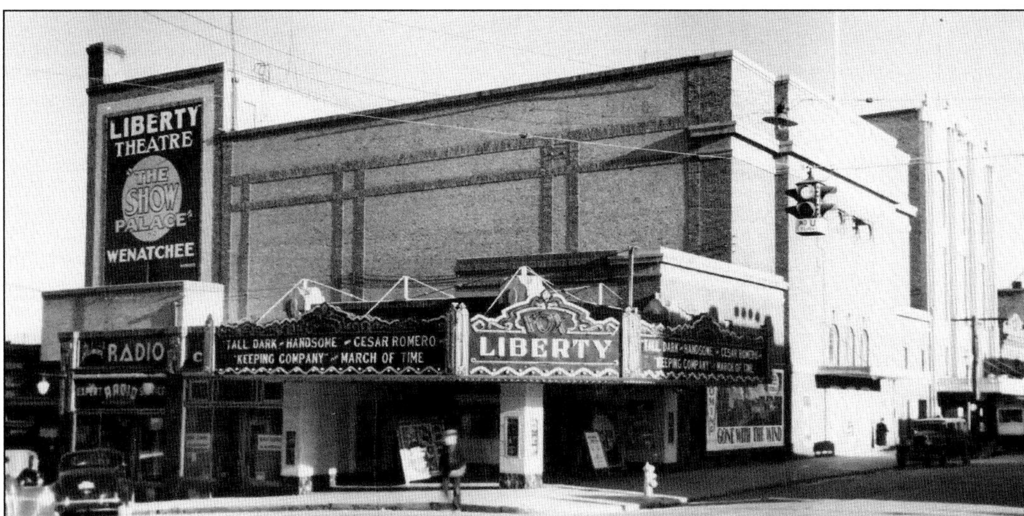

The marquee of the Liberty Theatre on the corner of Palouse and Mission Streets proudly advertises three 1941 features. The Liberty opened in 1919 and quickly outpaced Wenatchee's other theaters by its size and its beautiful new Wurlitzer pipe organ, which accompanied silent films and entertained during intermission. The Liberty is still in business, but its lavish corner entrance has been replaced by a simpler door on Mission Street. (WVMCC 97-48-322, donated by Wenatchee Public Works.)

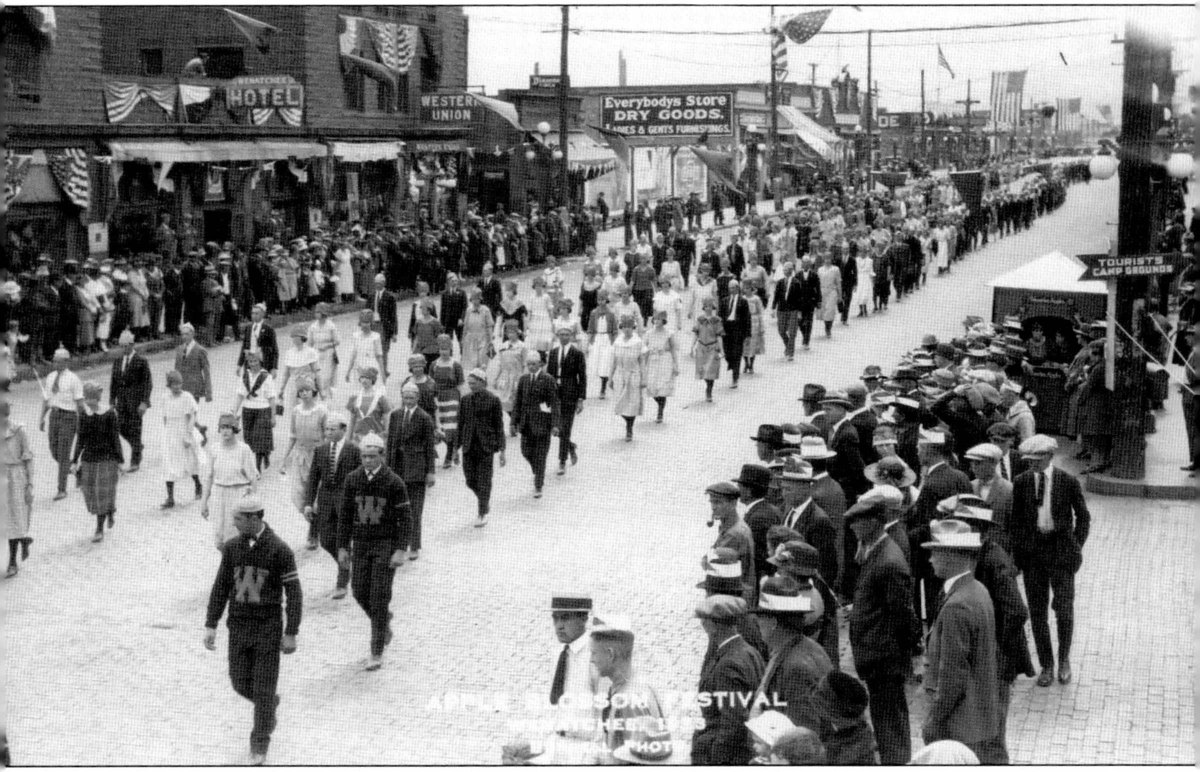

Hat-wearing students from Wenatchee High School march down Wenatchee Avenue in front of a large crowd during the 1923 Apple Blossom Festival parade. Looking south, the Wenatchee Hotel is a prominent landmark along with the Western Union office, Everybody's Store, and Wells & Wade Hardware (the DE is visible on the wall). At right, two young women sell winesap apples from a booth at the corner of Orondo and Wenatchee Avenues. A Saturday parade has been the highlight of the Washington State Apple Blossom Festival since 1921, the second year Wenatchee hosted a festival paying homage to the beauty of orchards in bloom. (WVMCC 74-48-3, donated by Lillian Lux Bellas.)

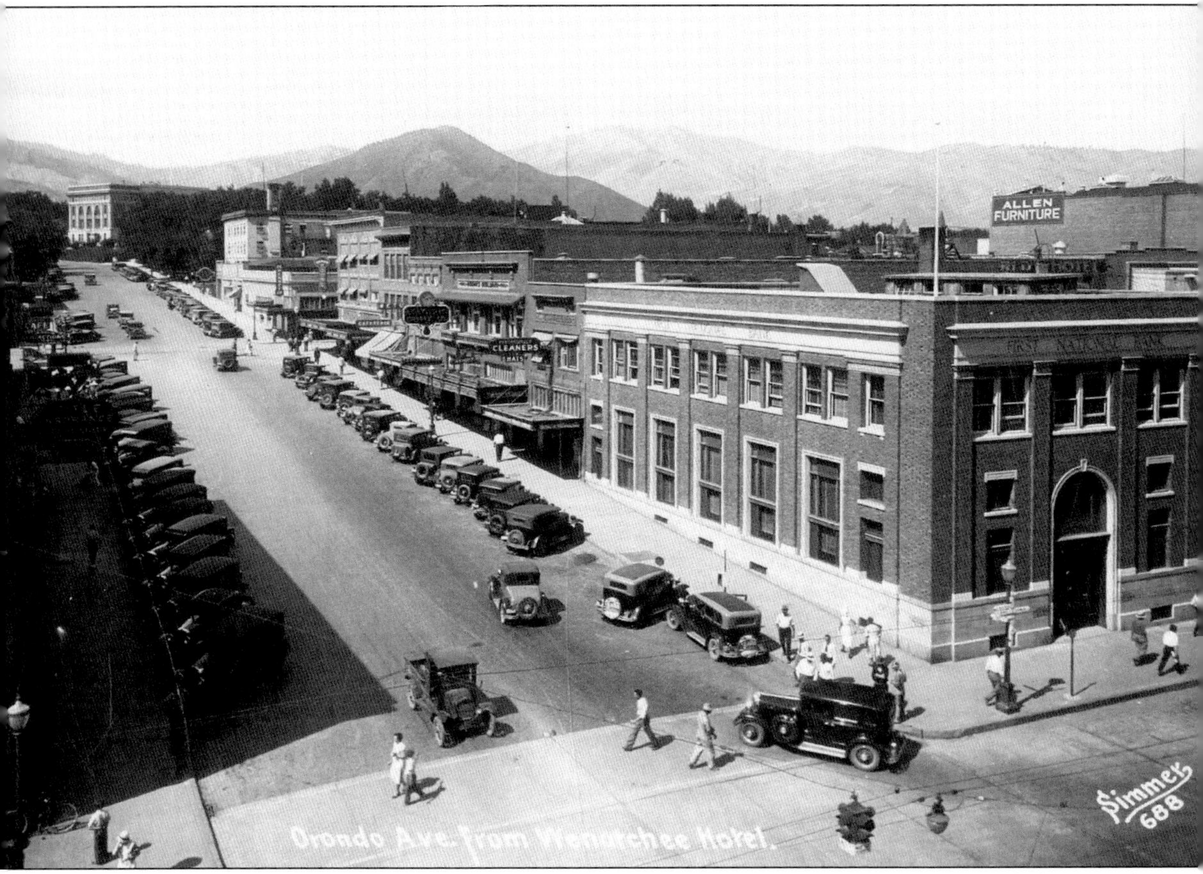

Looking up Orondo Avenue from its intersection with Wenatchee Avenue, this undated photograph shows the First National Bank, Nancekivell's Cleaners, Philips Building, Electric Supply Company, Women's Christian Temperance Union (W.C.T.U.), Harlin Hotel, J.C. Penney, Elks Building, and the Chelan County Courthouse. Across the street but not visible in the photograph is the Garland Building, a three-story apartment building with the Orondo Billiard Hall on the ground floor. Later known as the Orondo Recreation Club, this café was a popular hangout for members of the Wenatchee Chiefs minor-league baseball team. Many of them lived in the Garland Apartments; team photographs and baseball gloves are currently displayed on the walls of what is now called McGlinn's Public House. (WVMCC 86-24-444, donated by Wenatchee Chamber of Commerce.)

The Cascadian Hotel, built in 1929, is still Wenatchee's tallest building. Chambermaid Elsie Parrish worked there from 1933 to 1935; upon quitting, she presented the hotel with a bill for $216.19, the difference between what she had been and should have been paid according to Washington State's controversial minimum-wage law of $14.50 per week for men and women. The hotel refused, and Parrish sued. Wenatchee attorney C.B. Conner lost the case in the county superior court but won in an appeal to the state supreme court. Hotel attorneys took the case to the US Supreme Court, which ruled in Parrish's favor. Her victory on March 29, 1937, led Pres. Franklin D. Roosevelt to request and sign a national minimum-wage law. (Right, WVMCC 75-23-44, donated by Bertha Smith; below, 87-169-1, donated by *Women's World*.)

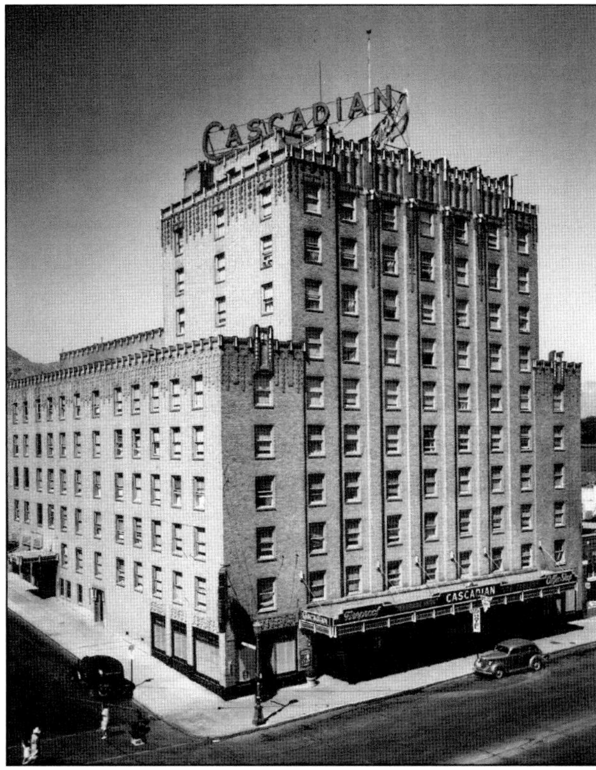

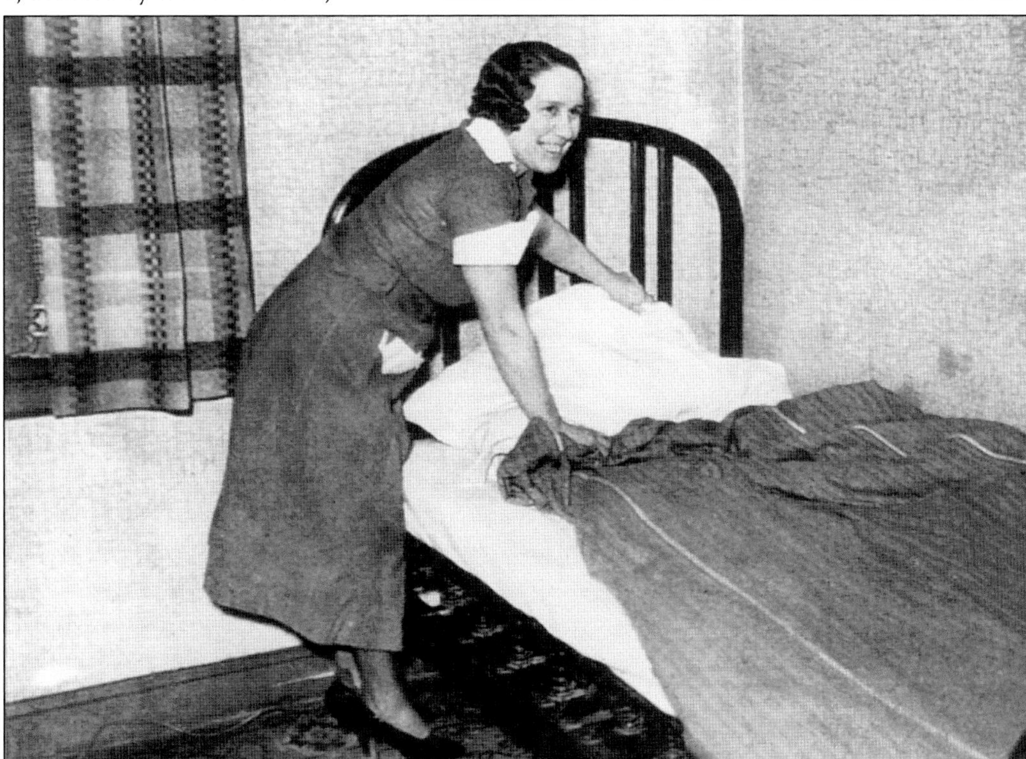

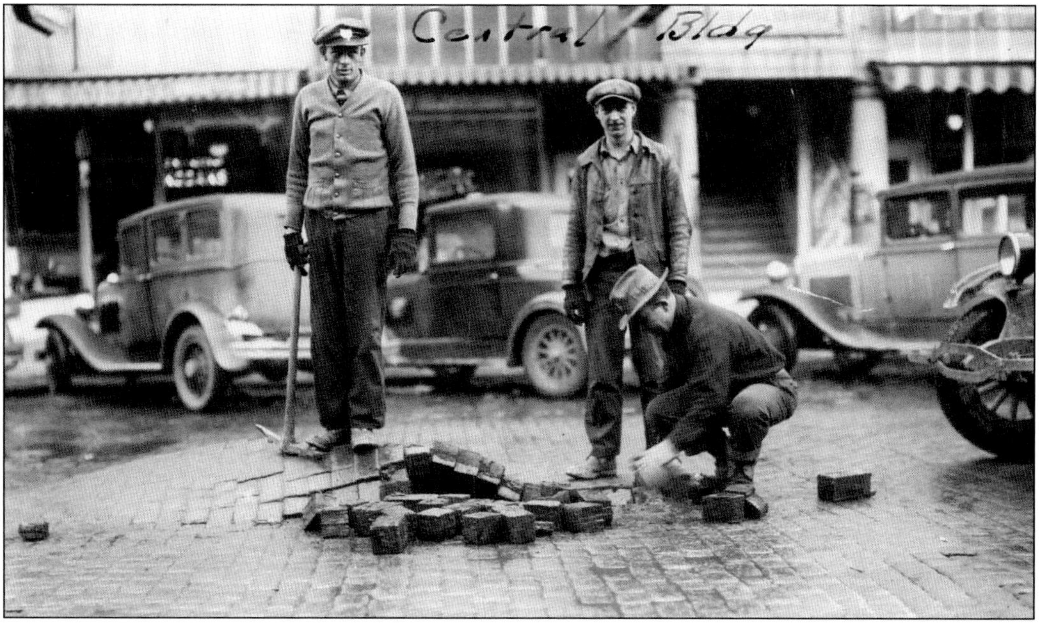

Above, city street department workers remove wooden blocks on Wenatchee Avenue near First Street in 1931. The blocks had been installed on a bed of gravel in 1913 as part of Local Improvement District 103, which called for paving the avenue between Bridge Street and Fifth Street. The blocks were a nuisance, expanding and contracting with changes in temperature and moisture to cause a safety hazard when blocks became dislodged. Quoted in the *Wenatchee Daily World* in December 1929, Conrad Rose declared, "The wood paving . . . is a disgrace. It is unsanitary, impossible to clean, and during the winter and wet seasons it is dangerous and expensive to keep in shape." Below, workers remove wooden blocks in the intersection of Orondo and Wenatchee Avenues, prior to a concrete surface being applied to "The Ave." (Both, WVMCC 82-105-24 and 82-105-4, donated by Norman Delabarre.)

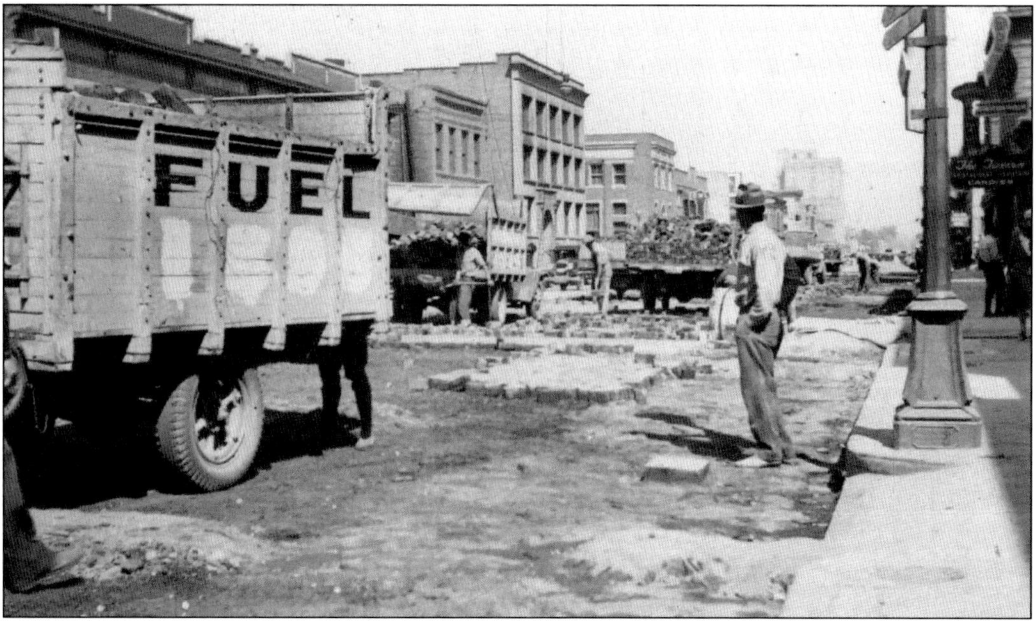

Six

Memorial Park

At the western edge of Wenatchee's commercial district is Memorial Park. The park occupies an irregular block bounded by Chelan Avenue, Orondo Avenue, Washington Street, King Street, and Palouse Street. Part of the land was set aside as Wenatchee's first public park when the city was incorporated and platted in 1892. Additional lots were purchased in 1922 and 1929 to expand the park to just under four acres.

With its lovely shade trees, the park was a popular place for families to gather on summer days and evenings. Residents of outlying areas who came to Wenatchee to shop would often eat their picnic lunches in the park. Wenatchee's town band played concerts on the grass and, after it was built in 1904, on the centrally located bandstand. Fourth of July ceremonies and Apple Blossom Festival activities drew community members together at the city park, as well.

Philanthropist Andrew Carnegie built one of his libraries on the eastern edge of the park, on Chelan Avenue. The park was known as Carnegie Park until June 1919, when its name was changed to Memorial Park in honor of US war heroes. It contains the following military memorials: a large monument dedicated to the Daniel McCook Post No. 25 and the Grand Army of the Republic 1861–1865 by Sons and Daughters of Union Veterans; a concrete bench also honoring the memory of Union veterans; and another monument dedicated to those who honorably served in World Wars I and II, Korea, Vietnam, and other conflicts.

The focal point of Memorial Park today is the stately Chelan County Courthouse, completed in 1924. In front of it are a rose garden and a rock monument dedicated to Judge Thomas Burke, a Seattle financier who contributed to Wenatchee's early development.

By 1939, the library outgrew its quarters. The Carnegie Building became the home of the brand-new North Central Washington Museum. With its displays of fossils and minerals, Native American artifacts, and pioneer memorabilia, the museum brought a new cultural dimension to Wenatchee. The museum moved to its current location in 1976. The Carnegie Building now holds the offices of the Apple Blossom Festival Association. The present public library opened in 1959 adjacent to Memorial Park.

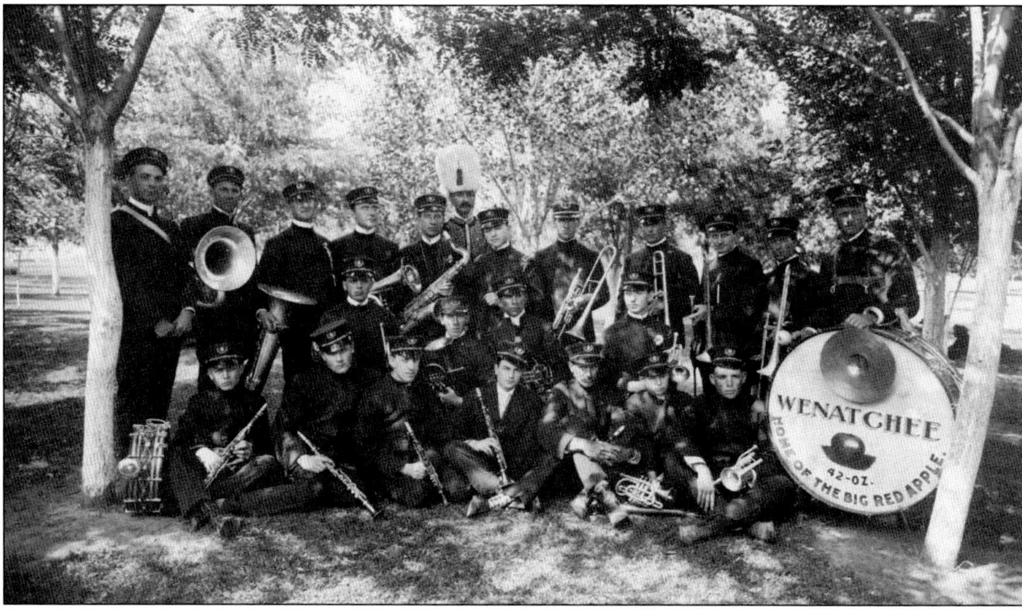

Wenatchee's town band started in 1897 as a 14-man brass band that played at local fairs, dances, steamboat excursions, and Independence Day celebrations. In 1905, it became known as the Wenatchee Military Band. By 1907, the band had added several members and wore smart-looking uniforms and hats. Above, members pose among trees in Memorial Park. Below, in front of the park's bandstand on July 4, 1907, are, from left to right, (first row) Charles Morse, Harvey Mills, Glenn Beal, Charles Dunning, Wellington Deitch, Otto Koehler, Leslie Wenner, and Fred Crollard; (second row) Dave Gellatly Sr., unidentified, and Bob Palmquist; (third row) Otto Anderson, Charles Buttles, Ormond Stocker, Gorham Humphreys, Frank Culp, drum major George Hauber, band director Louis Crollard, Paul Wenner, Frank Reeves, "Doc" Guthrie, Arthur Bousquet, and Pat Sherburne. Ed Ferguson is not pictured. (Both, WVMCC 78-218-48 and 78-218-49, donated by Mary Anderson.)

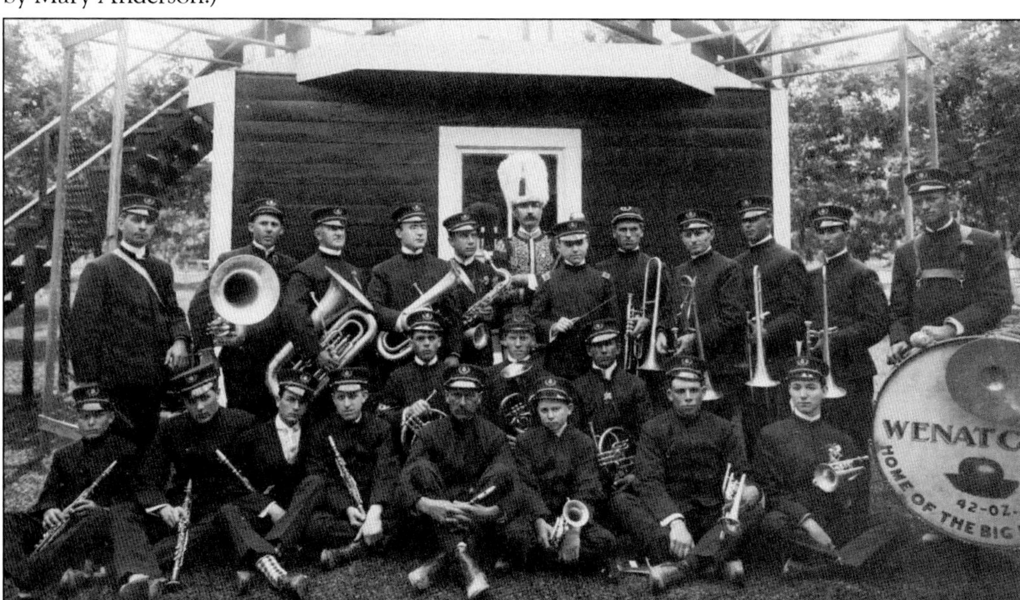

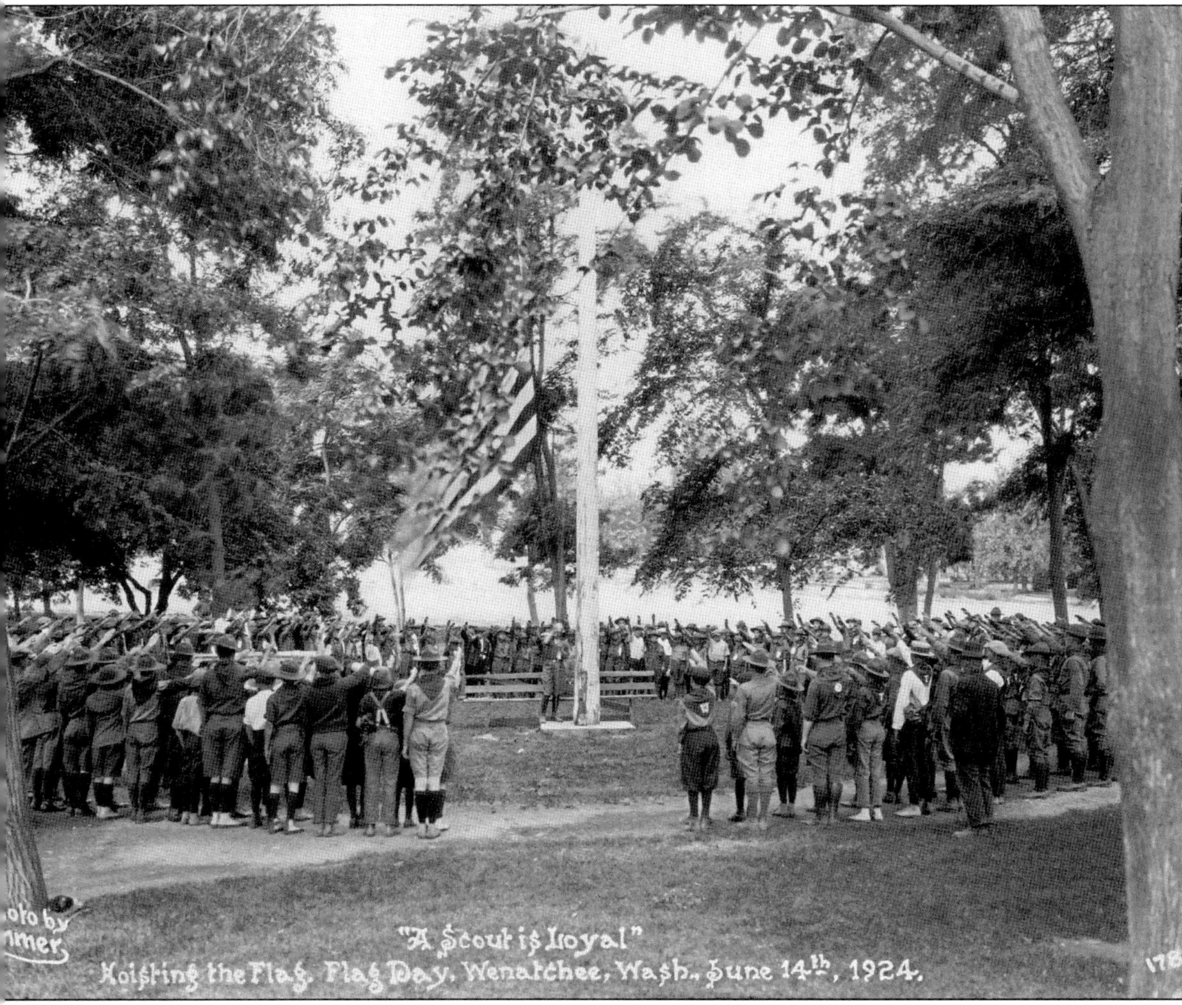

More than 350 Boy Scouts from throughout North Central Washington gathered in Wenatchee's Memorial Park on June 14, 1924, to celebrate Flag Day. They are shown here saluting Old Glory during a flag-raising ceremony that was one of many events held during the two-day rally. The Wenatchee Elks Club helped plan the program, the Elks Band provided musical entertainment, and wives of Elks Club members served dinner to the Scouts. Other events included a Flag Day parade, an oratorical contest, a street dance, and Scouting contests in bugling, archery, wall scaling, and water boiling. An inscription by photographer Al Simmer at the bottom of the photograph says, "A Scout is Loyal." Wenatchee's Boy Scout organization was formally incorporated on March 7, 1911. (WVMCC 86-24-2, donated by Wenatchee Chamber of Commerce.)

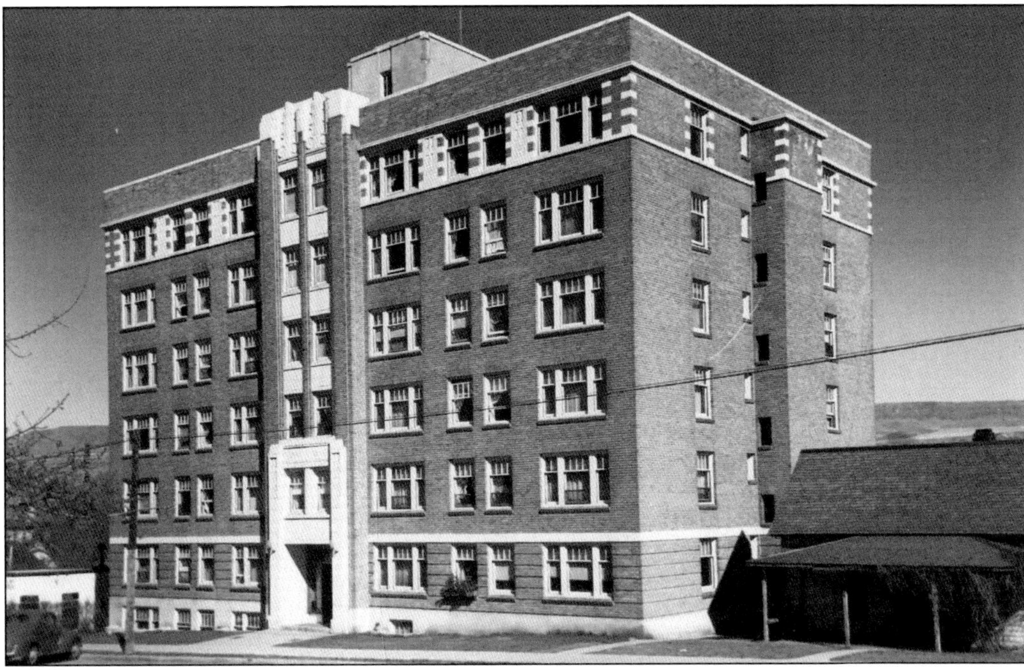

The Burke-Hill apartment building at 119 Okanogan Street, a block south of Memorial Park, was constructed in 1930. The six-story, 55-unit building illustrates the Beaux Arts form with Tropical Art Deco ornamentation. It was named after two men influential in Wenatchee's promotion and growth, Great Northern Railway's James J. Hill and developer Thomas Burke. The building was designed for bachelor apartments rather than family-living areas. (WVMCC 97-48-325, donated by Wenatchee Public Works.)

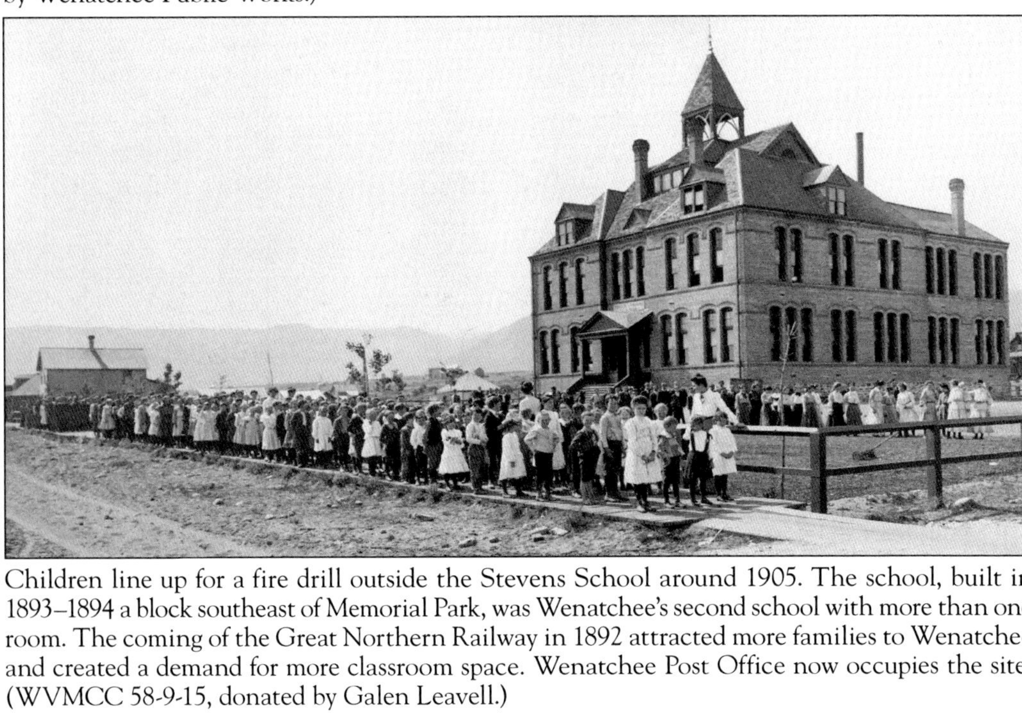

Children line up for a fire drill outside the Stevens School around 1905. The school, built in 1893–1894 a block southeast of Memorial Park, was Wenatchee's second school with more than one room. The coming of the Great Northern Railway in 1892 attracted more families to Wenatchee and created a demand for more classroom space. Wenatchee Post Office now occupies the site. (WVMCC 58-9-15, donated by Galen Leavell.)

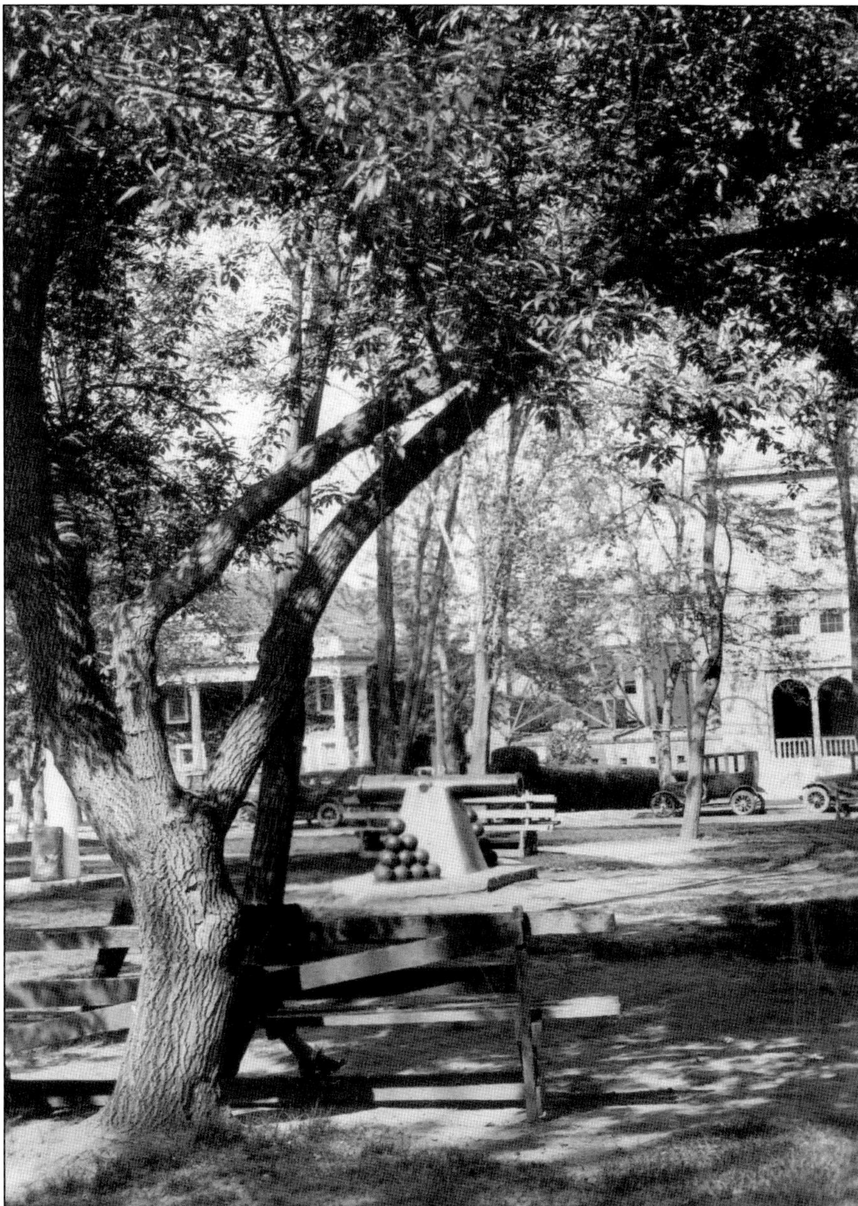

This field howitzer was made in 1855 by Cyrus Alger and Company of Boston. Thought to have been used during the Civil War, it was part of the federal inventory until the early 1900s. Washington State's US senator Wesley Jones and others arranged for the cannon to be donated to Wenatchee's Grand Army of the Republic post in 1914. Formal dedication ceremonies were held on September 11, 1915, in what later became known as Memorial Park, with more than 200 in attendance. The cannon originally was mounted on a wheeled carriage; this proved too tempting for mischief-makers, so it was remounted on a concrete pad flanked with two pyramids of cannon balls. These, too, occasionally fell prey to pranksters and were removed. In 1998, the howitzer was moved about 40 feet away, given a new foundation, enhanced with historical plaques, and rededicated. This photograph was taken in 1925; the Conrad Rose home and the Elks Temple can be seen in the background. (WVMCC 88-108-25, donated by Ileen Taylor.)

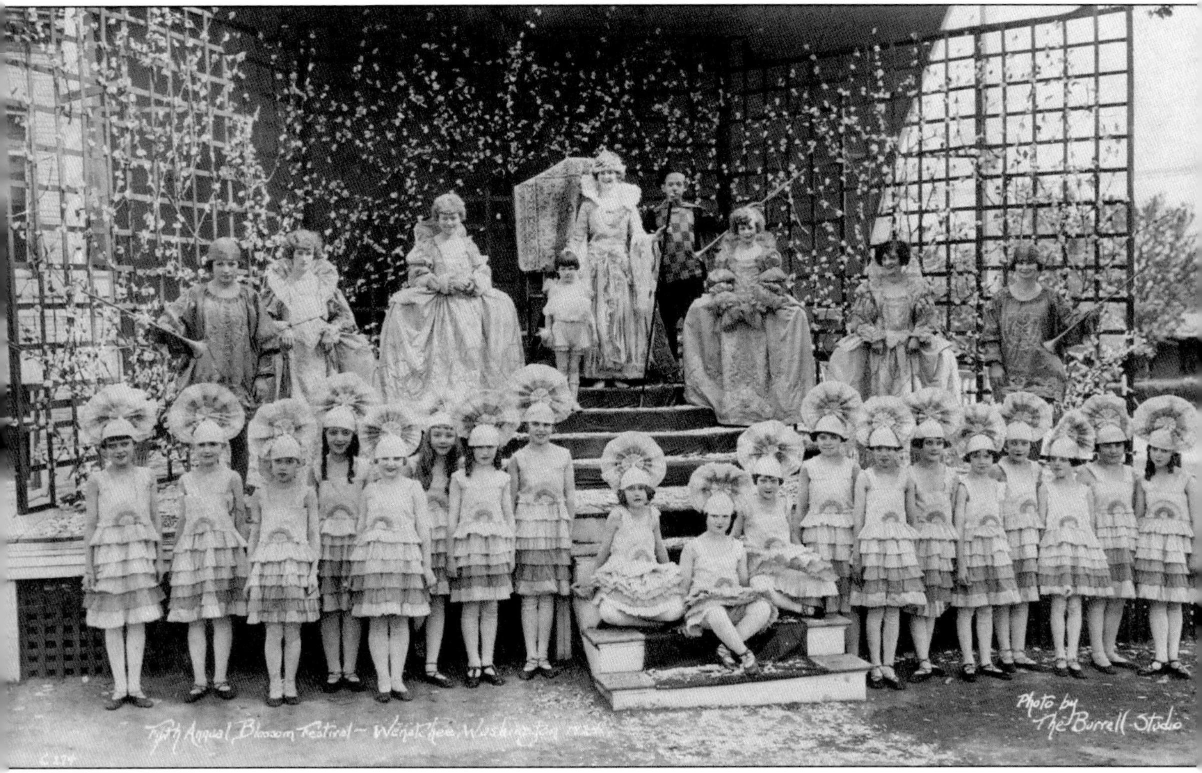

Apple Blossom Queen Rowena Burns (top, center) presides over her royal court in 1924. The temporary stage set up in Memorial Park was likely used for a pageant in addition to the royal crowning. Wenatchee's Apple Blossom Festival is Washington's longest-running major festival. It began as a one-day event in 1920, featuring concerts and a maypole dance in Memorial Park, a baseball game, an auto tour of orchards and scenic overlooks, and a street dance. A parade was added the following year and has been the highlight of the festival ever since. The Apple Blossom Festival now lasts 10 days and draws thousands of people to Wenatchee for the last weekend of April and first weekend of May. (WVMCC 79-18-3.)

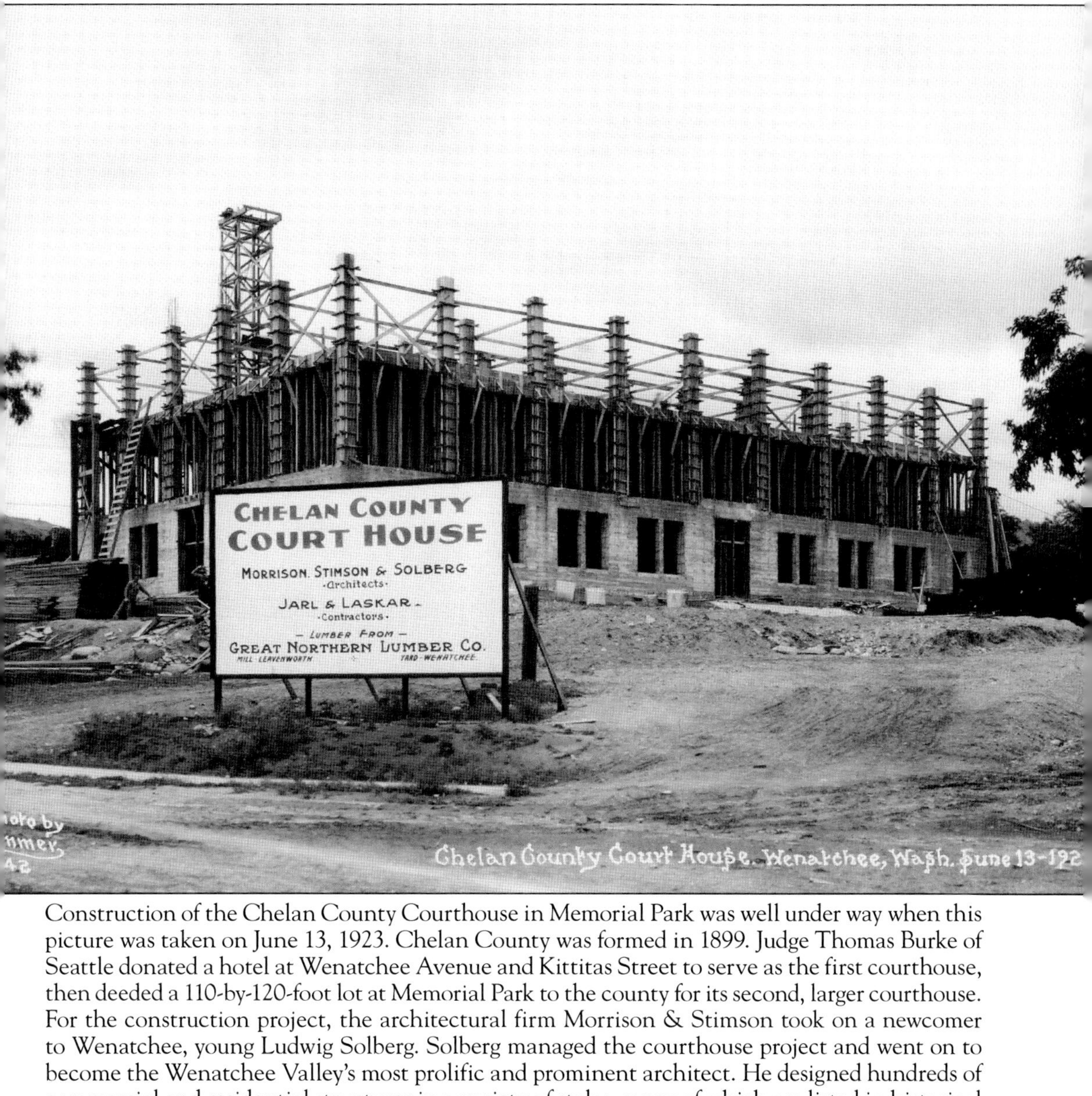

Construction of the Chelan County Courthouse in Memorial Park was well under way when this picture was taken on June 13, 1923. Chelan County was formed in 1899. Judge Thomas Burke of Seattle donated a hotel at Wenatchee Avenue and Kittitas Street to serve as the first courthouse, then deeded a 110-by-120-foot lot at Memorial Park to the county for its second, larger courthouse. For the construction project, the architectural firm Morrison & Stimson took on a newcomer to Wenatchee, young Ludwig Solberg. Solberg managed the courthouse project and went on to become the Wenatchee Valley's most prolific and prominent architect. He designed hundreds of commercial and residential structures in a variety of styles, many of which are listed in historical registers. (WVMCC 98-34-117, donated by Sandy Stoljer.)

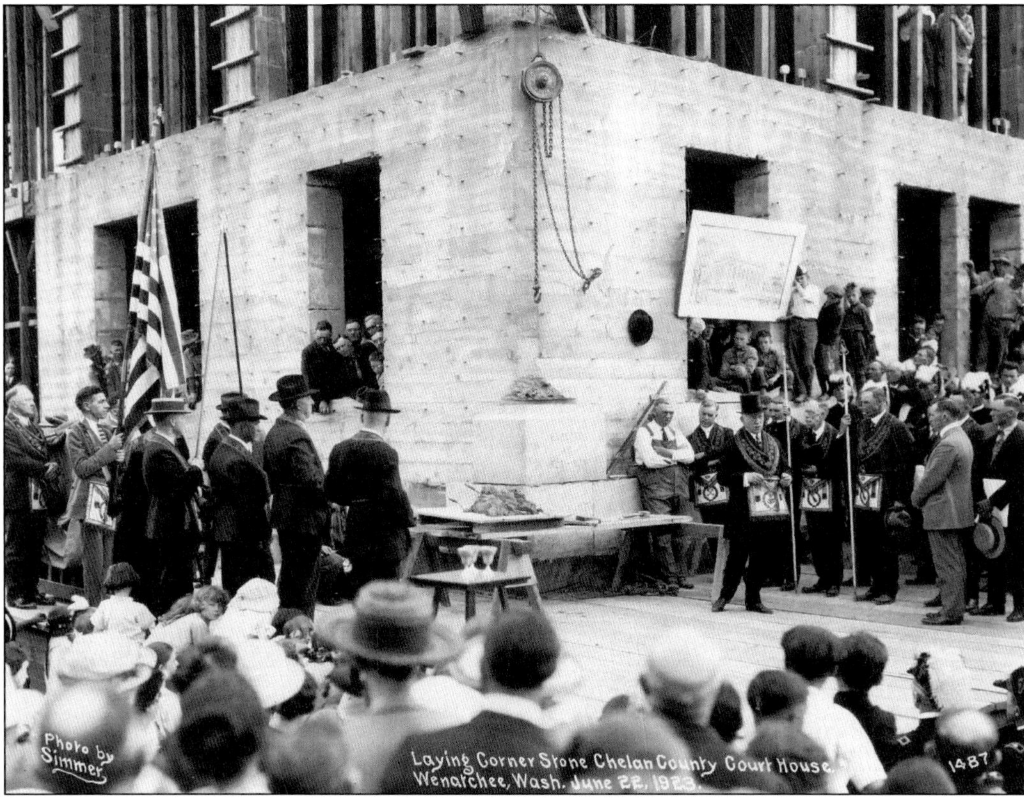

A large crowd gathered in Memorial Park on June 22, 1923, to observe the laying of the cornerstone of the county courthouse. Grand Master James McCormack of the Masonic Grand Lodge of Washington sealed up a box of records that were buried with the ceremonial stone on the southeast corner of the building. Granite blocks were then laid for the lower outside walls, with brick lining the upper two stories. Magnificent marble walls, floors, columns, and stairs grace the interior of the building. It was dedicated during the 1924 Apple Blossom Festival. The adjacent Law and Justice Building, built in 1983, houses courtrooms, offices, the county jail, and a café. Below, a monument to Judge Thomas Burke, who donated the courthouse land and helped finance the Columbia River Bridge, was dedicated in December 1923. (Both, WVMCC 98-34-115 and 98-34-114, donated by Sandy Stoljer.)

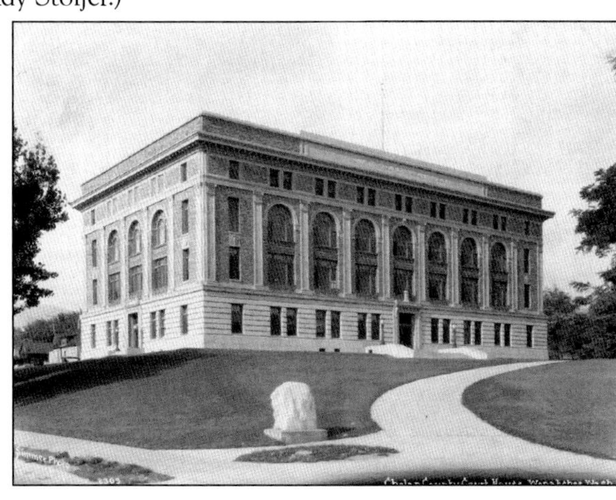

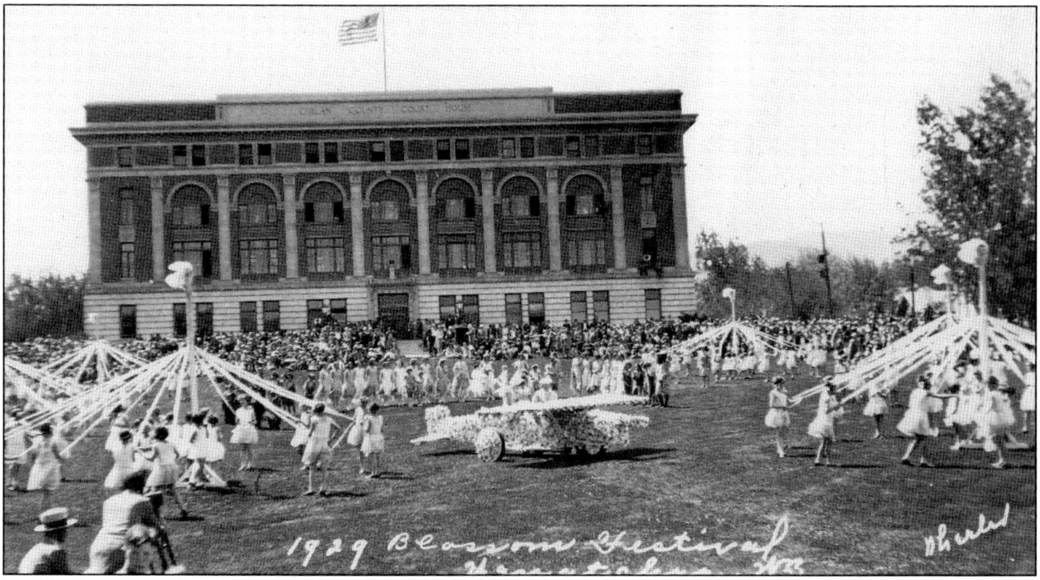

Maypoles spring from the lawn of Memorial Park during the 1929 Apple Blossom Festival. Children, dressed in their finest clothes, encircle the poles in this photograph by John D. Wheeler. A large number of people sit and stand in front of the courthouse, watching the festivities; several photographers may be seen in the lower-left corner of the photograph. In the center is one of the parade entries, a two-wheeled vehicle covered in flower petals to resemble an airplane (below). Rosella Corle was the Apple Blossom queen in 1929. (Both, WVMCC 010-27-114 and 010-27-9, donated by Leavenworth Public Library.)

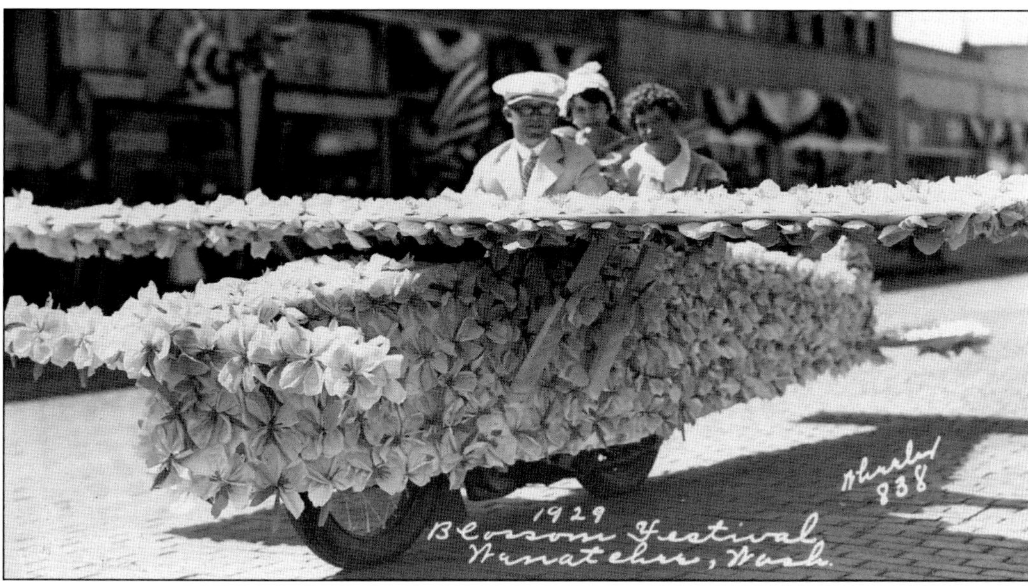

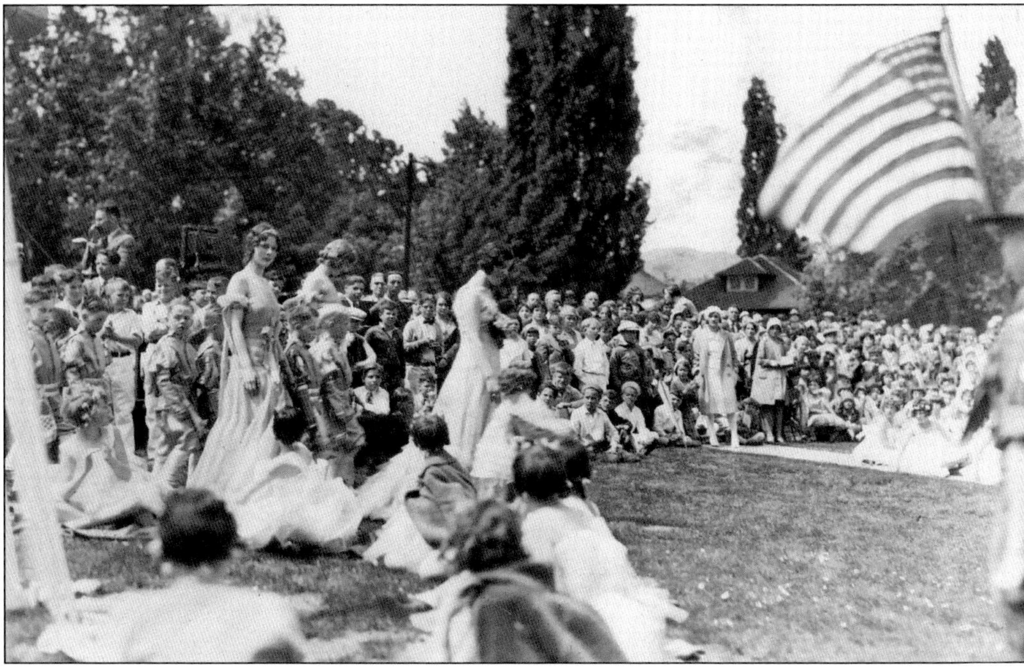

Preparing to be crowned as royalty of the 1930 Apple Blossom Festival, Queen Shirley Foster, Princess Margaret Bird, and Princess Helen Carol proceed up the lawn at Memorial Park to a stage specially built for the coronation and a children's pageant. The festival by this time was a three-day event with two parades, baseball games, band concerts, a carnival, and a Queen's Ball. A special feature in 1930 was "The Fire God," a pyrotechnic spectacle on the courthouse green presented on all three nights by Hitt Fireworks of Seattle and the Fanchon and Marcon musical revue. (Both, WVMCC 010-27-142 and 010-27-145, donated by Leavenworth Public Library.)

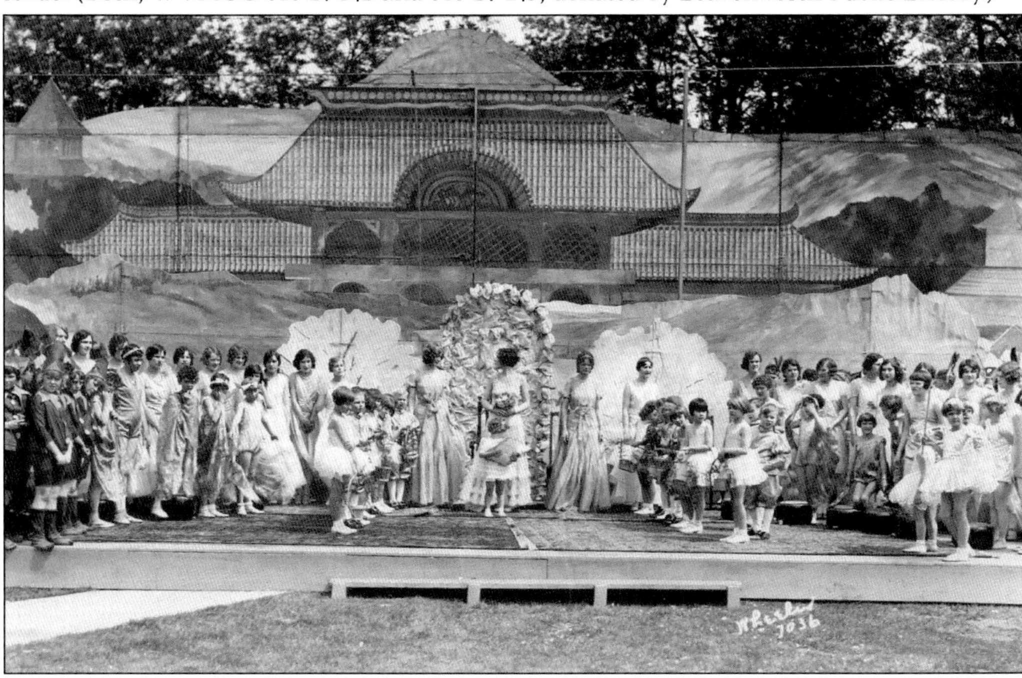

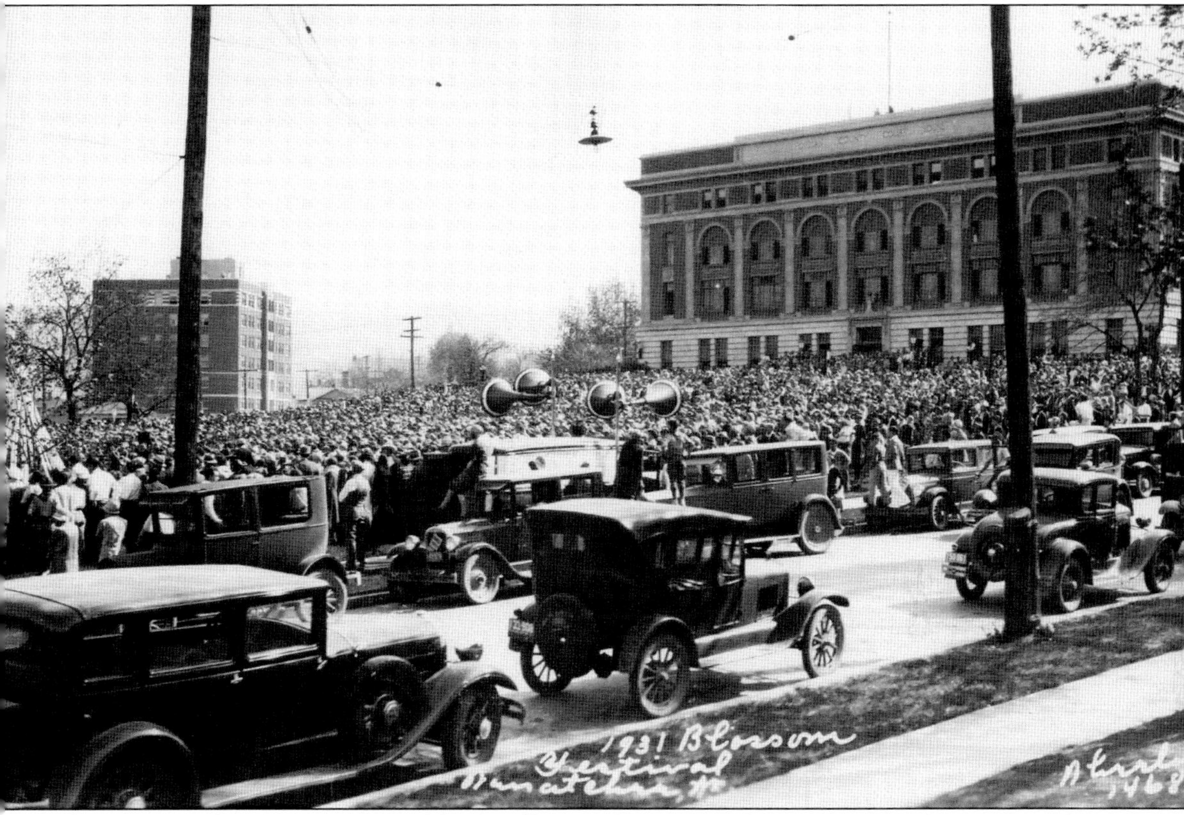

The 1931 Apple Blossom Festival broke all attendance records. An estimated 8,000 people jammed Memorial Park for the crowning of Queen Carol McGough and Princesses Jean Virmilya and Ovidia Lindston. The ceremony was followed by a pageant, titled "Builders of the Valley," presented by 600 children. Both were amplified by a sound system and broadcast throughout the park as well as on KPQ, Wenatchee's first radio station, which had entered the airwaves two years earlier. The grand parade drew record crowds, as well. The *Wenatchee Daily World* stated that 35,000 crowded the streets for a parade that stretched two miles long. Floats, bands, and princesses represented communities from all over the state at the 1931 festival. The springtime celebration has endured for more than 90 years and is the oldest major festival in Washington State. (WVMCC 010-27-400, donated by Leavenworth Public Library.)

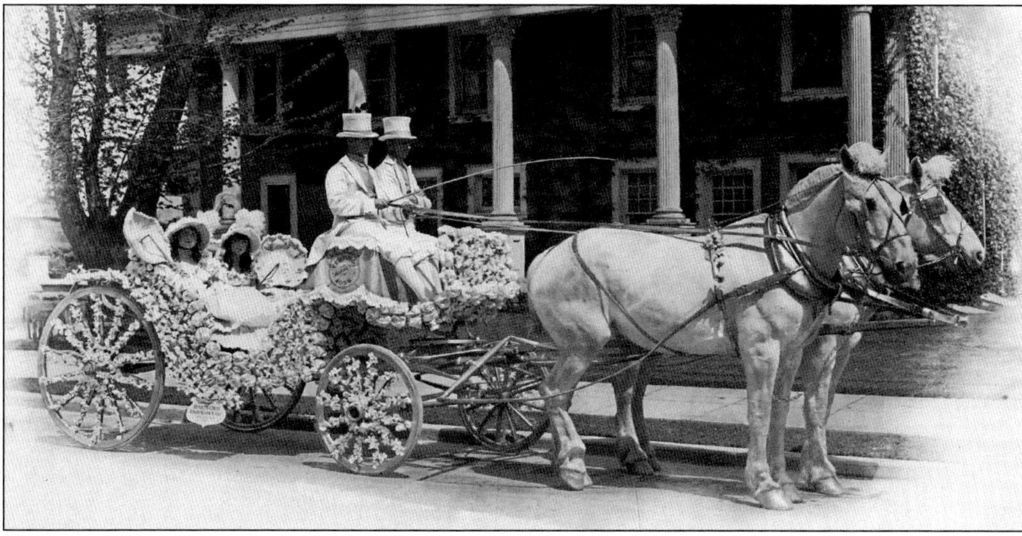

The stately home of Conrad and Elizabeth Rose stood across Chelan Avenue from Memorial Park. Built in 1906, the two-story brick building was designed in the Georgian Revival style with six Corinthian columns in front. The home, one of the finest mansions in Wenatchee, was sold to David Jones, who converted it into the Jones and Jones Funeral Home. In this 1924 photograph, two horses pulling the Ferguson-Ross Agency float in the Apple Blossom Parade stop in front of the home. (WVMCC 74-48-46, donated by Lillian Lux Bellas.)

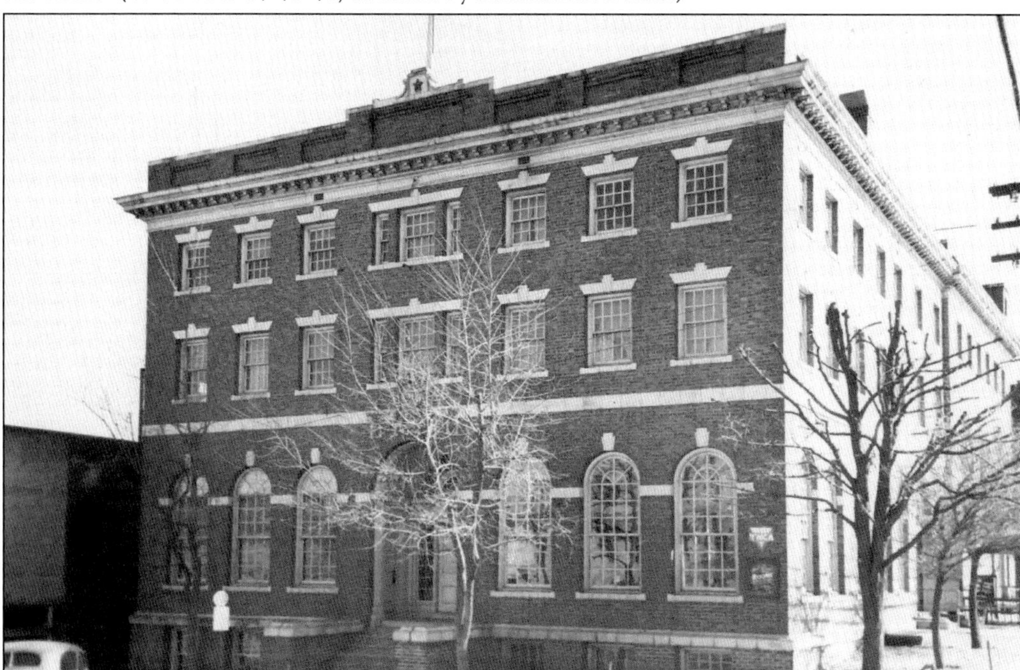

The Wenatchee chapter of the Young Men's Christian Association (YMCA) was founded in 1910, and its three-story building was completed in 1914. The upper two floors held dormitory rooms, furnished by different individuals, organizations, and church groups. A large gym on the ground floor and an indoor swimming pool in the basement made the Y an attractive recreational venue for boys and young men. (WVMCC 97-118-18.)

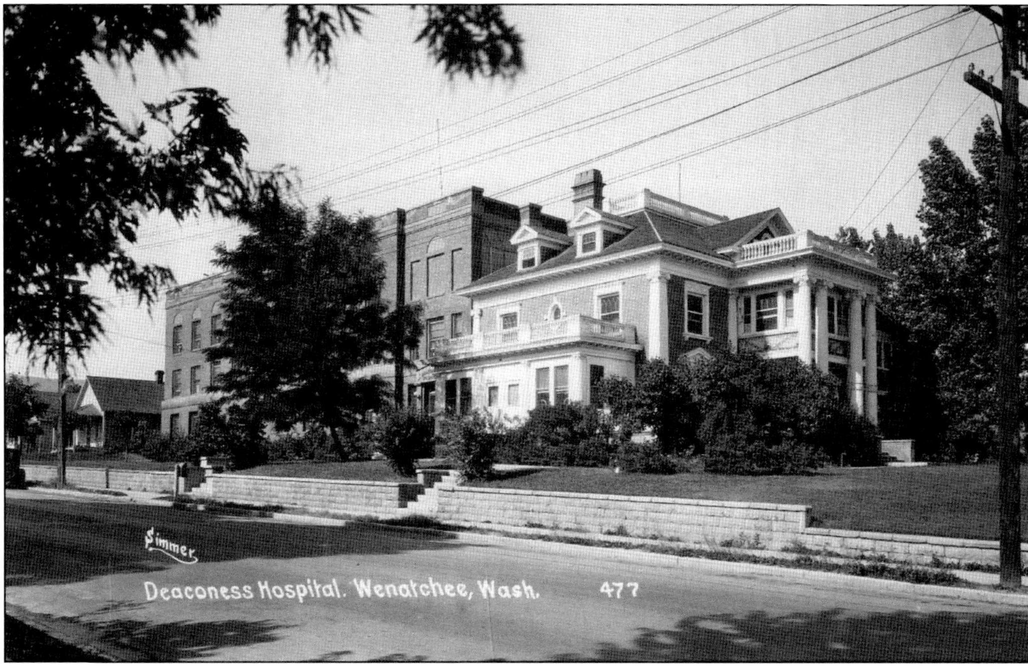

Wenatchee mayor and businessman John Gellatly built a beautiful three-story brick home at 312 Okanogan Street in 1908. It boasted the first hot water–heating plant and the first lawn-sprinkling system in Wenatchee. The Gellatlys donated this building to the Central Washington Deaconess Hospital Association, formed in 1915 by the First Methodist Church and other community members. The home was fitted with 25 beds, two operating rooms, sterilization-scrub rooms, a laboratory, and a laundry. A four-story hospital addition behind the house was completed in 1923, and the Gellatly building (which is no longer standing) was converted to the Deaconess School of Nurses. Wenatchee's two hospitals, Deaconess and St. Anthony's, merged in 1974 to become Central Washington Hospital. Below in 1956, from left to right, Frank Case and Gellatly (1869–1963) were past presidents of the Wenatchee Chamber. (Above, WVMCC 94-65-3, donated by Cathryn Comer; below, 86-24-263, donated by Wenatchee Chamber of Commerce.)

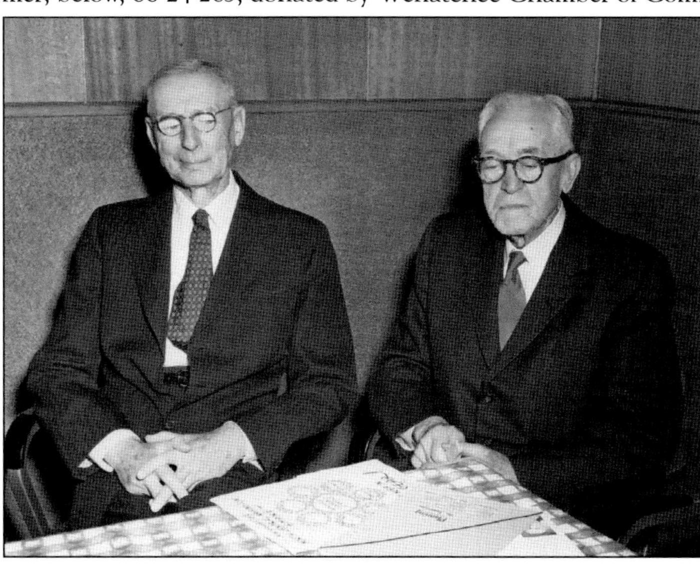

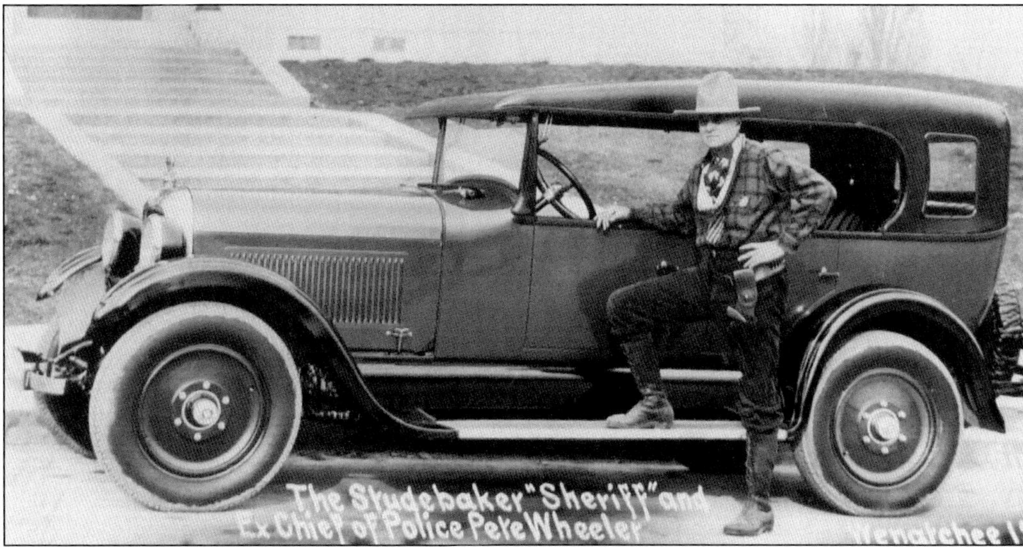

Chelan County sheriff Pete Wheeler, nicknamed "the Studebaker Sheriff," poses by the county courthouse in the mid-1920s. Wheeler, son of an 1885 homesteader, had served as a Wenatchee marshal in the early 1900s. He was elected sheriff in 1926 in the midst of Prohibition. Moonshining and bootlegging were prevalent in the county, as were arrests for liquor-related offences. Wheeler was credited with breaking up 50 distillery operations and bringing in thousands of dollars in fines from liquor violations. (WVMCC 83-84-152, donated by John A. Brown.)

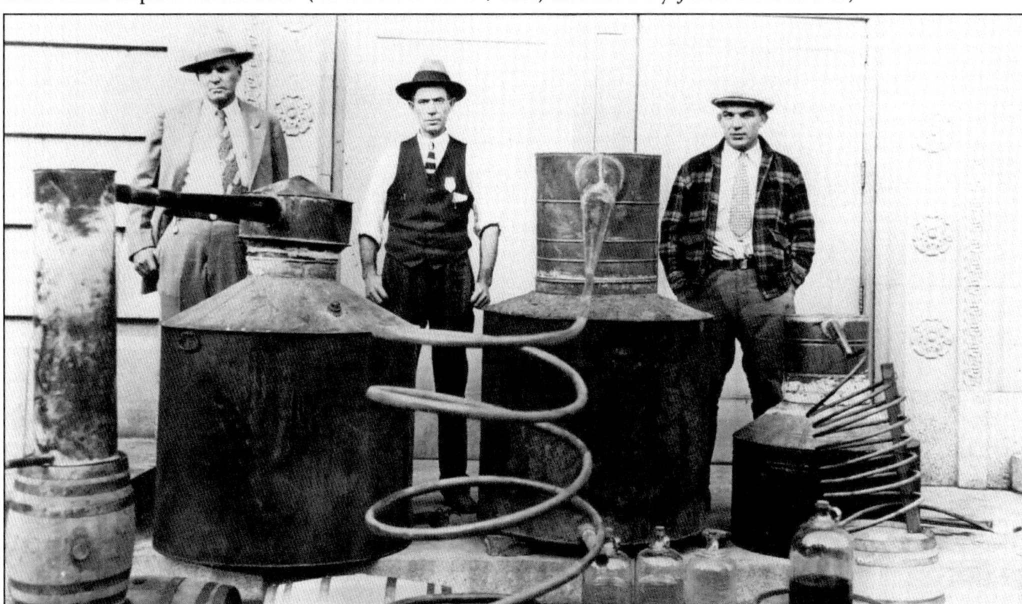

From left to right, Sheriff Pete Wheeler and deputies Noland Bagwell and Ralph Hand pose by the Washington Street entrance to the courthouse with a 60-gallon still confiscated from a moonshining operation several miles up the Blewett Pass Highway around 1927. Wheeler was later suspected of accepting protection money from bootleggers and even manufacturing and distributing whisky himself. He faced 31 liquor-related charges in federal court, but a deadlocked jury in 1931 caused the judge to dismiss charges. (WVMCC 83-84-151, donated by John A. Brown.)

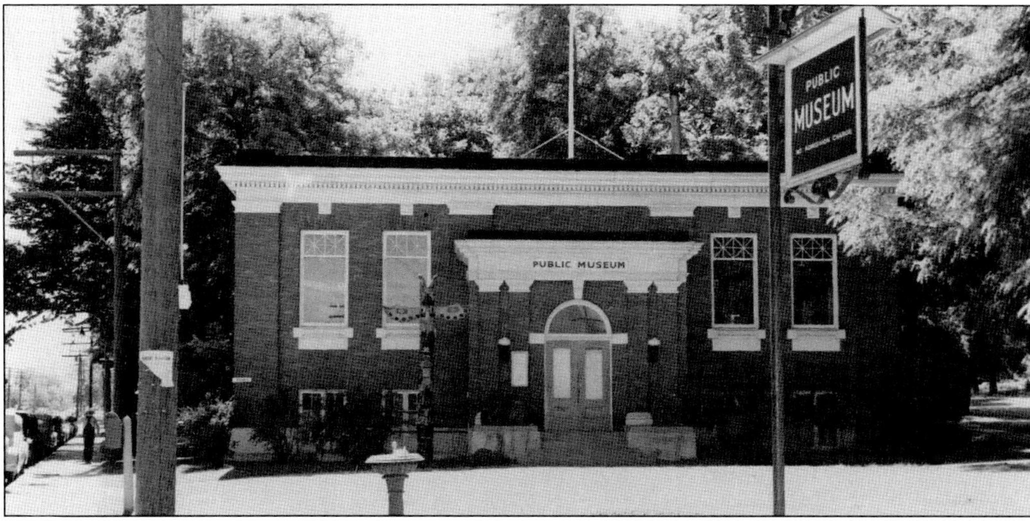

Scottish American businessman and philanthropist Andrew Carnegie donated money for the construction of more than 1,600 libraries in the United States from the 1880s through the 1920s. Wenatchee was one of the communities selected to receive such a library. Carnegie's office approved Wenatchee's plans and specifications in 1910 and donated $10,000 for the library's construction on Chelan Avenue at Memorial Park. In 1939, members of the Columbia River Archaeological Society (founded in 1920) and other community leaders established the North Central Washington Museum in the Carnegie Building. A.V. Shepard was the first curator. A totem pole carved by British Columbian Indians was presented to the museum in 1947 and stood by the front door. Below, newspaper publisher Rufus Woods (third from left) stands with friends inside the museum in 1940. (Above, WVMCC 86-24-859, donated by Wenatchee Chamber of Commerce; below, 82-46-1, donated by Bernice Gellatly Greene.)

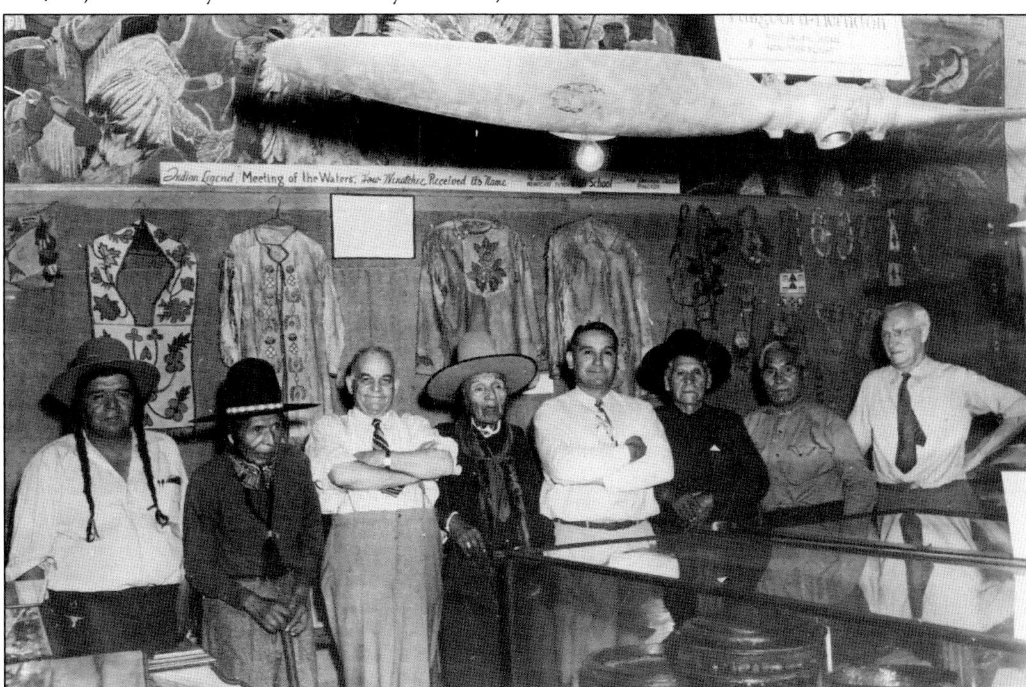

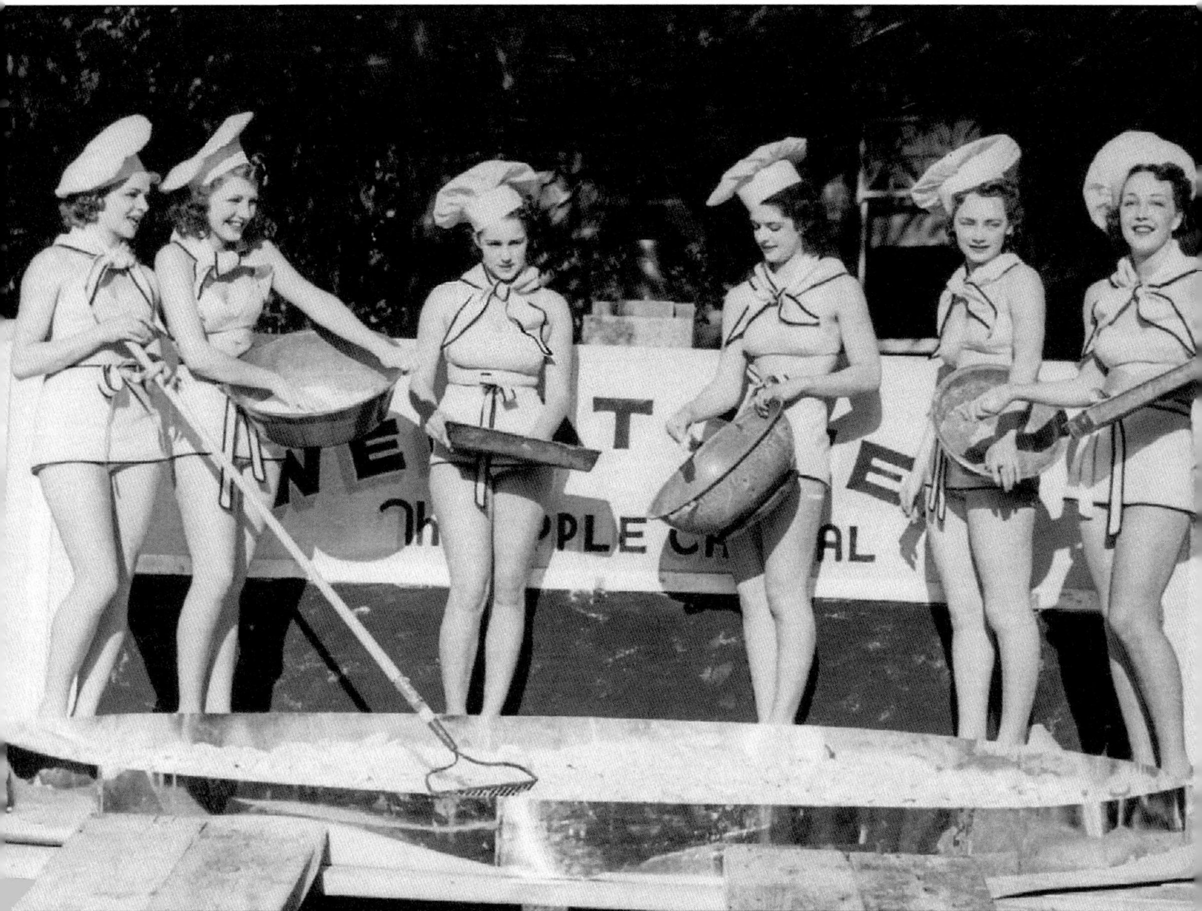

The Wenatchee Chamber of Commerce staged a publicity stunt for National Apple Week in October 1938 to advertise Wenatchee and its apples to the world. Don Kenaston was chairman of the planning committee. Volunteers built an oven and baked a one-ton apple pie in Memorial Park, using two tractors to haul the pie in and out of the oven. The pie used 85 boxes of apples (3,400 pounds raw) and measured 10 feet in diameter. Two thousand people got to eat the pie, an estimated one-pound slice per person. From left to right, Irma Gutzwiler Russell, Mildred Brownlow Nicholson, Orabelle Graham, Virginia McWhirter Dodson, Helen Boddy Shafer, and Lois Christenson pose by the pie. A sign proclaiming Wenatchee as the Apple Capital is visible behind them. Three newsreel cameramen recorded the event for national viewing in movie theaters. (WVMCC 976-18.)

Seven

TRIANGLE PARK

A county fair was held in Wenatchee in September 1901 on vacant land west of the city limits along Miller Street and Orondo Avenue. In 1909, four Wenatchee businessmen purchased about seven acres of this property and converted it to a park, building a fenced grandstand for baseball games and planting trees and lawn. The park provided ample room for fairs, circuses, baseball games, and picnics. Ten years later, voters approved purchase of the land, creating the city's Recreation Park. The rest of the land, which came to be known as Triangle Park, was also used for informal ball games.

The American Legion youth baseball league started using Recreation Park in 1929. The Wenatchee Chiefs, a professional minor-league team that was part of the Western International League, played there from 1937 to 1965. Their home games were among Wenatchee's most popular entertainment, as were occasional exhibition games played by major-league traveling teams that brought up-and-coming stars to town, including Satchel Paige, Bob Feller, and Grover Cleveland Alexander.

The city opened a "tourist camp" southeast of Recreation Park in 1922. With better roads being built and automobile use increasing, Wenatchee citizens felt it prudent to encourage motorists to drive to Wenatchee and camp in comfort. Pioneer Middle School and the city pool now occupy this site, along Yakima Street.

Wenatchee's first organized hockey league began playing in January 1931 on a boardless rink formed by flooding Recreation Park. Five to eight local teams played games until 1935, when the league folded; warm weather often interfered with ice quality. Competitive youth hockey began again in the mid-1960s, when the city turned the old Hughes Memorial Swimming Pool at the foot of Fifth Street into a refrigerated outdoor rink.

Triangle Park was formally acquired by the city in 1934. Parts of Recreation and Triangle parks were sold to the Wenatchee School District in 1956 for construction of Pioneer Middle School. This included the Apple Bowl, where Wenatchee High School football games are now played. The remainder of the two parks was traded to the school district in 1991.

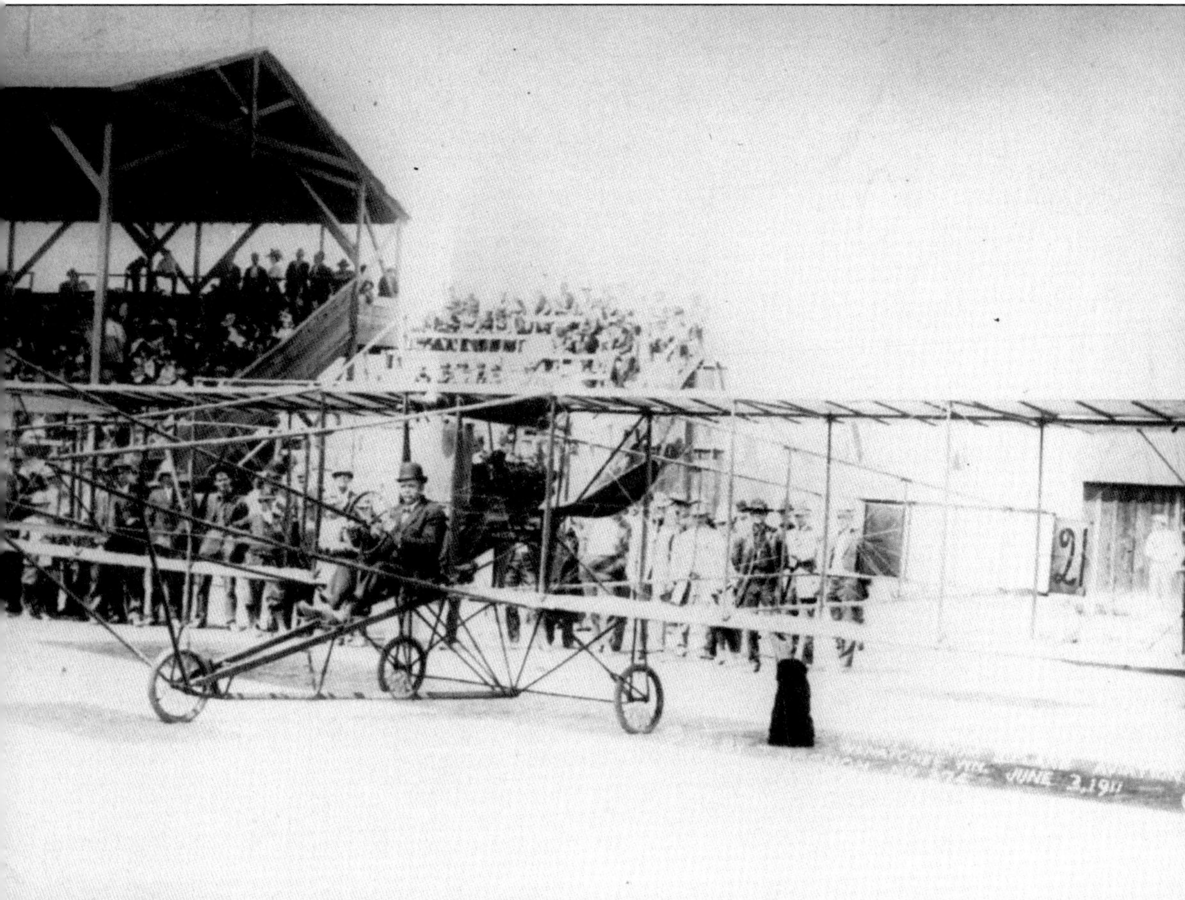

Charles F. Walsh was the first aerialist to visit North Central Washington. Local promoters arranged for him to give two shows in Recreation Park on June 3 and 4, 1911, selling tickets for 50¢ each (25¢ for children). Walsh flew his Curtiss-Wright-Farnum biplane flawlessly on Saturday, but strong winds on Sunday made it difficult to fly. He took off successfully and flew at 75 miles per hour almost to the mouth of Squilchuck Canyon and then turned back. The crowd observed the plane lurching up and down and knew the barnstormer was in trouble. When he began to lose power, Walsh made an emergency landing on Millerdale Road—narrowly avoiding a cherry orchard but striking a telephone pole and rolling one wheel into the irrigation ditch. He was not seriously injured, but the rest of his show was canceled. (WVMCC 86-24-279, donated by Wenatchee Chamber of Commerce.)

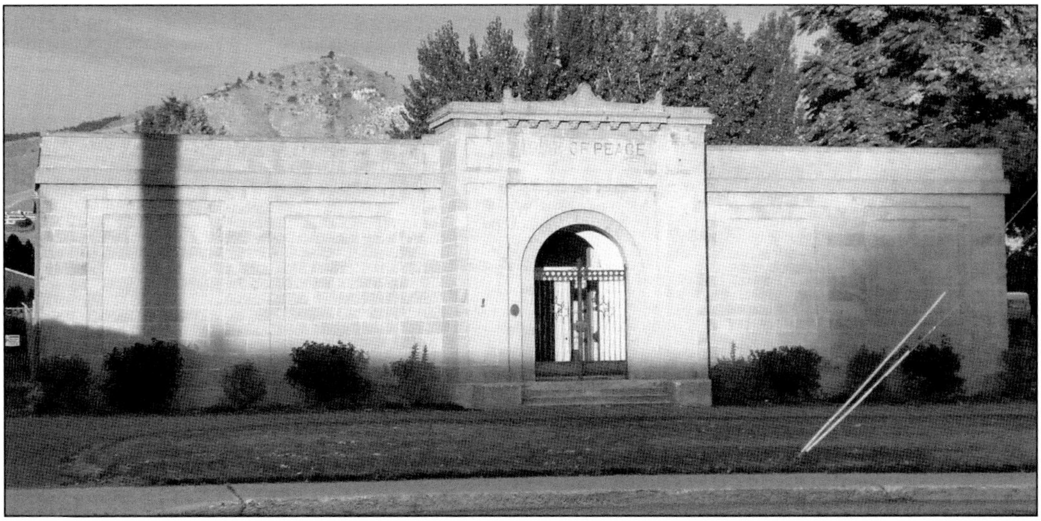

The Home of Peace Mausoleum on Miller Street, across from Pioneer Middle School, holds the remains of 208 people who were entombed between 1916 and 1938. Inspired by Fannie and Harry Wiester's sadness at having to bury their two-year-old son in the rural graveyard several miles from their home, orchardist Ed Russell donated property for construction of a resting place closer to town. The gray concrete Beaux Arts–style structure contains 195 marble-faced crypts—a few of which are shared, while others are empty. Many of the occupants were early Wenatchee settlers, Civil War and World War I veterans, and prominent citizens. Wiester, whose department store was on Wenatchee Avenue, and his wife had their son reinterred at the mausoleum and later joined him there. No entombments have been made since the early 1980s. (Above, courtesy of Chris Rader; below, WVMCC 85-0-197.)

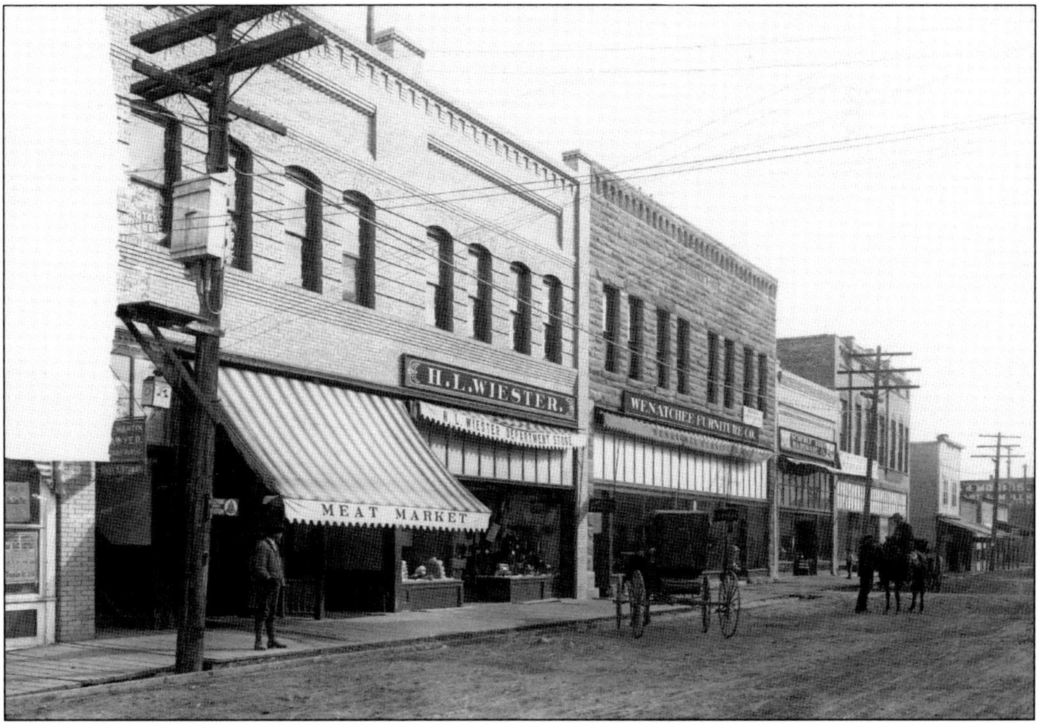

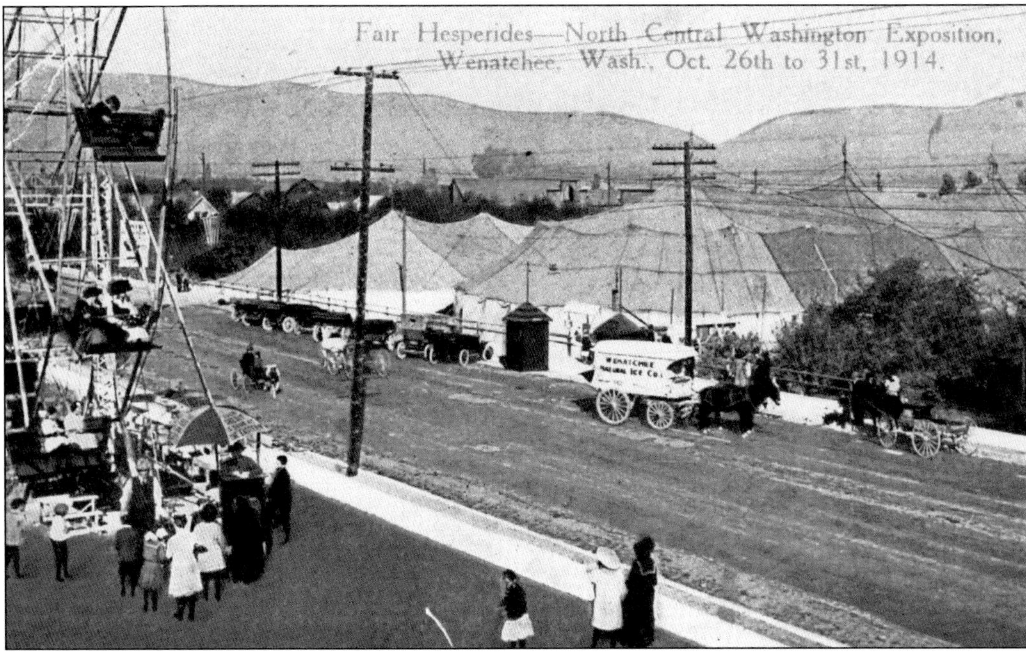

Wenatchee presented the Fair Hesperides October 21–25, 1913, and October 26–31, 1914. This 1914 postcard shows wagons and cars parked on Orondo Avenue with people riding a Ferris wheel in what later became Triangle Park and several tents erected in Recreation Park. The pennant is of blue felt with white lettering and a white apple centered between two gold apples. In Greek mythology, Hesperides were maidens who dwelt in a garden that grew perfect golden apples for the goddess Hera. Wenatchee's two fairs featured carnivals, parades, concerts, gymnastic and horse-riding exhibitions, box nailing and packing contests, horticultural displays, and a grand ball. (Above, WVMCC 73-73-18, donated by Lillian Lux Bellas; below, 010-62-41, donated by Donald Lester.)

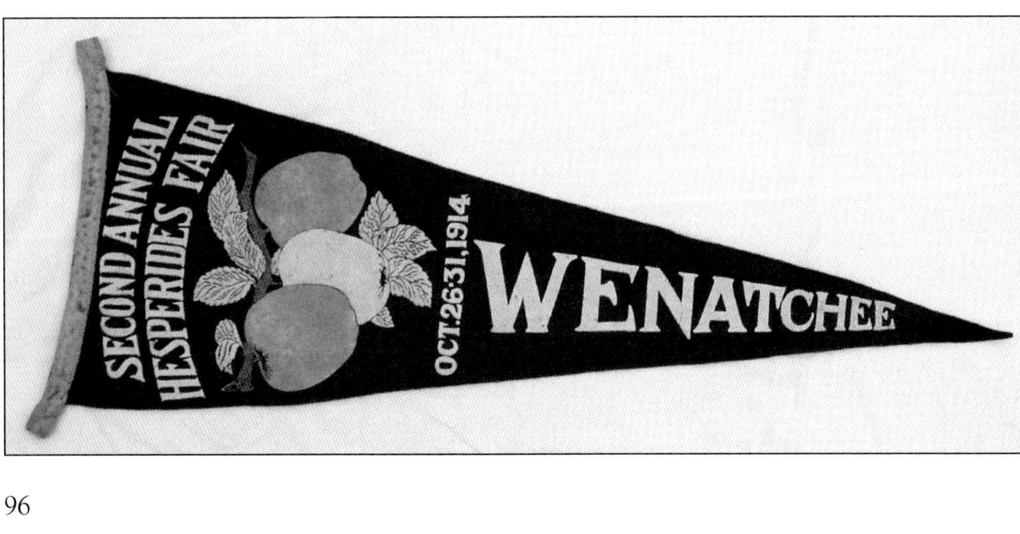

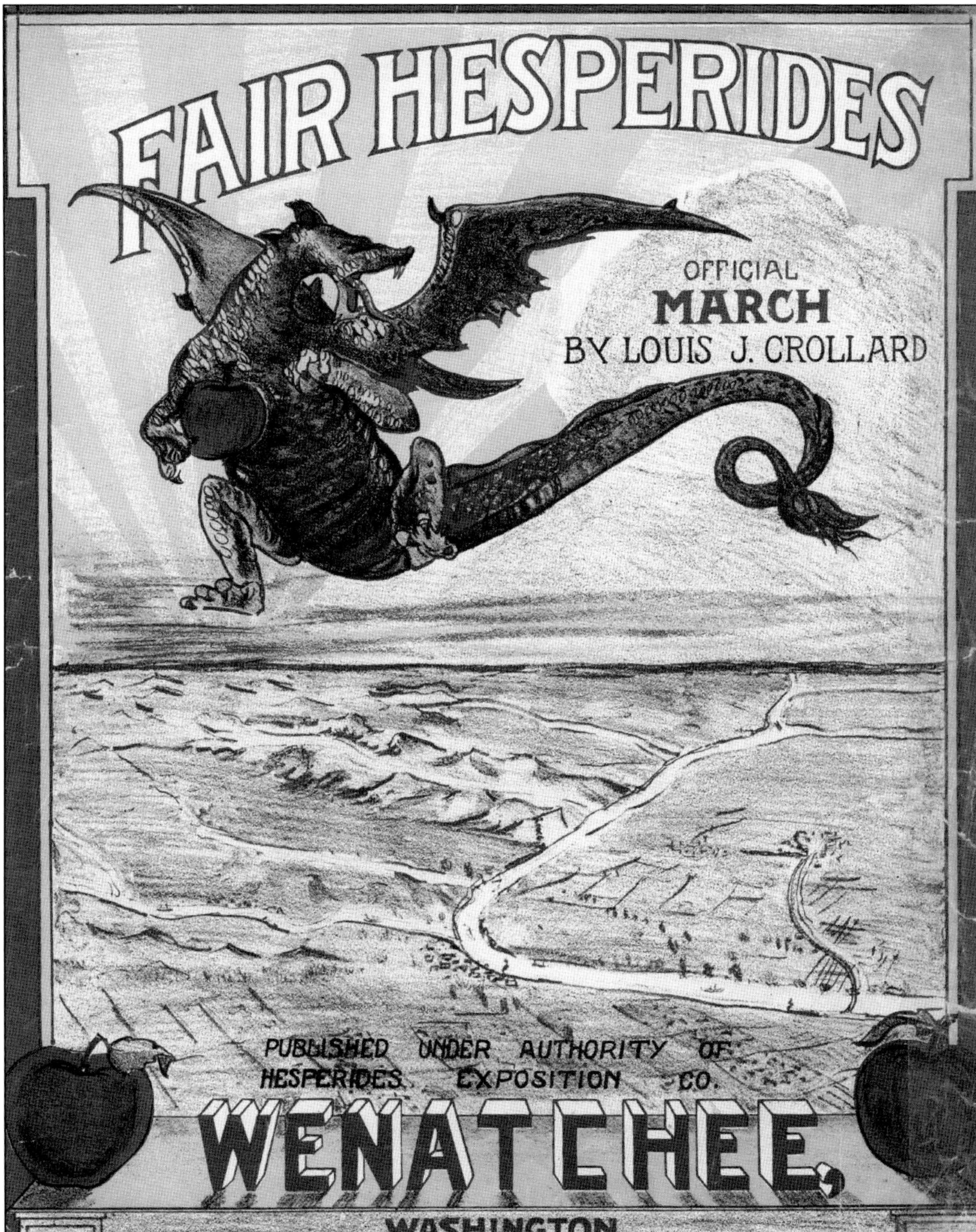

Louis Crollard, a popular Wenatchee attorney and leader of the town band, composed a march in honor of the Fair Hesperides. The sheet music cover pictured here features a winged dragon holding an apple as it flies over Wenatchee. Five pages of music were copyrighted in 1913 under the authority of Hesperides Exposition of Wenatchee. On opening day of the 1913 fair, a grand parade of veterans was led by the 14th US Infantry Band and the Wenatchee Military Band; it ended at the Fair Hesperides Gates, where the two bands played the march in unison. The gates were formally opened, and the Honorable Frank Reeves gave a welcome address. The *Wenatchee Daily World* reported the first fair a financial success, with 8,858 paid admissions. (WVMCC 78-133-1, donated by Mildred Valaas.)

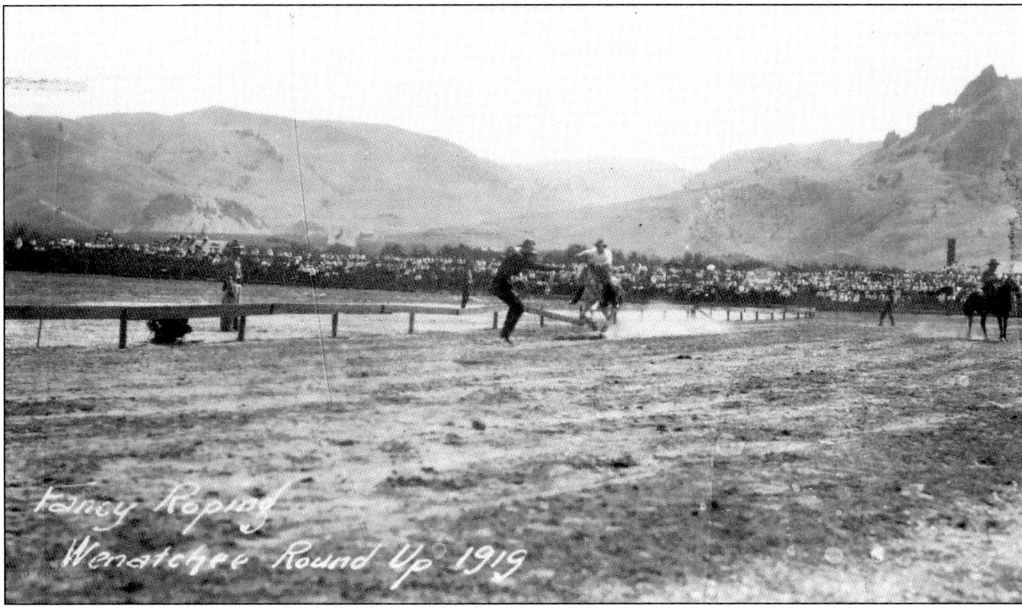

Recreation Park was the venue for several rodeos, including the Wenatchee Round-Up in 1919. Above, the cowboy at left twirls a lariat in hopes of snagging the foot of the horse in the fancy roping competition. A large crowd is seated on bleachers. Part of Saddle Rock is visible in the background. Below, two horseman watch as Tunk Creek Smith mounts the jumping horse Red Pepper. Note spectators sitting on the roof of a nearby building. (Above, WVMCC 75-52-1; below, 75-52-2.)

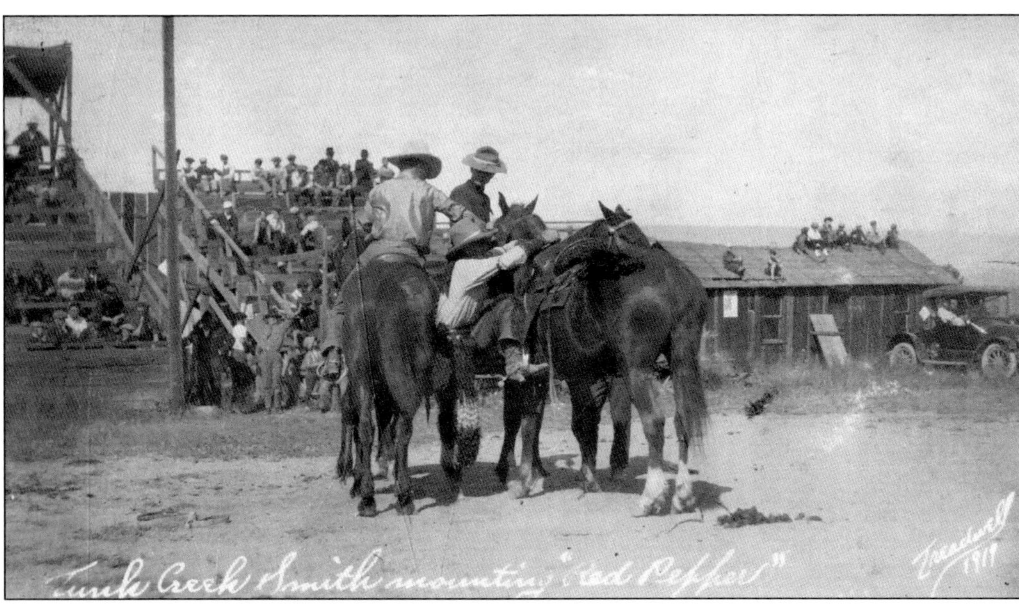

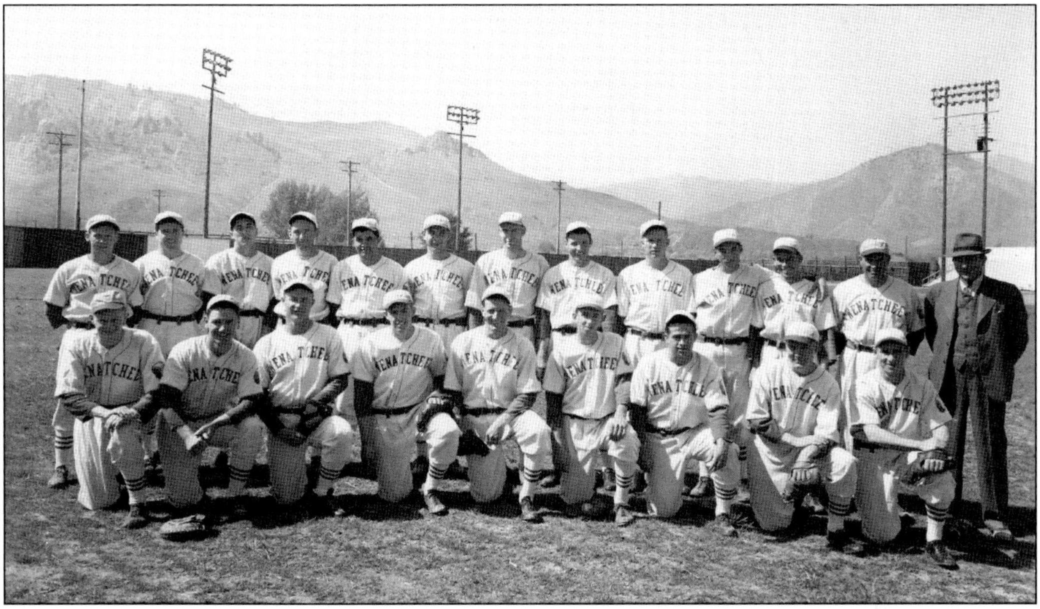

The Wenatchee Chiefs were a professional minor-league team that played in Recreation Park from 1937 to 1965. They were charter members of the Western International League, playing teams from Spokane, Yakima, Tacoma, and Lewiston, Idaho, and Vancouver, British Columbia. In 1955, the Chiefs joined the Northwest League and won two pennants. The 1939 club pictured here, probably the best in Chiefs history, was a farm team for the New York Yankees. It led the league in hitting (.300) and home runs (170) and won the pennant with ease. Six of its players went on to play for major-league teams. Owner Charles Garland, second from right in the second row, helped finance the Chiefs; he insisted that his role not be publicized. Right, "Big Jim" Nicholson played third base for the 1939 Chiefs. (Above, WVMCC 007-33-50, donated by Carole Verch; right, 007-34-9, donated by Ray Long.)

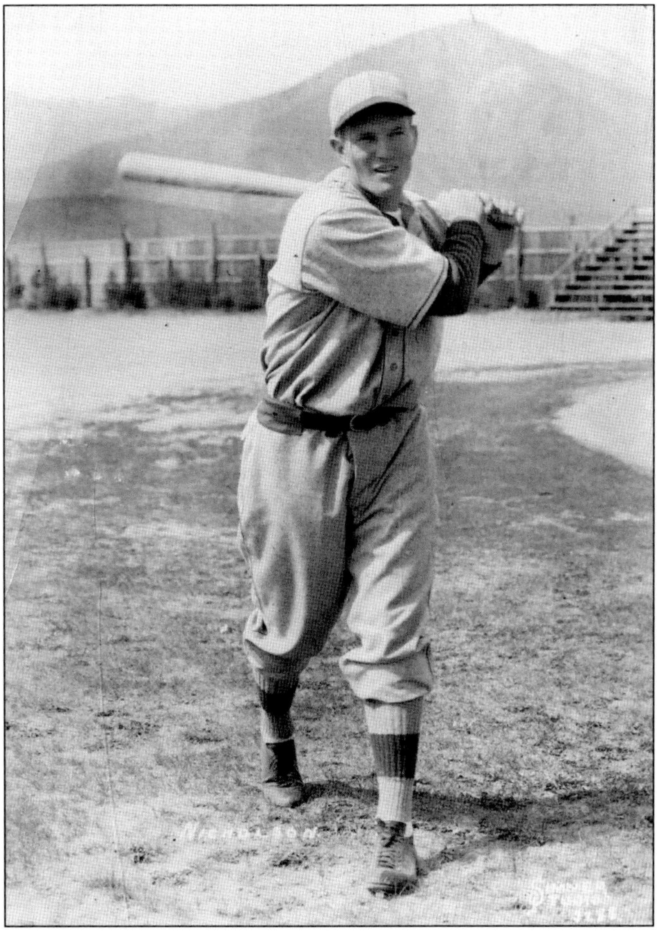

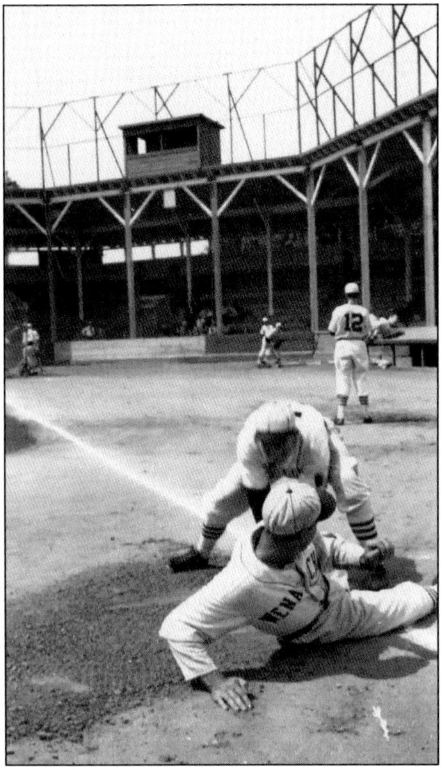

Shortstop Bill Skelly slides into third base at Recreation Park as the Wenatchee Chiefs warm up for a game in 1939. The Recreation Park grandstand was rebuilt in 1974; there is no longer an announcer's box, as shown in this photograph. Skelly led the league in hitting at .366 and hit 28 home runs that year. Glenn Wright, below, was the team's popular manager. Long a baseball-loving town, Wenatchee was an ideal location for a minor-league team. Informal town teams had been playing teams from Leavenworth, Waterville, and other communities since 1895, drawing large crowds to Sunday afternoon games. By the 1930s, Wenatchee had a healthy American Legion youth baseball league and an adult league, with teams representing clubs, churches, and businesses like Morris Hardware and Bakelite Bakery. (Left, WVMCC 007-33-66, donated by Carole Verch; below, 007-34-1, donated by Ray Long.)

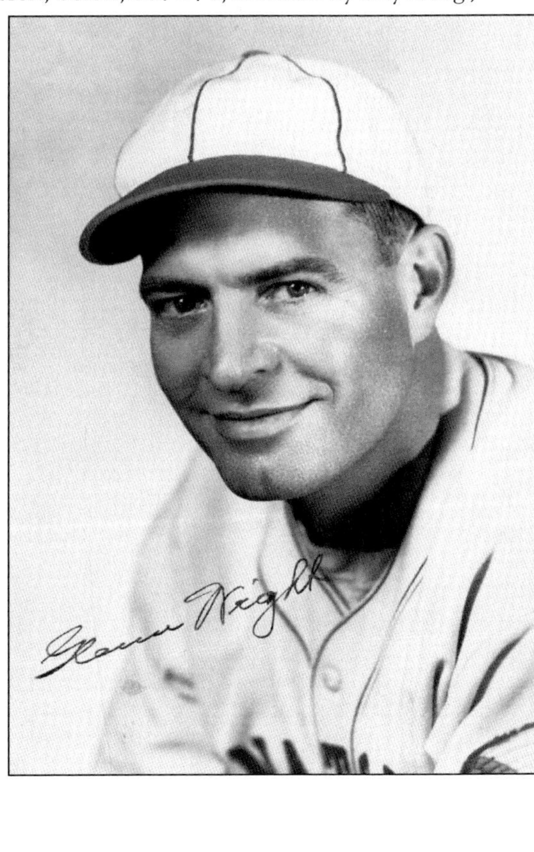

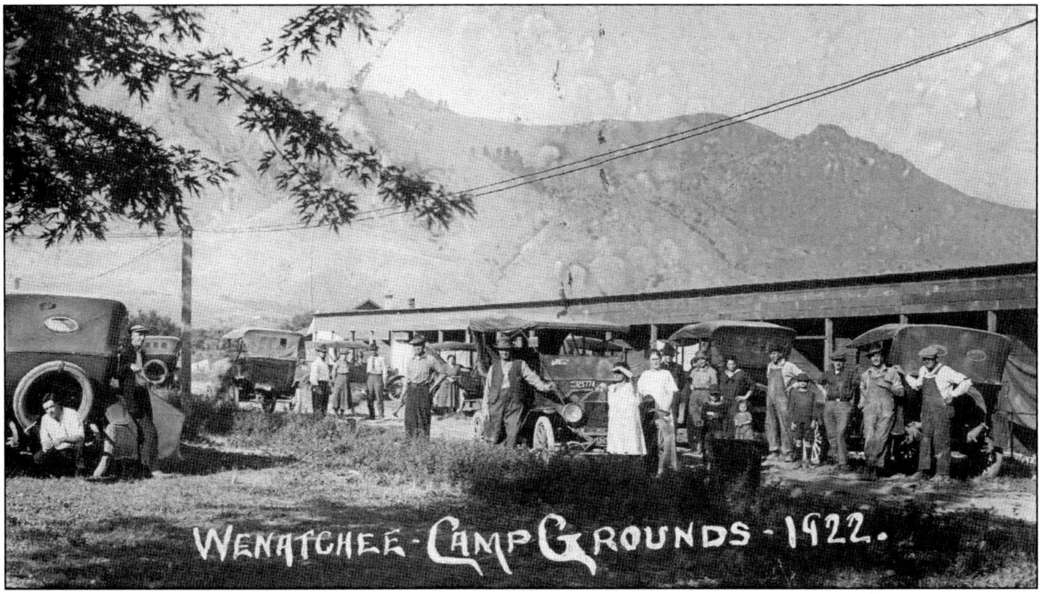

With the rapid increase of automobile use and better road construction, Wenatchee opened a tourist camp just south of Recreation Park in 1922. The five-acre camp sported three tennis courts, restrooms, firewood, and stalls where visitors could wash clothes, cook food, and store their belongings. By the following summer, the camp was so popular that the city increased fees from 25¢ to 50¢ a day. Pioneer Middle School and the city pool now occupy this site. (WVMCC 85-0-134.)

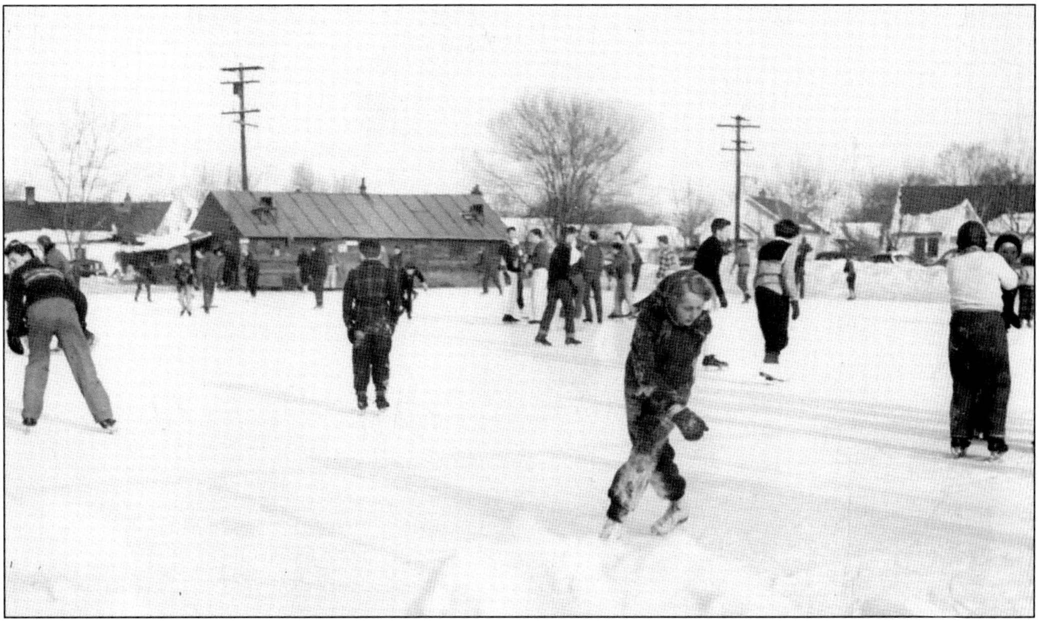

Ice-skaters enjoy a winter day on a makeshift rink in Pioneer Park in 1949. Skaters graduated to a better rink in the 1960s, when the city turned the Hughes Memorial Swimming Pool into a refrigerated outdoor rink with board walls constructed by volunteers. This was replaced in the early 1980s by an indoor facility with two rinks. Wenatchee skaters now use the Town Toyota Center. (WVMCC 97-48-250, donated by Wenatchee Public Works.)

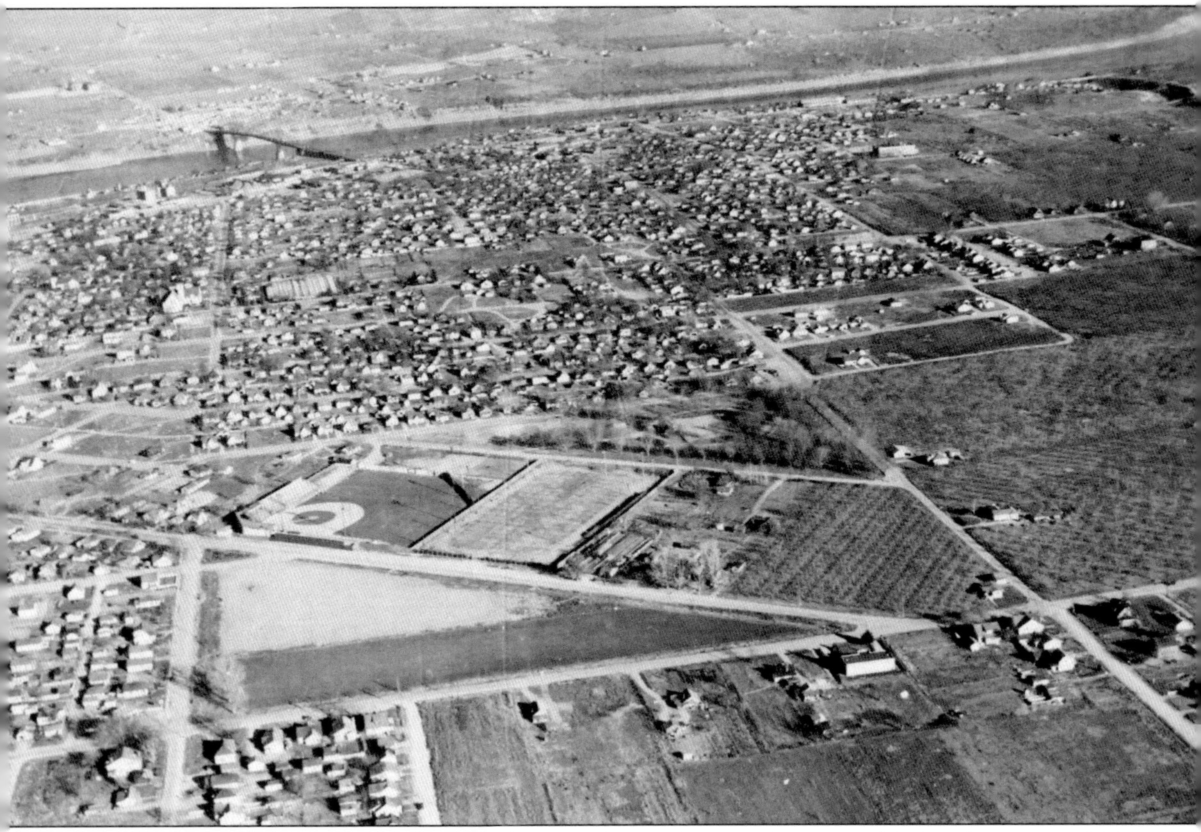

The date of this east-looking aerial photograph is unknown, but it was likely taken in the 1930s or 1940s. The well-defined baseball diamond is Recreation Park, where the Wenatchee Chiefs held sway. Below Recreation Park and across Orondo Avenue is the unimproved Triangle Park, bounded by Cherry Street (at left) and Miller Street (below). The treed triangle-shaped area at center was the tourist camp; it appears to have been out of use by the time the photograph was taken. Orchards dominated the landscape south and west of the city until recent years. The western end of Orondo Avenue was closed to automobile traffic in 1992 as part of a land swap between the city and Wenatchee School District. (WVMCC 86-24-290, donated by Wenatchee Chamber of Commerce.)

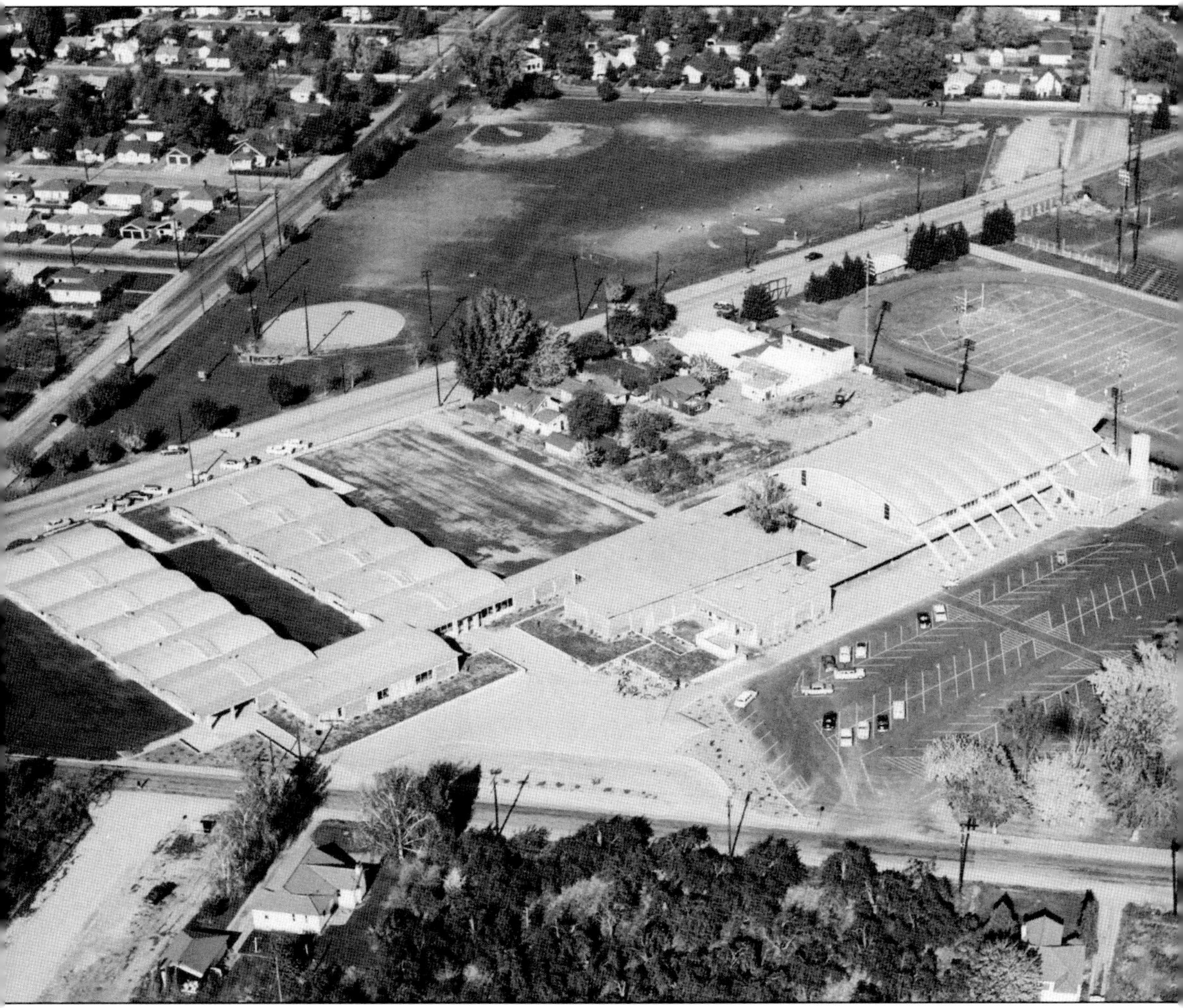

This north-looking photograph, taken on September 28, 1958, shows the new Pioneer Junior High School; Triangle Park, with its three baseball diamonds, is in the background. Orondo Avenue still ran from Cherry Street (upper right) to Miller Street (middle left), making it clear how Triangle Park got its name. The school opened in 1956. It was the first stand-alone junior high in Wenatchee; the H.B. Ellison Junior High had been built as an add-on to the old high school. The current Wenatchee High School at the corner of Miller and Millerdale (just off the lower left of this photograph) was built in 1972. High school football games are played on the field shown at upper right; it now has aluminum bleachers and is called the Apple Bowl. (WVMCC 86-24-895, donated by Wenatchee Chamber of Commerce.)

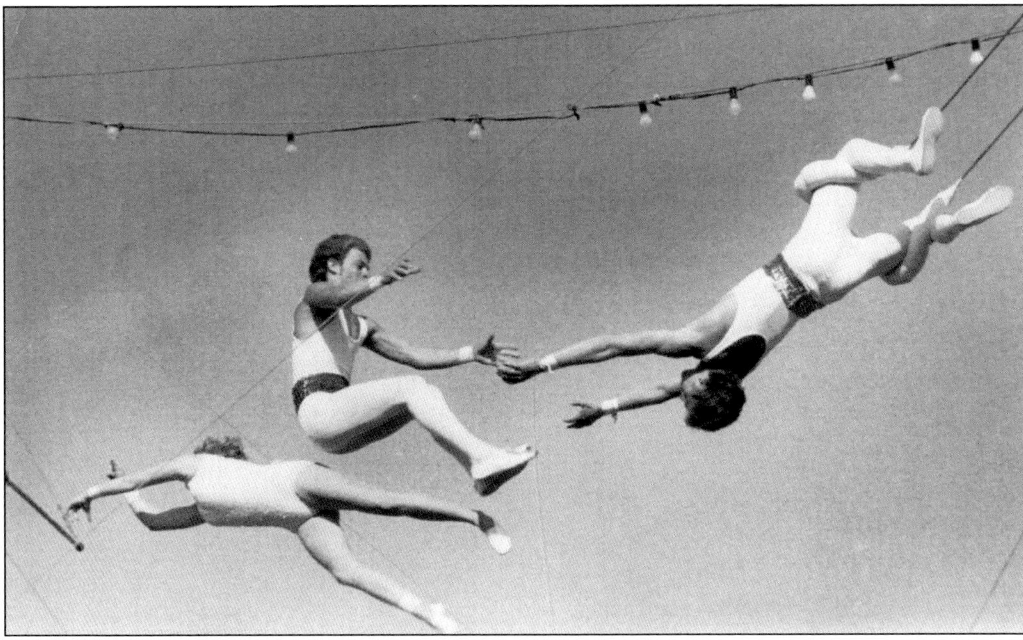

The Wenatchee Youth Circus began in 1952 as an extracurricular tumbling group for middle school boys and girls. School advisor Paul Pugh coached the kids, imbuing them with confidence and enthusiasm. More acts were added in the next few years, and the performance quality continued to improve. Before long, the youth circus grew to about 85 children, aged five to 18, who toured the western United States from June through August. They practiced and performed in Recreation Park and the Apple Bowl during the summer months. In winter, they used the Orchard Junior High gym to work on trampoline, tumbling, fire eating, and low-wire acts; high-wire rigging was set up outdoors in spring. (Both, WVMCC 007-37-464 and 007-37-428, donated by Robert Loffelbein.)

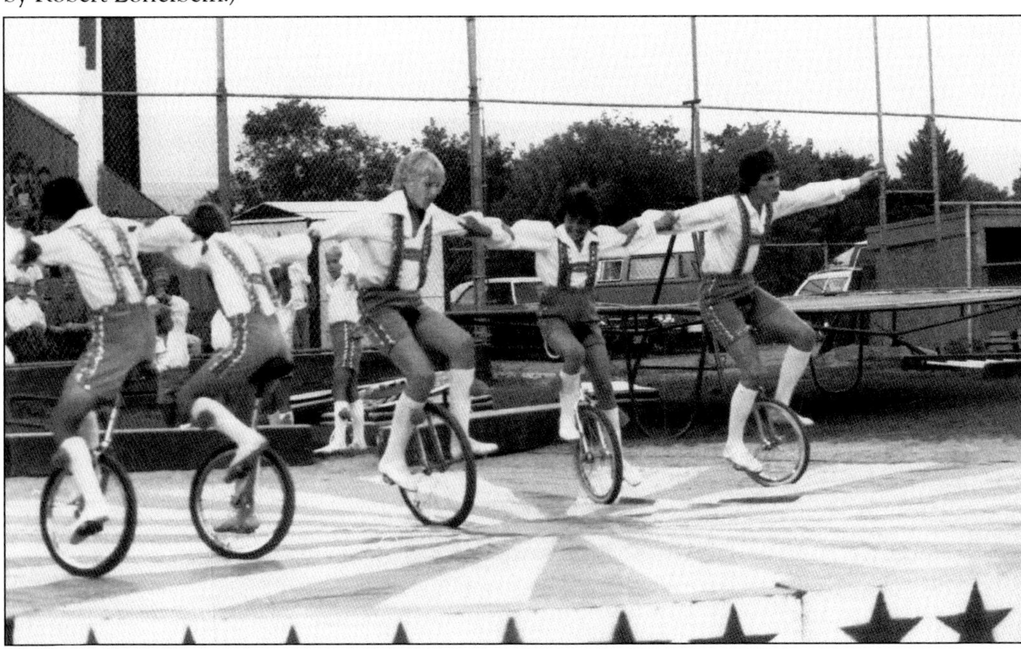

Randy Meyer rides a unicycle on the high wire in a Wenatchee Youth Circus performance in the early 1960s. As the circus grew, so did its equipment, costume, and volunteer needs—usually filled by parents of the performers. Specially designed circus wagons carried the ropes, cables, tents, canvas backdrop, costumes, band instruments, children's gear, kitchen equipment, and food. The wagons were hauled on a huge flatbed truck to distant "away" performances. (WVMCC 86-24-381, donated by Wenatchee Chamber of Commerce.)

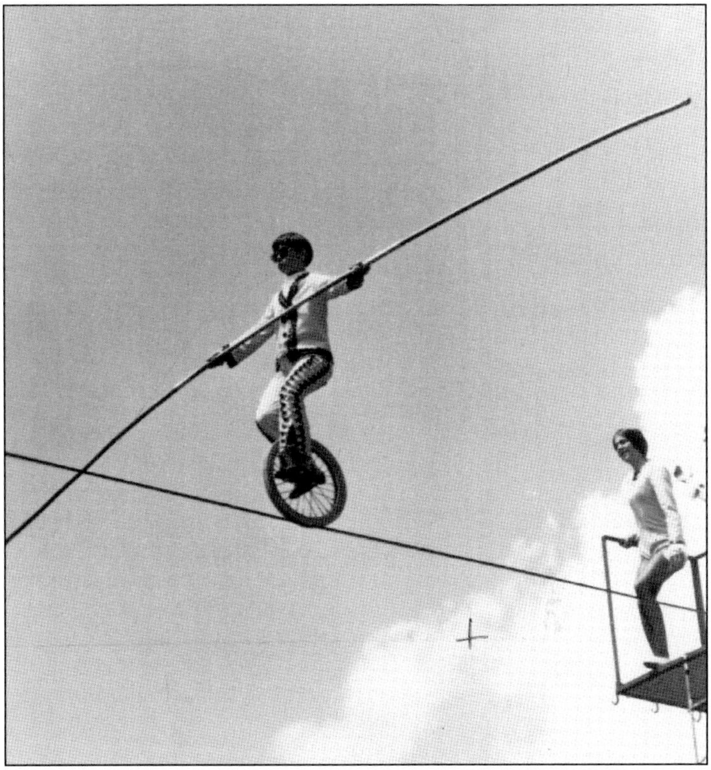

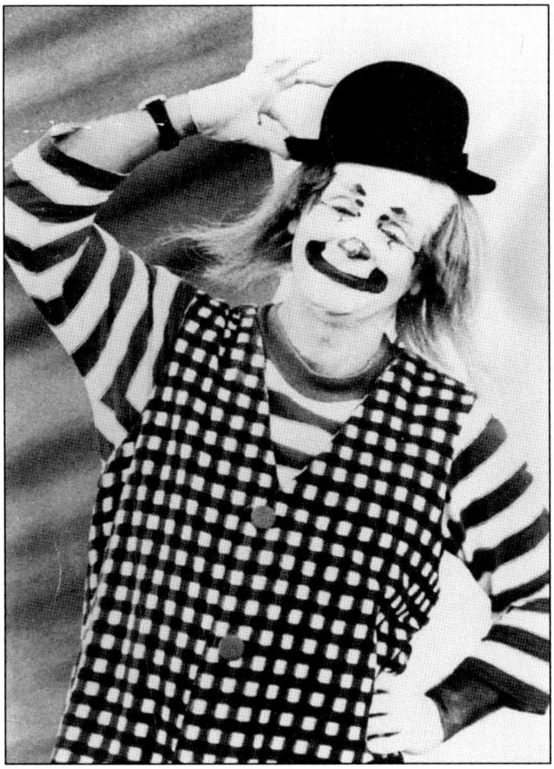

Youth circus founder and manager Paul Pugh was not only a coach, mentor, promoter, bean counter, and volunteer coordinator but also a performer, known as Guppo the Clown. The Wenatchee Youth Circus is still going strong in its 60th year at the time of this book's publication. It has been rated one of the four top nonprofessional troupes in the United States. (WVMCC 007-37-468, donated by Robert Loffelbein.)

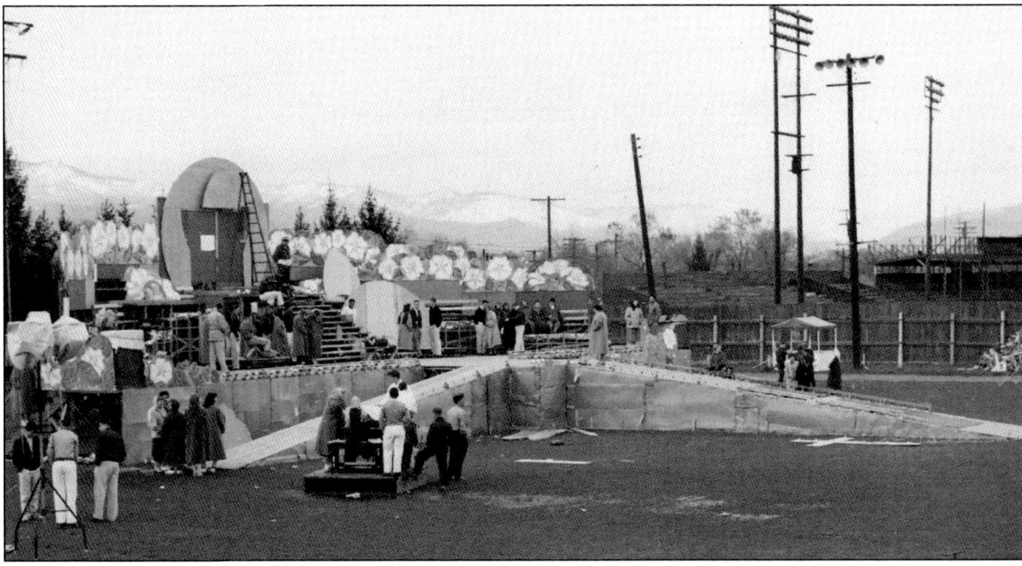

Workers put finishing touches on the stage being constructed for the coronation of 1955 Washington State Apple Blossom Festival royalty at Wenatchee Apple Bowl. Recreation Park is visible in background. The annual parade begins at the Apple Bowl and proceeds down Orondo Avenue to downtown. (WVMCC 79-4-57, donated by Dorothy Herr.)

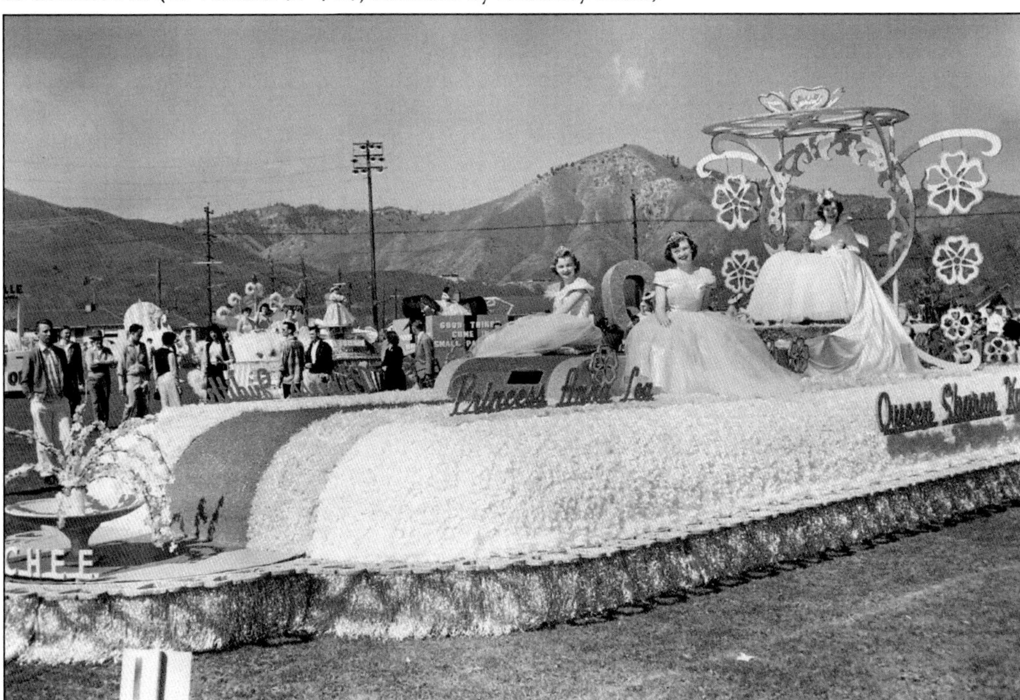

Sitting left to right on Wenatchee's Apple Blossom Festival float are Princesses Judy Emerson and Anna Lea Batterman and Queen Sharon Kay Redlinger. The float waits at Triangle Park in preparation for beginning of the 1955 parade. Triangle Park has long been the staging ground for the annual Grand Parade, now held on the first weekend of May. A kids' parade marches along a slightly shorter route the previous weekend. (WVMCC 79-4-60, donated by Dorothy Herr.)

Eight

Appleyard, South Wenatchee

Before the Great Northern Railway Company connected Wenatchee to the rest of the United States in 1892, the only route into Wenatchee was over Colockum Pass from Ellensburg. Several of Wenatchee's first pioneers chose to homestead on land at the foot of the Colockum, south of Wenatchee itself. Among these was Harmon Simmons, a pharmacist from Missouri who arrived with his wife and daughter in 1886 and settled on 160 acres near Squilchuck Creek with frontage on the Columbia River. Other settlers trickled in, forming a small neighborhood known as South Wenatchee. A two-room school served children in first through eighth grades.

Great Northern purchased some of Simmons's land for a terminal yard when it moved its Cascade Division headquarters from Leavenworth to South Wenatchee in 1922. "Appleyard" was a busy place, with 14 short sets of tracks, an office, a roundhouse for servicing steam engines, an icehouse, an electrical shop, a storehouse, a sand house, a water tank, an oil tank, and a turntable with a movable track that could feed engines into various stalls of the roundhouse.

With the influx of railroad workers, some of whom had families, the community grew. Its main street was the north-south road between Wenatchee and Malaga. The commercial area included a grocery store and gas station at the junction with Viewdale Street to the north, a meatpacking plant, a retail meat market, two cafés, two hotels, a shoe repair shop, a barbershop, and a combined post office and grocery store. The post office was first called "Delicious," after the apple variety, but changed to South Wenatchee in 1925. A larger brick school was built in 1924.

The Appleyard/South Wenatchee community was struck by the following tragedies: a flash flood in 1925 that killed 16 people and a railroad tank car explosion in 1974 that killed two and injured 66. The railroad terminal was damaged by both incidents, but repairs were made, and trains continued to be serviced at Appleyard until 1986. With the demise of the terminal yard, the delivery of mail by the Wenatchee Post Office, and the assimilating of the school (now called Mission View) into the Wenatchee School District, South Wenatchee's separate identity is now a thing of the past.

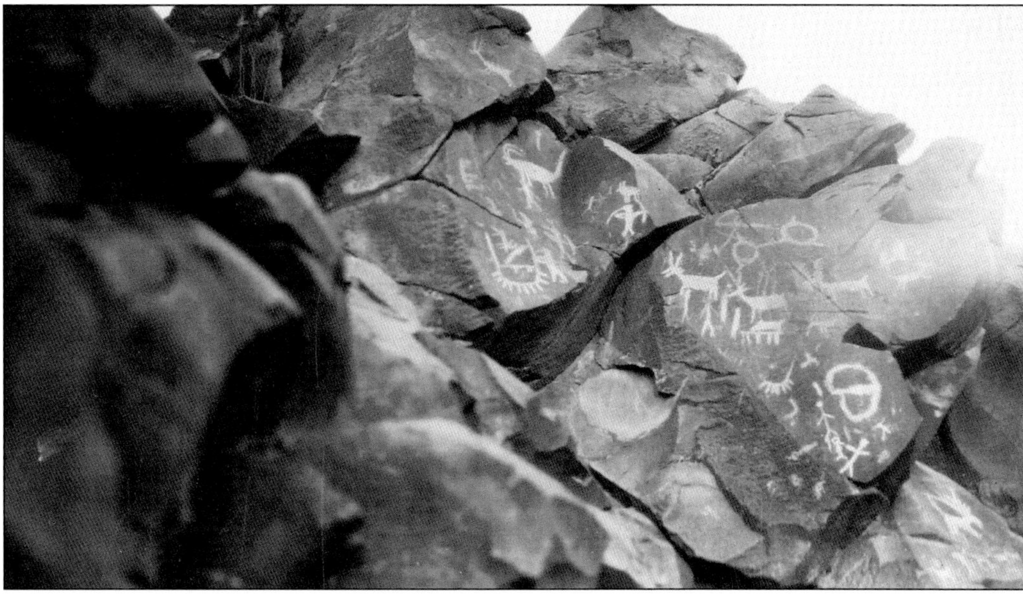

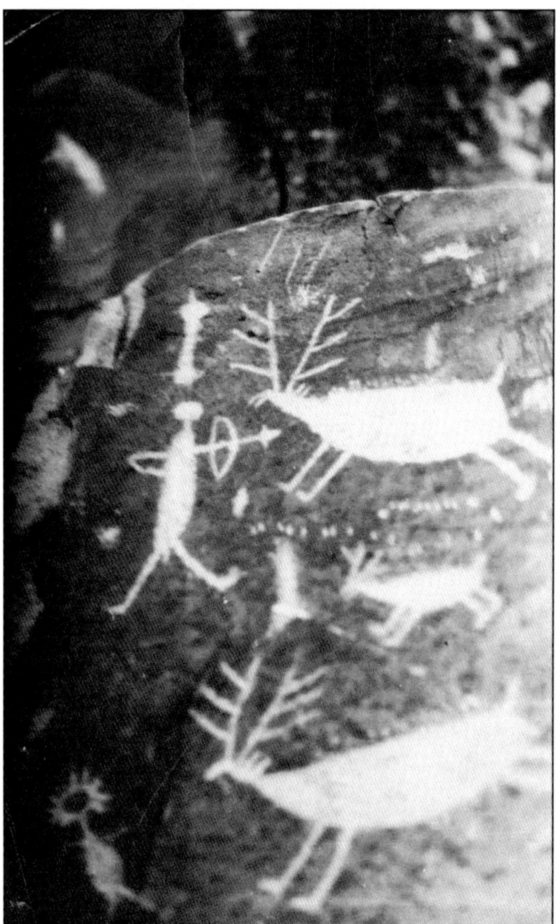

Native Americans lived all up and down the Columbia River long before white explorers and settlers came to the Pacific Northwest. Some of them carved line drawings into rock, an art form called petroglyphs; pictographs are painted onto rock. The above photograph of petroglyphs was taken about 1921 south of Wenatchee, near present-day Rock Island. It depicts animals, probably a bighorn sheep and several deer; a man with a bow and arrow; and, at bottom right, possibly a woman giving birth while another figure raises his arms in joy. The petroglyph at left shows a hunter and several deer. When Rock Island Dam was completed in 1933, it raised the level of the Columbia River and covered hundreds of petroglyphs. Some were excavated and donated to the Wenatchee Valley Museum and Cultural Center. (Both, WVMCC 86-30-134 and 86-30-133, donated by John J. Browne Jr.)

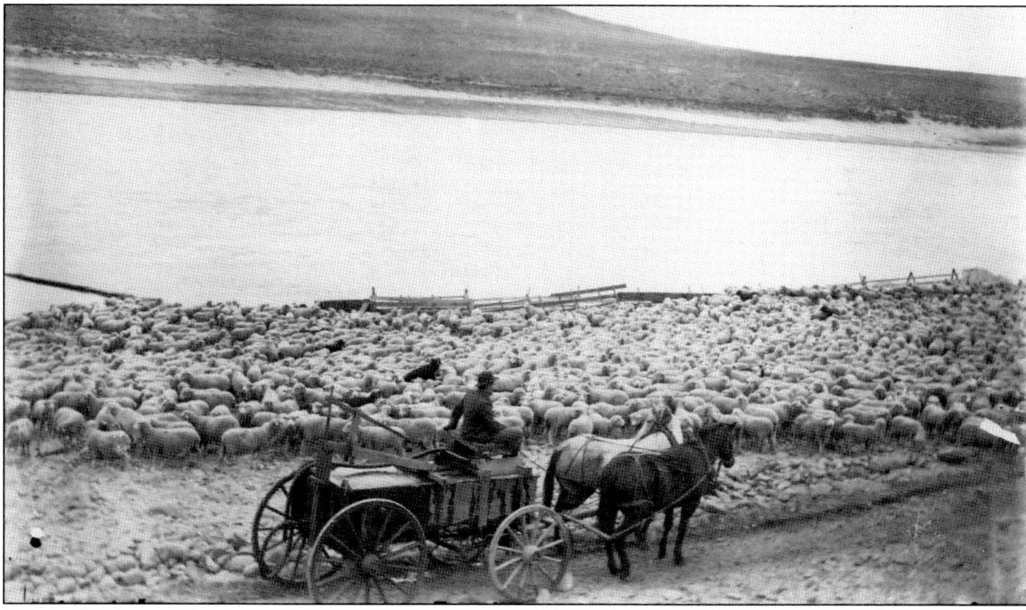

Large flocks of sheep were herded through the Wenatchee, Entiat, and Cascade Mountains during the first few decades of the 20th century. Old-timers today remember sheep being massed at Appleyard and then driven up the Colockum Road into the Wenatchee Mountains. Sheep also grazed in the high country above Leavenworth and were ferried across the Columbia River to Douglas County for the winter. In this c. 1890 picture, two horses pull a man on a water wagon alongside a flock of sheep by the Columbia. (WVMCC 94-31-14, donated by Eleanor Spangler.)

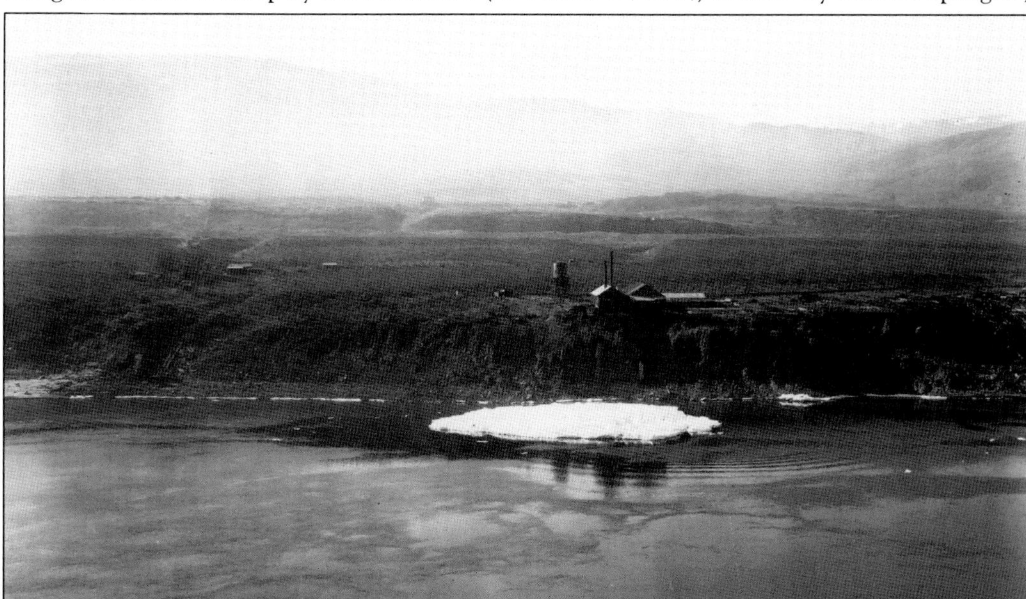

Landreth Brothers Lumber Company operated a sawmill on Stemilt Hill from 1910 to 1924, then moved it to the mouth of Stemilt Creek on the Columbia River. Logs accumulated in an eddy above the mill, a cable system lifted them to the mill, and train cars hauled the finished lumber a mile upriver to Appleyard. This 1930 photograph shows ice floating near the Columbia River shore with logs at right and tracks behind the mill. (WVMCC 85-0-84.)

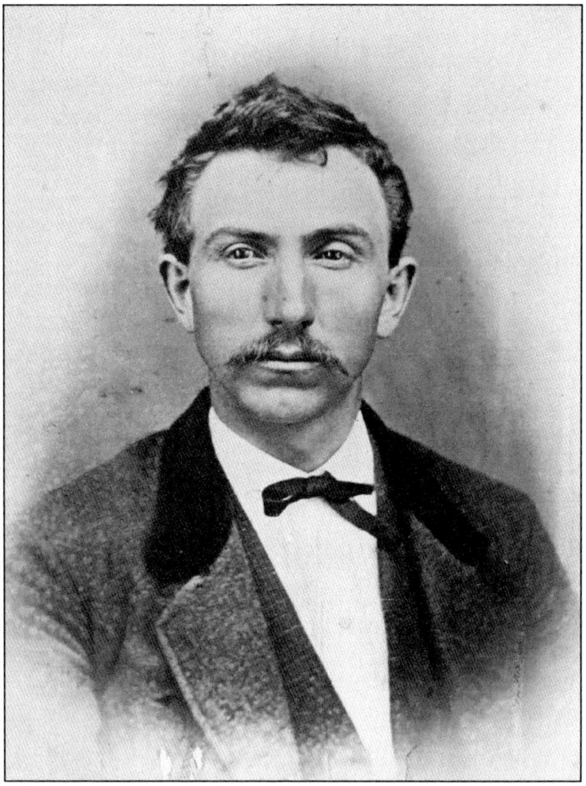

Harmon Simmons (1848–1932) arrived in Wenatchee in 1886 with his wife, Mattie, and three-year-old daughter, Minnie. He purchased 160 acres of Billy Smith's homestead in South Wenatchee and put in a large orchard of walnuts, apricots, peaches, cherries, pears, and apples. He also grew alfalfa. Over the years, he sold parts of his land to neighboring farmers and Great Northern Railway. Harmon and Mattie's second daughter, Mabel, born in South Wenatchee in 1890, is thought to be the first white girl born in the Wenatchee area. In the c. 1900 photograph below, Simmons family members pose on the porch of their large house on Boodry Street. They are, from left to right, Harmon, Mattie, Minnie, and Mabel. Considered a go-getter, Harmon was well liked and known as "Dad Simmons" throughout the South Wenatchee community. (Both, courtesy of Preston and Jill Simmons.)

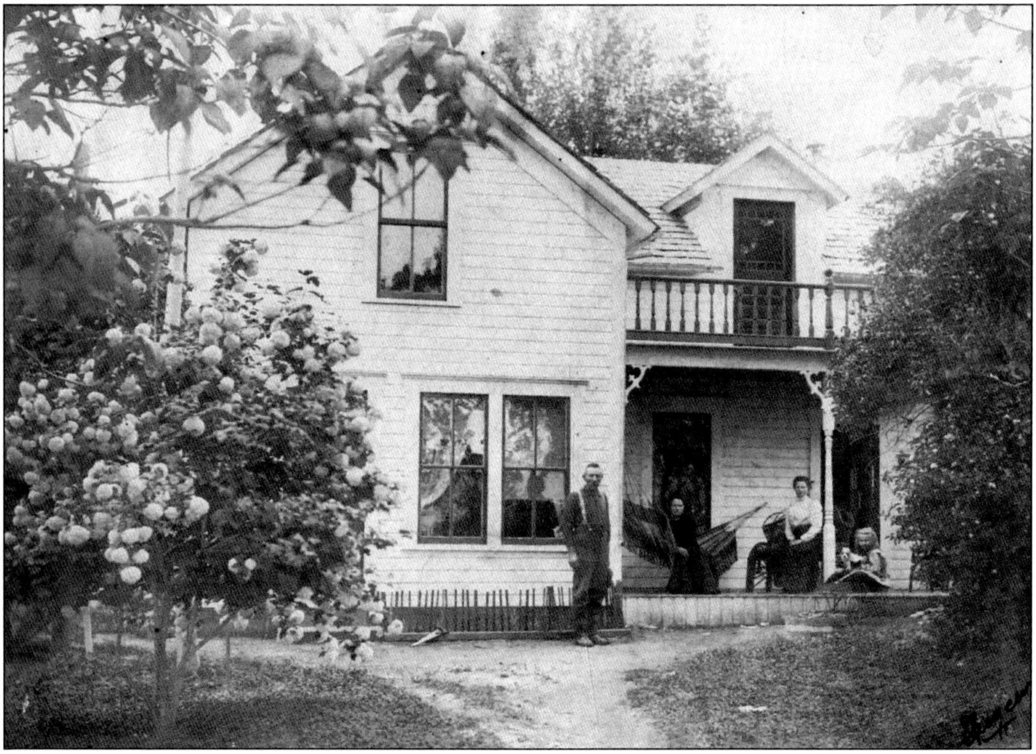

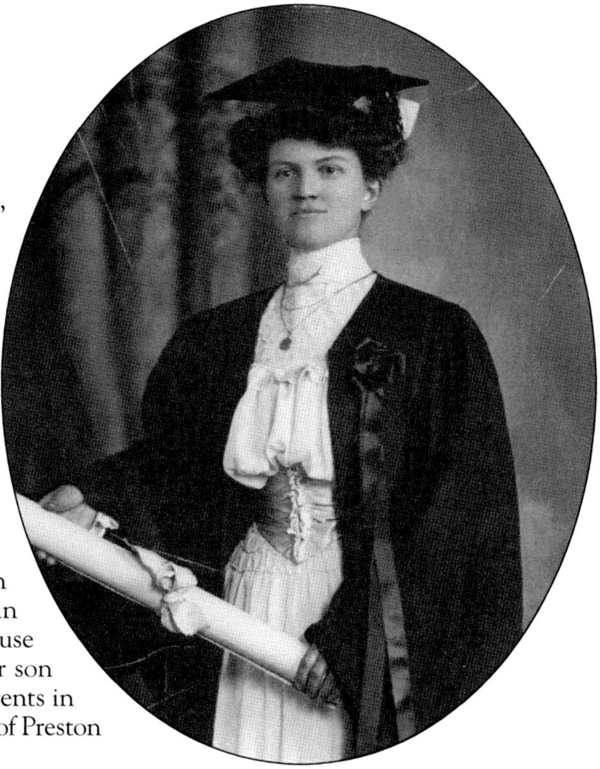

After finishing high school in Wenatchee, Minnie Simmons (1883–1945) attended Vashon College and then earned a medical degree from Barnes Medical College in St. Louis. She is shown here in her Barnes graduation photograph in 1905. She and her husband, Alex Seibert, established a joint practice in Wenatchee from 1911 to 1917 and had what was said to be the most modern X-ray machine in the Pacific Northwest. They divorced in 1919. Thought to be Wenatchee's first female physician, "Dr. Minnie" specialized in diseases of women and children. She maintained an office in downtown Wenatchee and also made house calls in South Wenatchee. She and her son Preston, shown below, lived with her parents in the Boodry Street home. (Both, courtesy of Preston and Jill Simmons.)

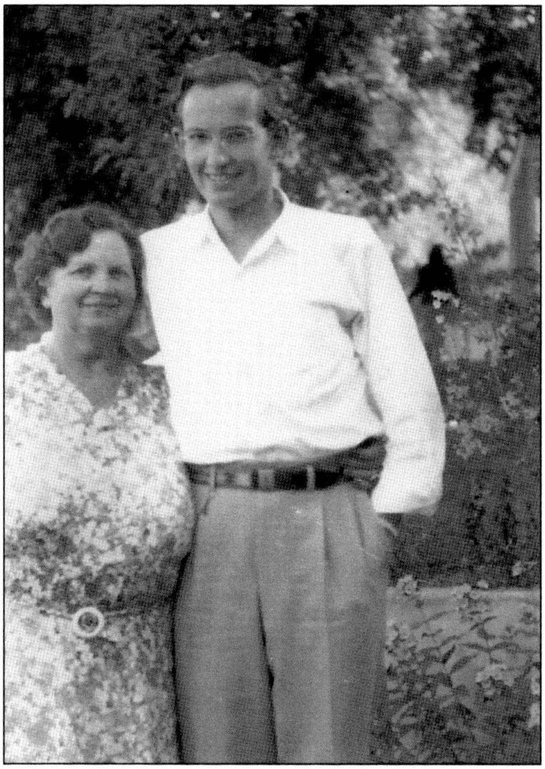

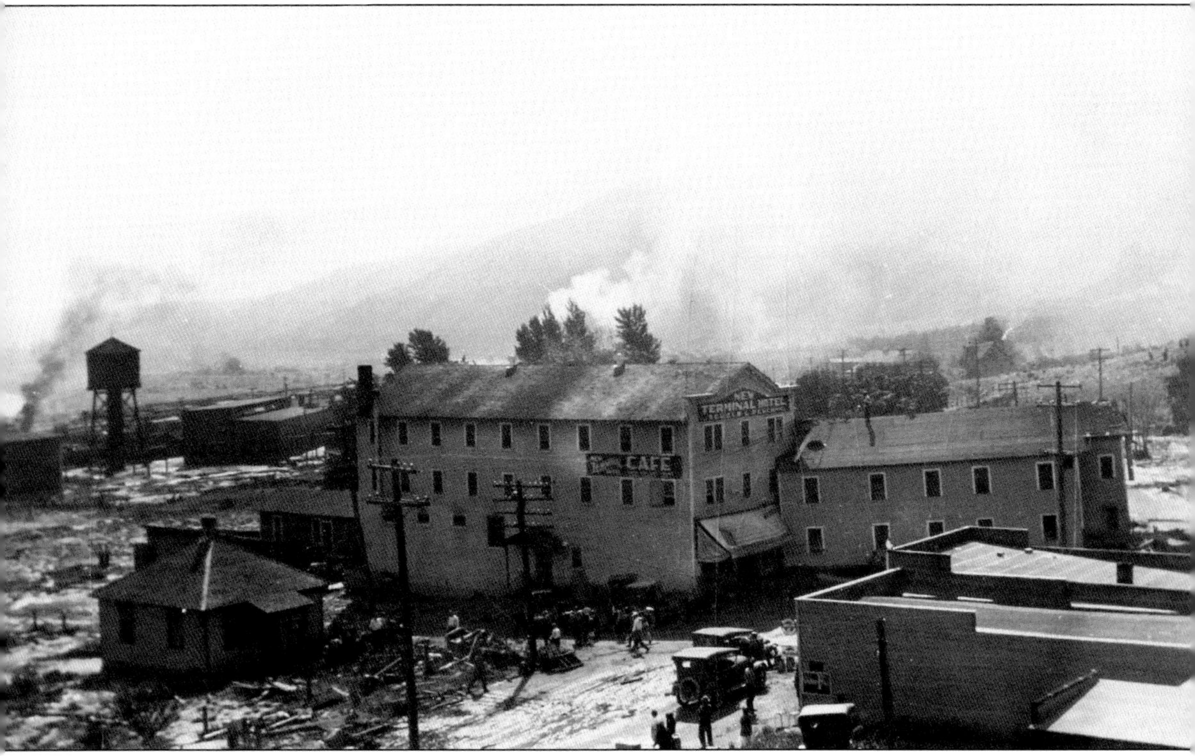

A cloudburst high above the Wenatchee Mountains on September 5, 1925, caused a 15-foot wall of water to roar down Squilchuck Creek to the Appleyard railroad terminal. The flash flood picked up tree stumps and one-ton boulders, turning the creek into a raging river. In the flood's path were four homes and two hotels used by railroad men, the New Terminal and the Springwater. The torrent demolished the homes and swept four children away to their deaths. As it reached the Springwater, the flood splintered the entire first floor and pushed the two upper floors 60 feet across the road into the New Terminal Hotel. Twelve more people were killed and a dozen injured. The entire flood incident took only 90 minutes, but its devastation was immense. The hotels were restored and homes rebuilt, but South Wenatchee/Appleyard never really recovered from the tragedy of the 16 deaths. (WVMCC 86-24-291, donated by Wenatchee Chamber of Commerce.)

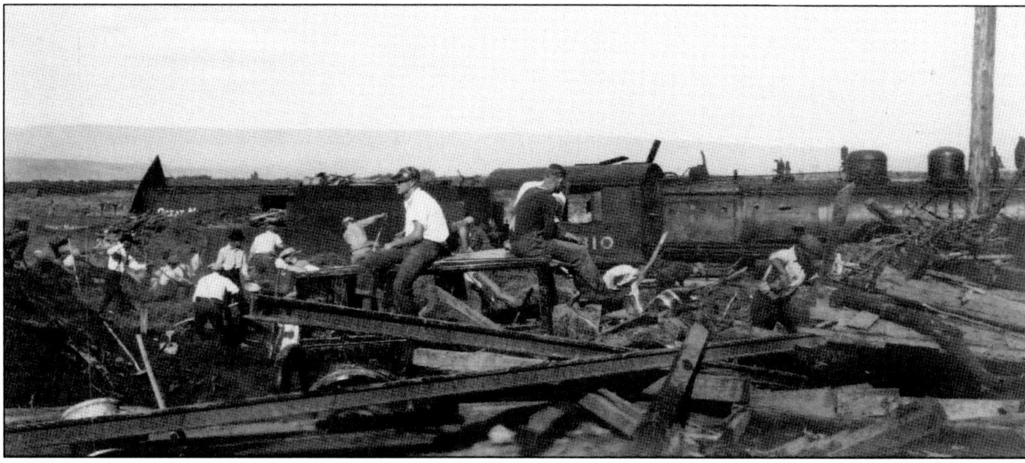

Above, three Great Northern Railway employees rest on a displaced table at Appleyard amid the destruction of the 1925 flash flood while others poke through the rubble. Steam locomotive No. 3310 escaped major damage, though its windows were cracked. The flood took out sections of track, twisted rails, overturned several cars, and covered much of Appleyard with mud and debris. Wreckage along the tracks extended for a half mile. Below, people (possibly employees) sit outside the repaired New Terminal Hotel and Confectionery about 1930. The popular "Uncle Joe" Beuzer owned the hotel and pool hall for 40 years, holding an open house for Appleyard children every Sunday afternoon with free candy, popcorn, soda, and ice cream. Beuzer evacuated some 20 people from the Springwater and spent days digging Appleyard out following the 1925 flood. (Above, WVMCC 88-108-1750, donated by Ileen Taylor; below, 85-0-212.)

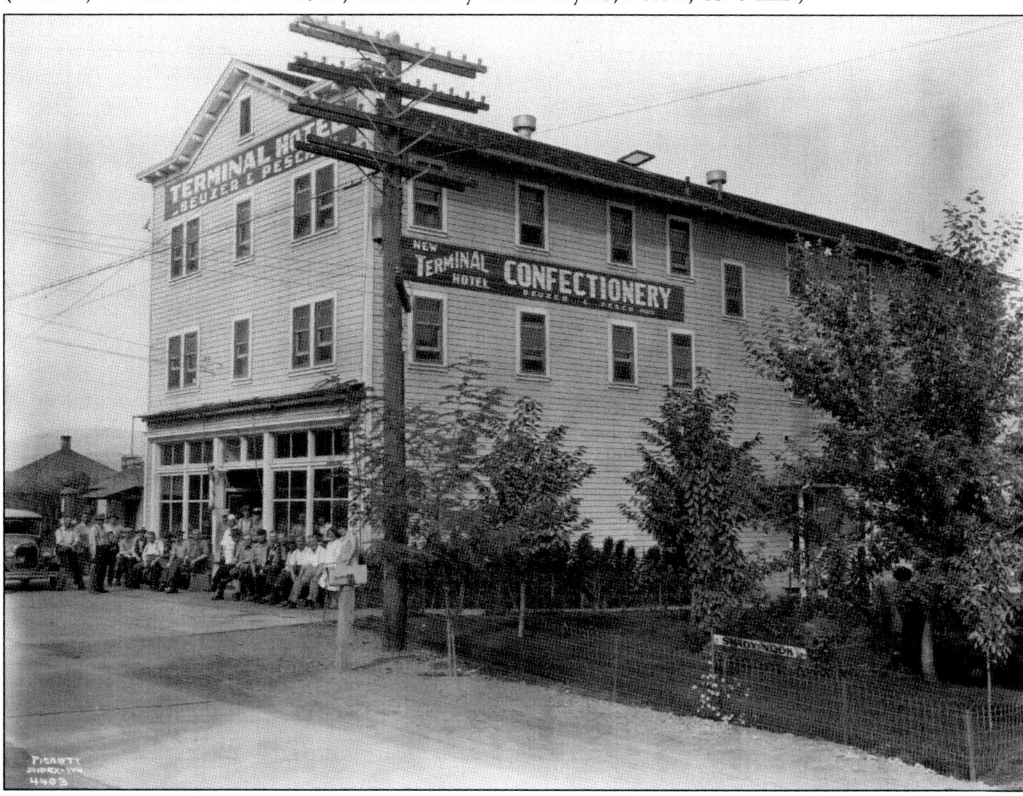

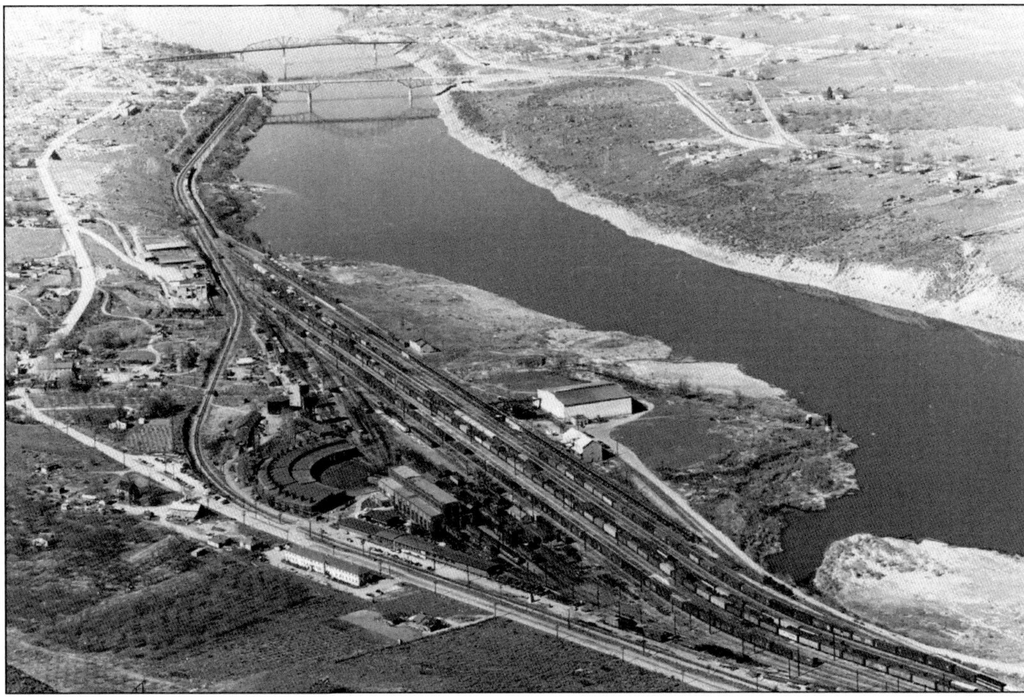

This aerial photograph of Great Northern Railway's Appleyard, looking northward from the train yard, was taken around 1952, shortly after the George Sellar Bridge replaced the pipeline bridge in the state highway system; both are visible in the distance. At left center is the remainder of the small South Wenatchee commercial district bisected by the Malaga-Alcoa Highway. Boodry and Beuzer Streets intersect with this main road at the edge of the photograph. The large white building at center is the icehouse. (WVMCC 75-23-71, donated by Bertha Smith.)

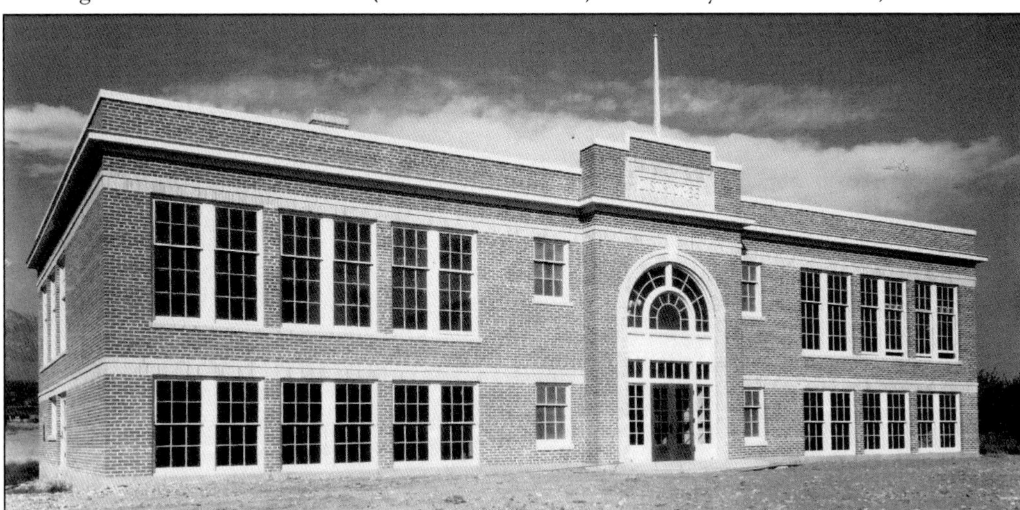

Squilchuck School District No. 66, formed about 1900, included a few one-room schools that consolidated when the South Wenatchee School (pictured) was built on Terminal Avenue in 1924. The school, designed by architect Ludwig Solberg, went to the eighth grade. The district was annexed into the Wenatchee School District in 1944. Mission View Elementary School now occupies that location. (WVMCC 98-34-65, donated by Sandy Stoljer.)

A mushroom cloud arises over South Wenatchee just after noon on August 6, 1974, when a Burlington Northern chemical tank car at the Appleyard terminal exploded. The blast demolished buildings, destroyed railroad cars, and hurled burning wreckage over a mile-wide radius. It shattered windows as far as three miles away and started large grass fires nearby and across the river in East Wenatchee. The damage to the rail yard, railroad equipment, and nearby vehicles, homes, and businesses was estimated at $7.5 million. Sixty-six people were injured, but remarkably, only two people were killed—Burlington Northern switch foreman David Jones and a transient later identified as Lindell Messer of Alabama. (Both, WVMCC 88-108-641 and 88-108-1531, donated by Ileen Taylor)

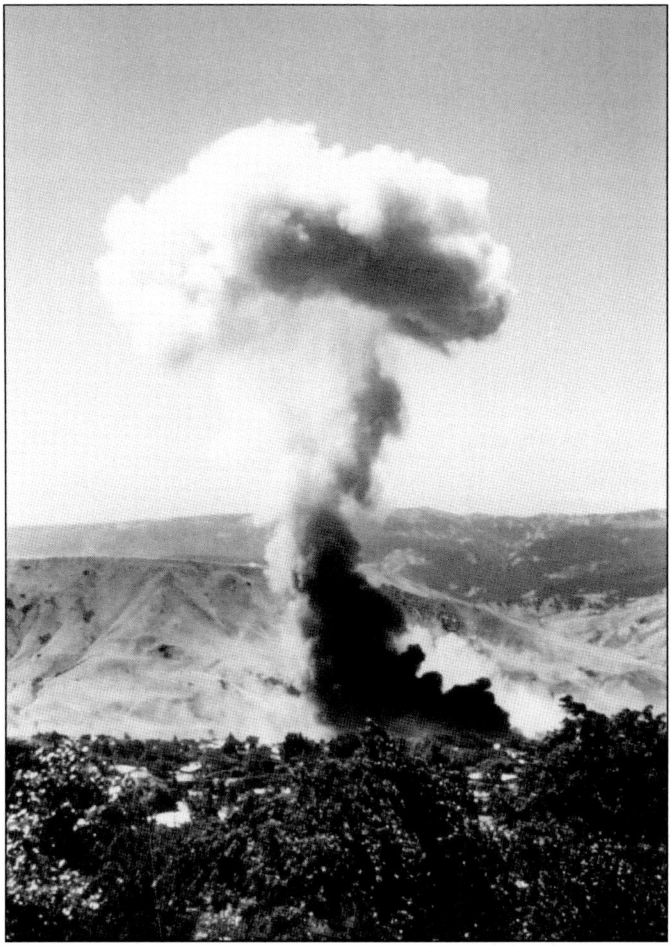

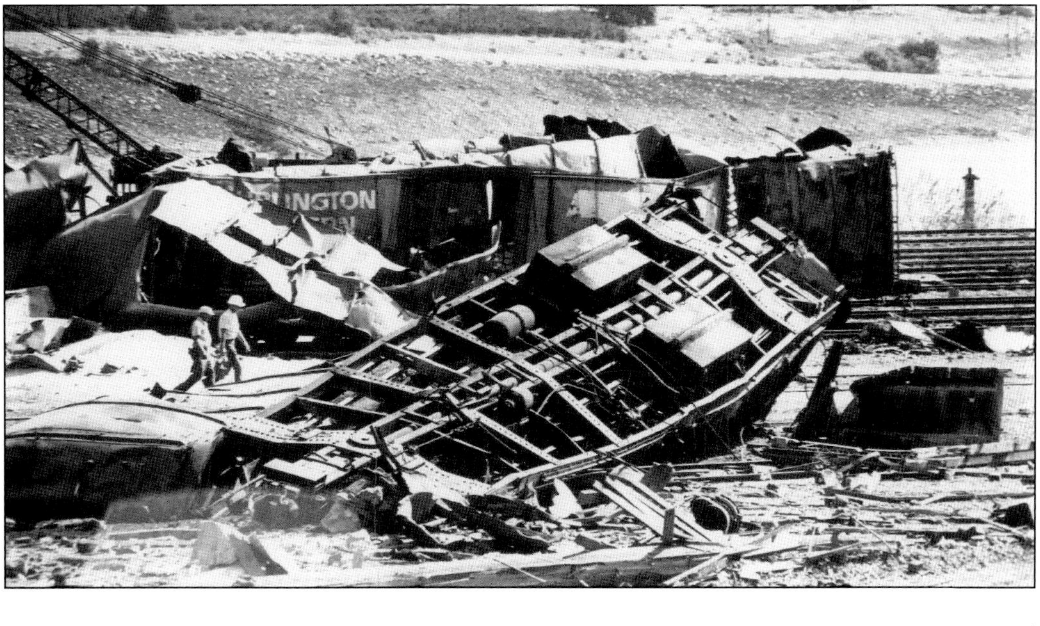

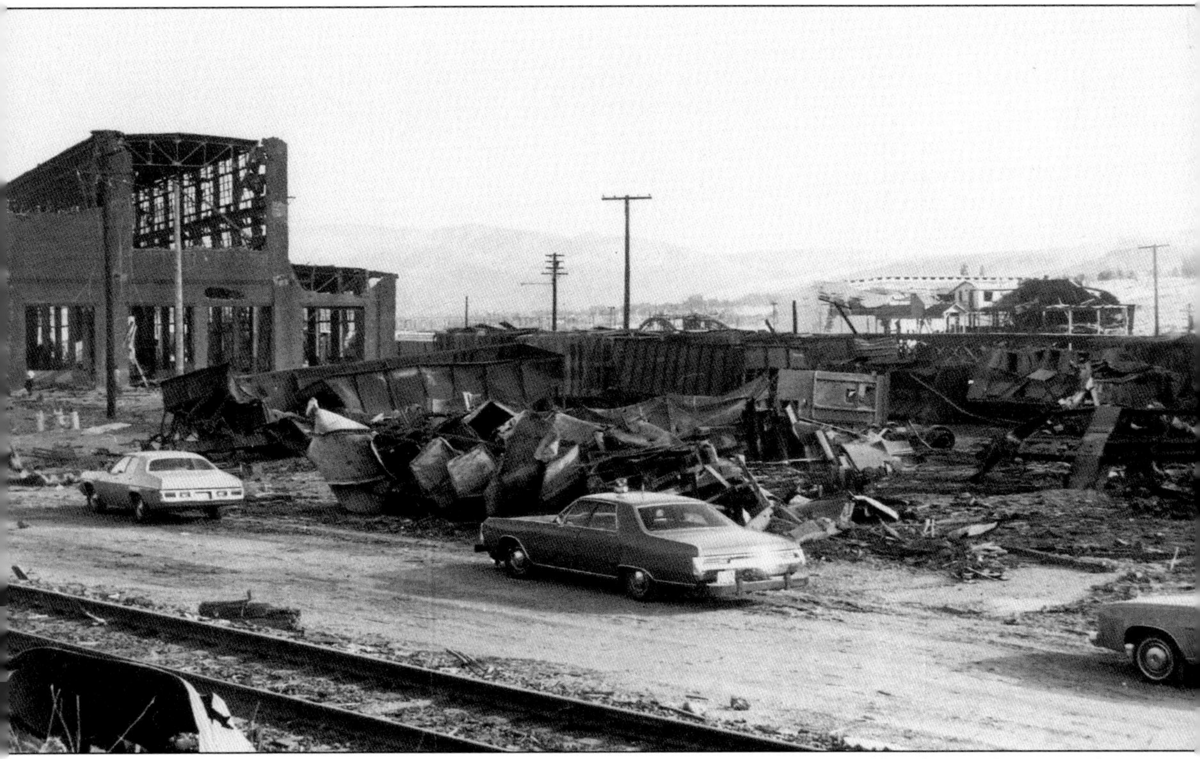

The electric shop at Appleyard was one of six railroad buildings gutted by the explosion. Fifteen nearby houses were heavily damaged, and the Cedergreen Food Corporation's cold storage warehouse 150 feet away lost four million pounds of frozen vegetables when shrapnel ripped holes into the side of the building, destroying the refrigeration system and filling the facility with ammonia and debris. Seeing the yellow cloud of smoke rise above Appleyard from miles away, off-duty police and fire personnel immediately rushed to the scene, as did doctors, nurses, and ambulances. Three Forest Service aircraft dropped fire retardant on the flaming buildings and smoldering rolling stock. Some two dozen fire trucks and crews from surrounding fire districts helped bring the conflagration under control, and railroad crews began pulling undamaged freight cars, some containing explosive materials, to safety. After an 18-month investigation, the National Transportation Safety Board was unable to determine what initiated the explosion. (WVMCC 88-108-1543, donated by Ileen Taylor.)

Nine

Fancher Heights

The City of East Wenatchee was incorporated in 1935. Prior to that date, the growing community across the Columbia River was considered part of Wenatchee, though it had its own small commercial district along Ninth Street and Grant Road. Harry Patterson was the first white settler to stake a homestead claim in what is now East Wenatchee in 1888. Other settlers trickled in. The flow increased after the Columbia River Bridge was completed in 1908; it carried a large pipeline with enough water to irrigate some 4,000 acres of potential orchard land. The bridge also facilitated wagon and automobile traffic, soon replacing the cable ferry.

East Wenatchee had several elementary schools, but its high school students had to cross the bridge to Wenatchee to attend school until 1955, when East Wenatchee voters approved a bond to build Eastmont High School. The earlier students were called "bridge walkers," sometimes with disdain. Wenatchee's first airfield was located on a plateau above East Wenatchee. Named after Maj. Jack Fancher, this unpaved airfield became the landing place for a flight that catapulted Wenatchee/East Wenatchee into the international spotlight.

Clyde Pangborn, a native of Douglas County, was one of America's better-known barnstormers. He and fellow pilot Hugh Herndon set out in the summer of 1931 to set an around-the-world record. Circumstances intervened, and Pangborn and Herndon changed their goal to making the first nonstop flight across the Pacific Ocean. They left Misawa, Japan, on October 2 in the *Miss Veedol*, a single-engine Bellanca adapted to carry a heavy load of fuel. After jettisoning the landing gear to lighten the plane, the pilots landed at Fancher Field in East Wenatchee on October 5 after 41 hours and 15 minutes of flying. A small crowd observed the belly landing, and soon the rest of the world knew of the Misawa-Wenatchee flight that earned its pilots a $25,000 prize.

A larger airport, named after Pangborn, was built outside of East Wenatchee in 1941. Fancher Field is now a housing development and racetrack, but a memorial to the Pangborn-Herndon flight overlooks the valley near the landing place of East Wenatchee's most famous event.

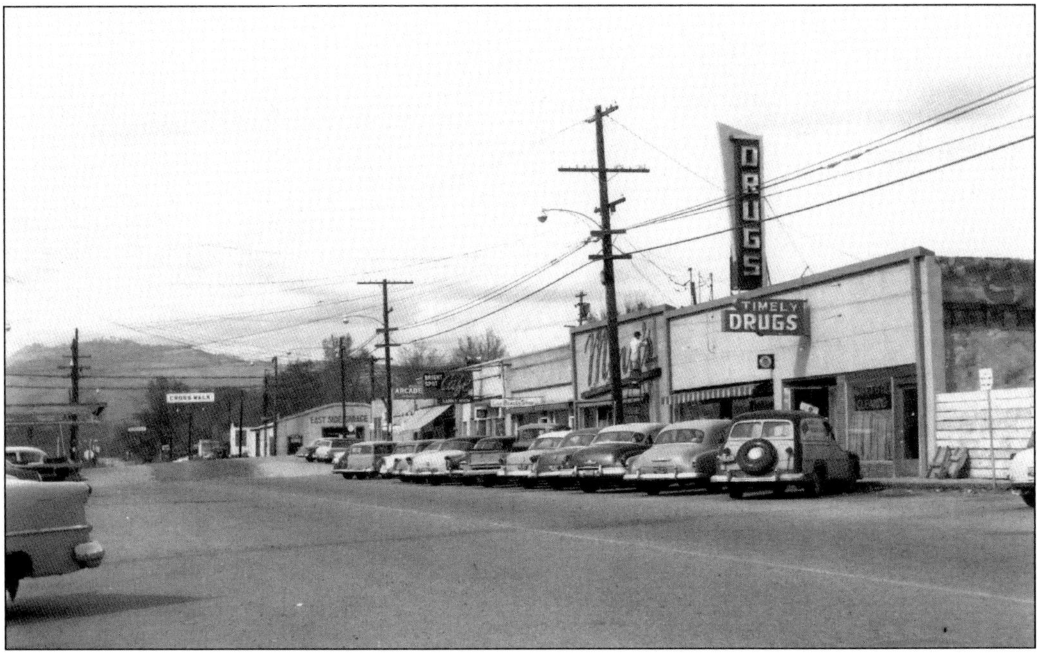

A worker touches up the sign above Minn's Tavern on East Wenatchee's main street, now called Valley Mall Parkway, around 1955. Other businesses on that block include Timely Drugs, Lois's Beauty Shop, Bright Spot Café, and The Arcade. The East Side Garage is across Ninth Street, with Burch Mountain in the background. Postwar affluence created a housing and business boom in East Wenatchee in the 1950s. (WVMCC 008-64-1, donated by Douglas County Museum.)

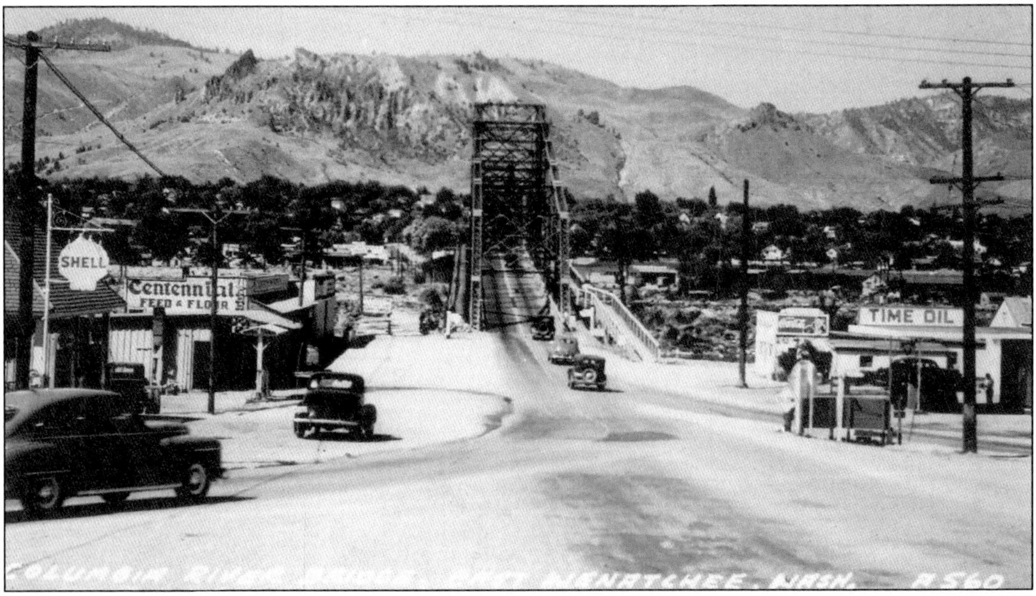

Cars cross the Columbia River Bridge from East Wenatchee around 1945. An irrigation pipeline can be seen on the south side of the bridge; pedestrians, including East Wenatchee students heading to high school, used the walkway on the bridge's north side. Saddle Rock is visible on the horizon. Businesses near the bridge entrance include the Shell gas station, Time Oil station, and Centennial Flour and Feed. (WVMCC 008-14-1, donated by Wilma Stellingwerf.)

This undated aerial photograph of Fancher Field, looking northeast, shows the Waterville Plateau in the background. In 1928, Army major "Jack" Fancher and fellow aviators put on a thrilling show above the field during the Apple Blossom Festival, featuring daredevil stunts and an aerial bombing display. Attempting to detonate three leftover bombs after the show, Fancher was killed when one exploded. Wenatchee later named the airfield after him. (WVMCC 86-24-849, donated by Wenatchee Chamber of Commerce.)

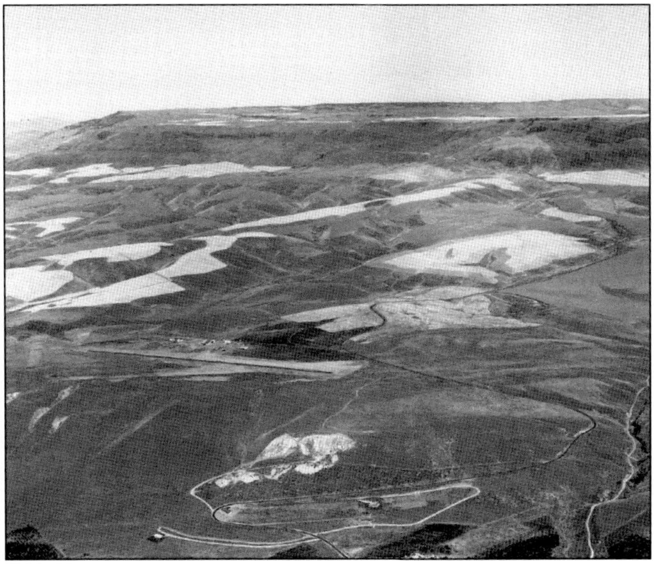

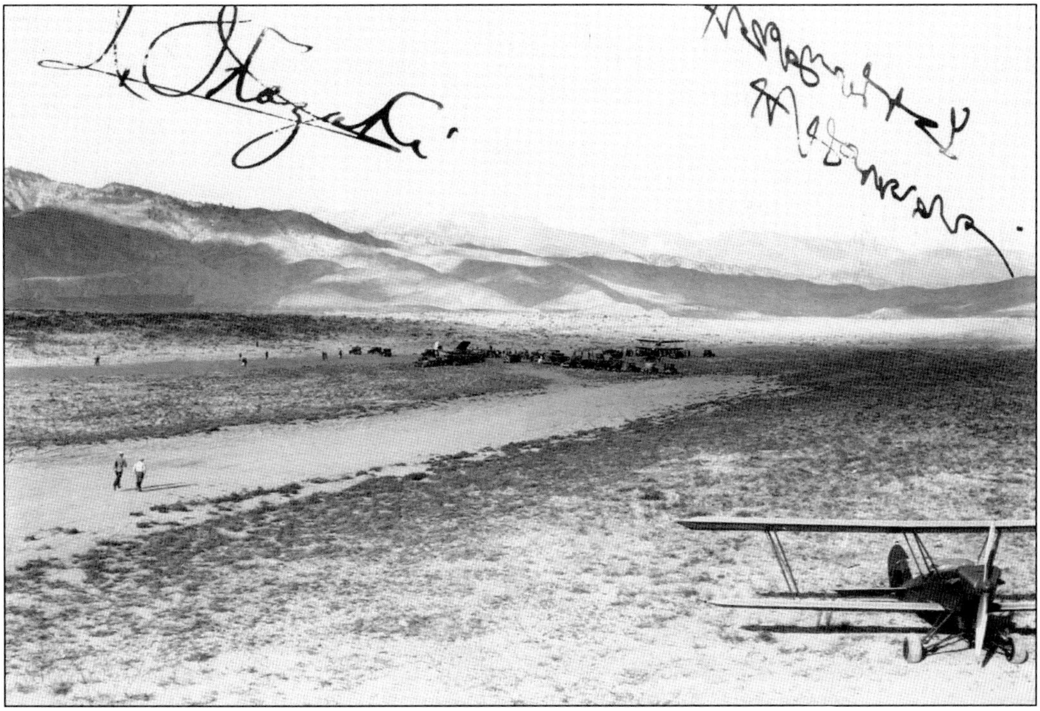

The Wenatchee airfield was a barren and somewhat desolate spot but flat enough for a long landing strip. Clyde Pangborn was familiar with Wenatchee's airstrip and chose to land the *Miss Veedol* here in October 1931 when clouds obscured other Northwest airports. Cars, onlookers, and two biplanes gather near the *Miss Veedol* in this photograph, taken a few days after the famous landing. (WVMCC 80-56-272, donated by Carl Cleveland.)

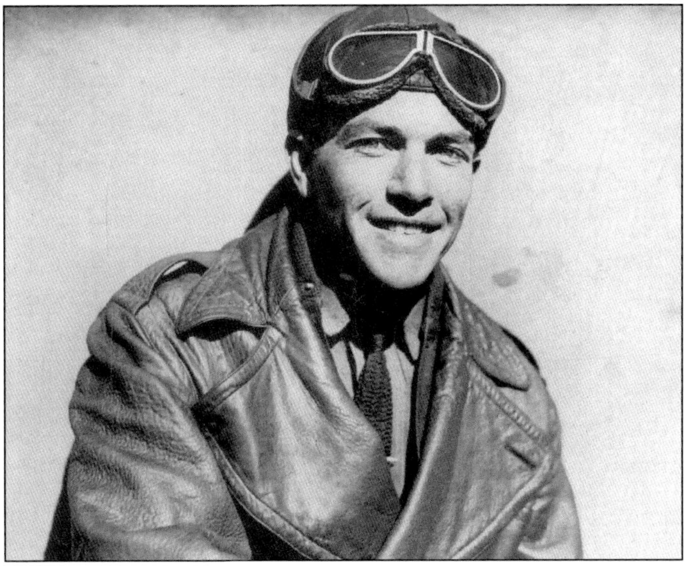

Clyde Pangborn (1894–1958) was born upriver from Bridgeport and grew up in Idaho. In 1921, he helped form the Gates Flying Circus, performing aerial shows for rural audiences across the country. His daredevil barnstorming tricks included changing planes in mid flight, jumping from a car onto a plane's ladder, and flying upside-down. New federal safety laws discouraged barnstorming by 1930, so Pang looked for a new challenge. (WVMCC 80-56-81, donated by Carl Cleveland.)

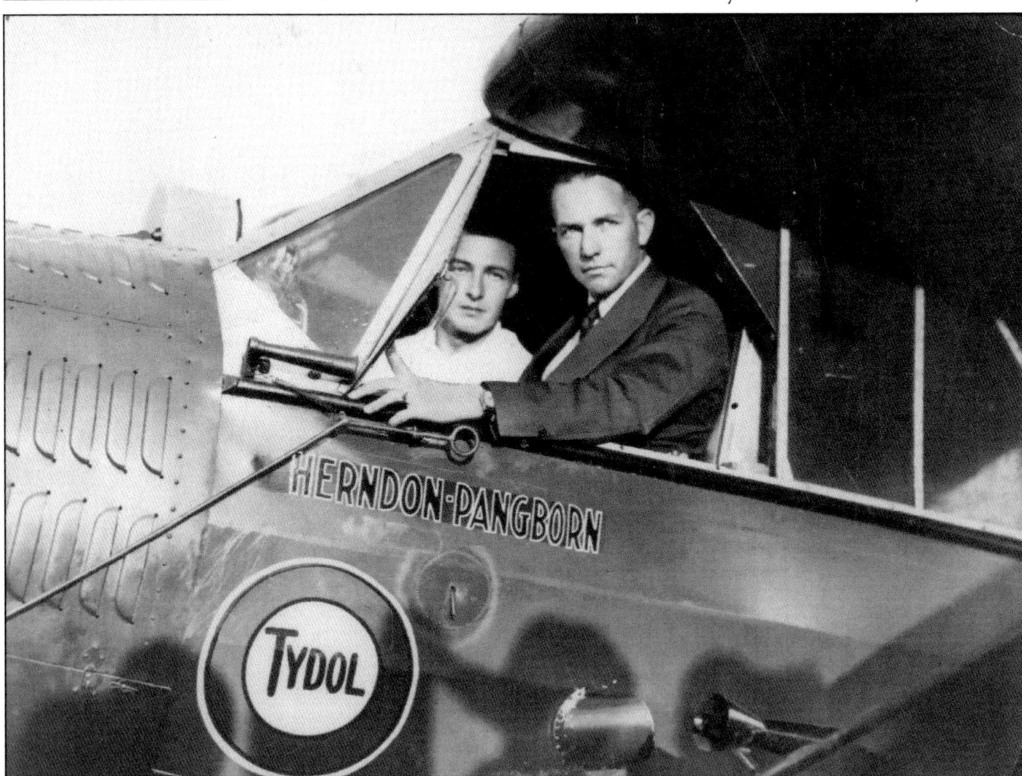

Pangborn (right) and copilot Hugh Herndon look from the cockpit of the *Miss Veedol* on July 29, 1931, preparing to depart New York to beat Wiley Post and Harold Gatty's round-the-world flight record. The single-engine plane had no radio, and navigation was difficult. Bogged down in mud on a Siberian runway and then mistaken for spies and arrested by the Japanese government, the pilots set a new goal of the first nonstop flight across the Pacific. (WVMCC 80-56-262, donated by Carl Cleveland.)

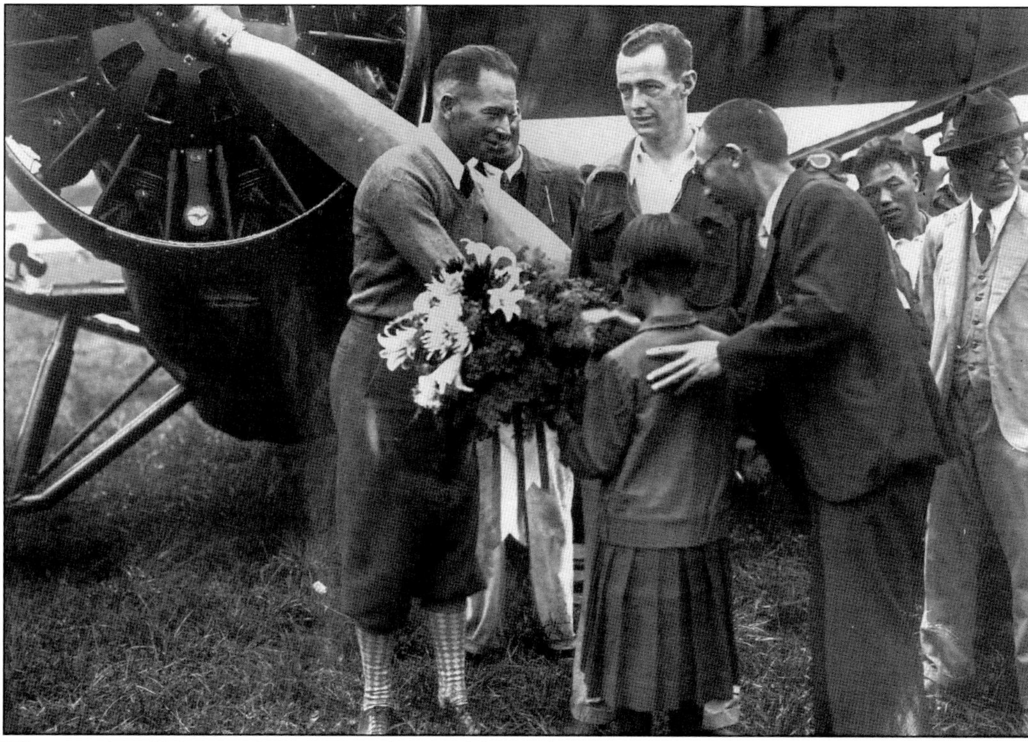

The people of Misawa, Japan, were hospitable to the American pilots and helped pack the sand on the Sabishiro Beach runway for *Miss Veedol*'s takeoff. Here, a young girl and her father present flowers to Pangborn, left, and Herndon as they prepare for the flight. (WVMCC 001-32-17, donated by Mary Jo Harbold.)

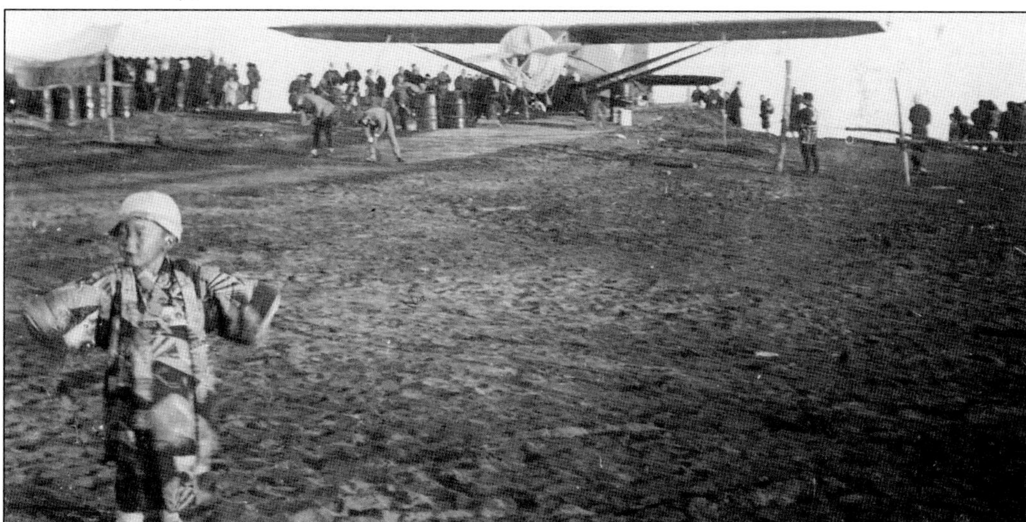

A kimono-clad boy stands on the sand in front of *Miss Veedol* as others observe the plane prior to takeoff. The plane was outfitted with belly and "chin" tanks to hold more fuel. To lighten the plane, the pilots dropped the landing gear in the ocean after takeoff, but the drag struts hung up on the fuselage. At 14,000 feet, the daring Pangborn climbed outside the aircraft and freed the struts. (WVMCC 80-87-2, donated by Kojiro Kido.)

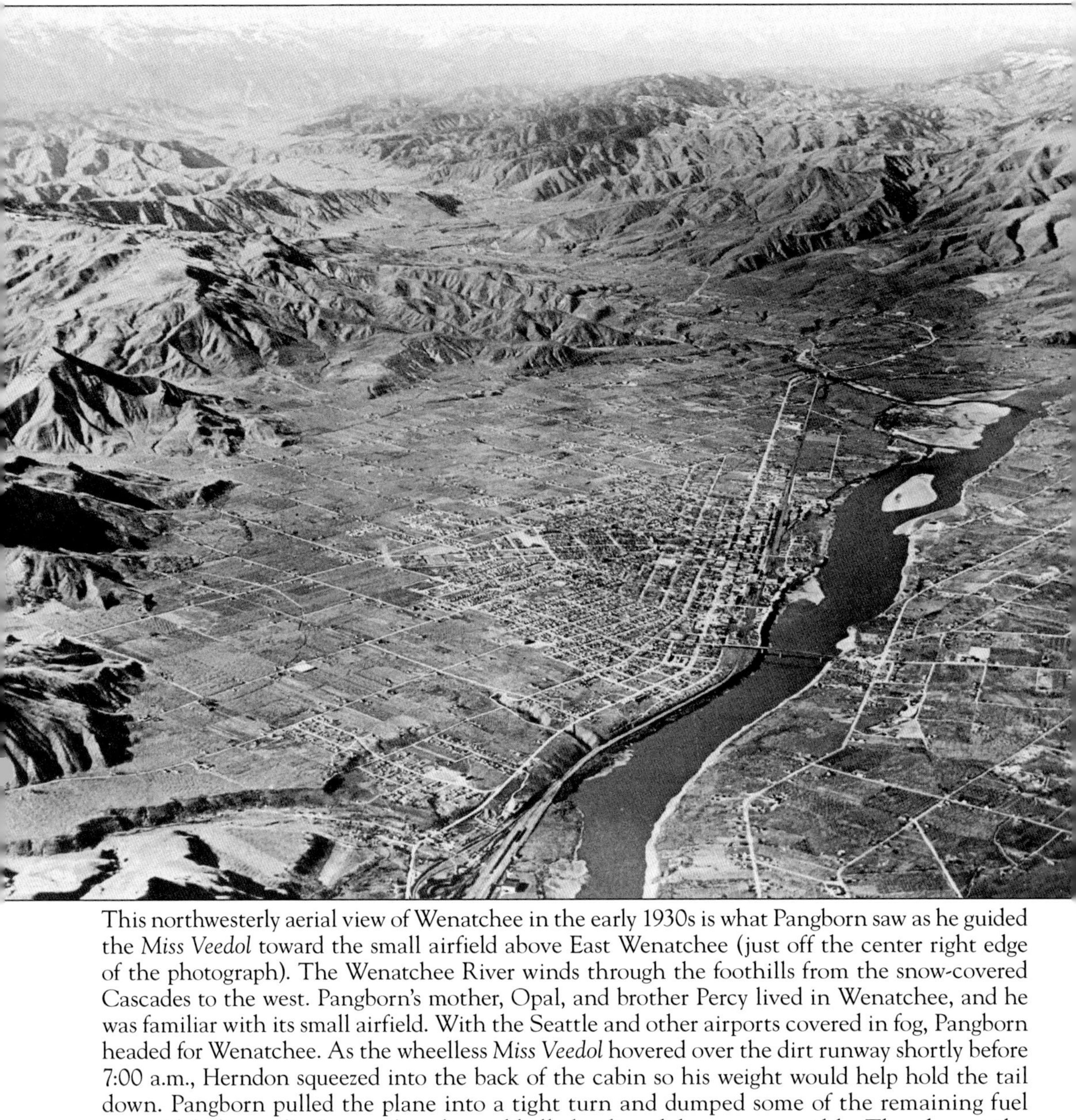

This northwesterly aerial view of Wenatchee in the early 1930s is what Pangborn saw as he guided the *Miss Veedol* toward the small airfield above East Wenatchee (just off the center right edge of the photograph). The Wenatchee River winds through the foothills from the snow-covered Cascades to the west. Pangborn's mother, Opal, and brother Percy lived in Wenatchee, and he was familiar with its small airfield. With the Seattle and other airports covered in fog, Pangborn headed for Wenatchee. As the wheelless *Miss Veedol* hovered over the dirt runway shortly before 7:00 a.m., Herndon squeezed into the back of the cabin so his weight would help hold the tail down. Pangborn pulled the plane into a tight turn and dumped some of the remaining fuel to avoid fueling a fire in case his planned belly landing did not go smoothly. Then he cut the ignition and lowered the plane slowly and safely to the ground. (WVMCC 75-23-46, donated by Bertha Smith.)

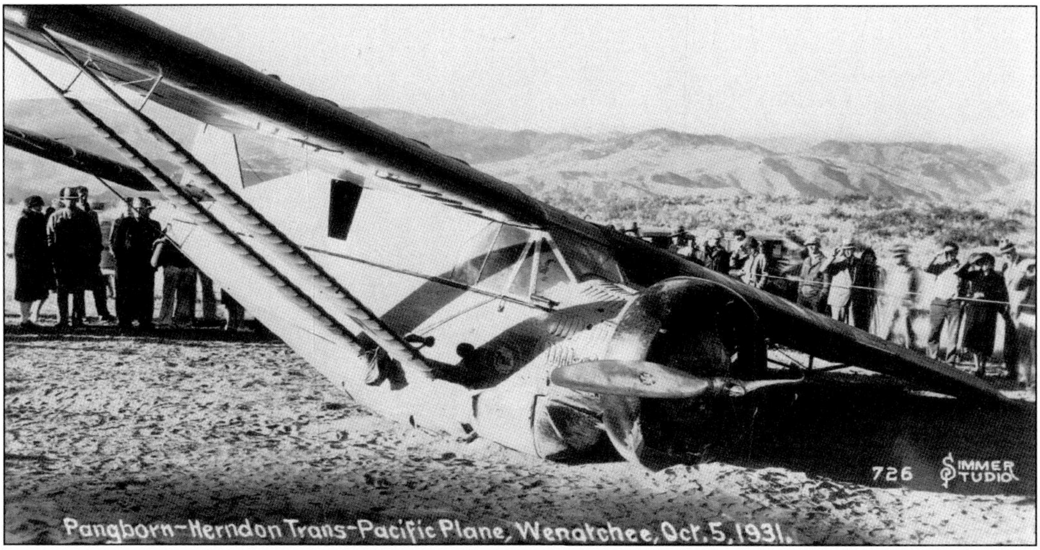

About 30 people had kept vigil in the tiny airport above East Wenatchee the night of October 4 and 5, 1931, in hopes that Pangborn and Herndon would land there. International news had announced their successful departure from Misawa two days (and an international date line) before. The plane landed safely on its belly, tipping onto its left wing and bending the propeller. (WVMCC 80-56-274, donated by Carl Cleveland.)

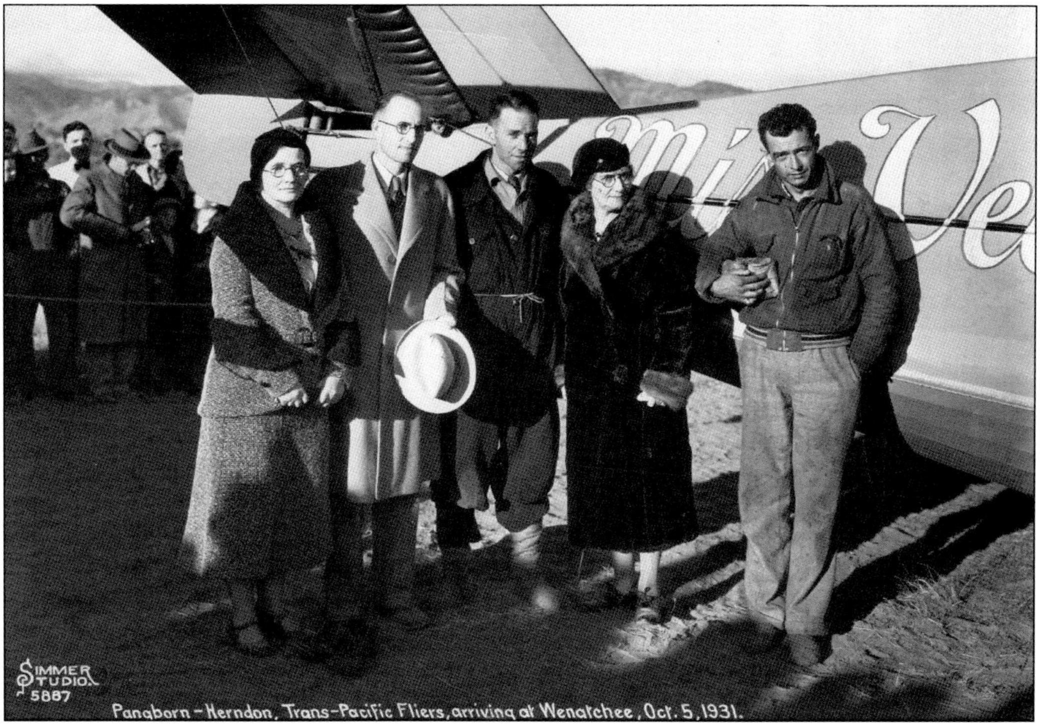

The Pangborn family was among those who were on hand to greet Clyde and his copilot with relief and joy following the successful flight. Standing by the *Miss Veedol* are, from left to right, Doris Pangborn, Percy Pangborn, Clyde Pangborn, Opal Pangborn, and Hugh Herndon. (WVMCC 80-56-257, donated by Carl Cleveland.)

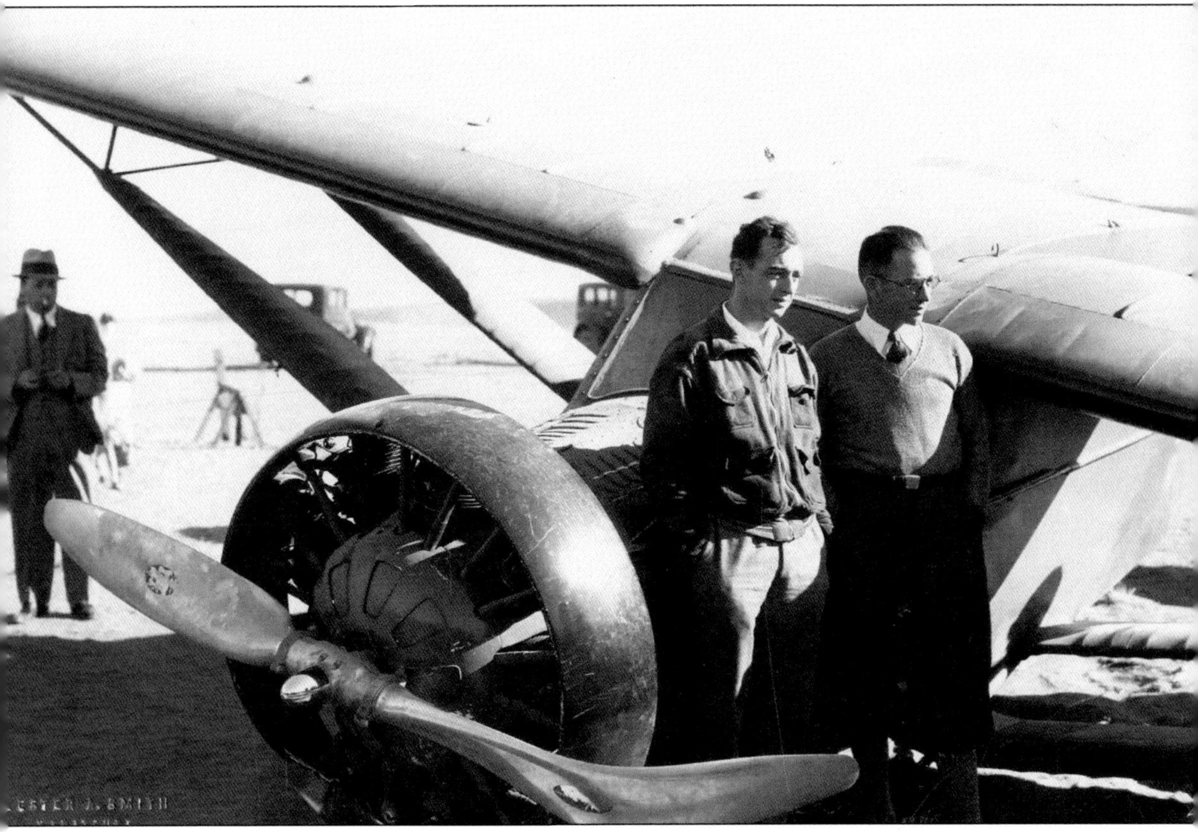

Looking tired but happy after the 41-hour flight, Herndon and Pangborn stand by the damaged propeller. They were hungry, too, having only brought along thermoses of tea (which froze at high elevation) and some sandwiches to save weight. The airmen were honored that afternoon with an impromptu parade and ceremony at Memorial Park. The world's first nonstop flight across the Pacific made Pangborn and Herndon famous and put Wenatchee's name on the international map. The propeller and other Pangborn memorabilia are on display at the Wenatchee Valley Museum and Cultural Center. (WVMCC 80-56-263, donated by Carl Cleveland.)

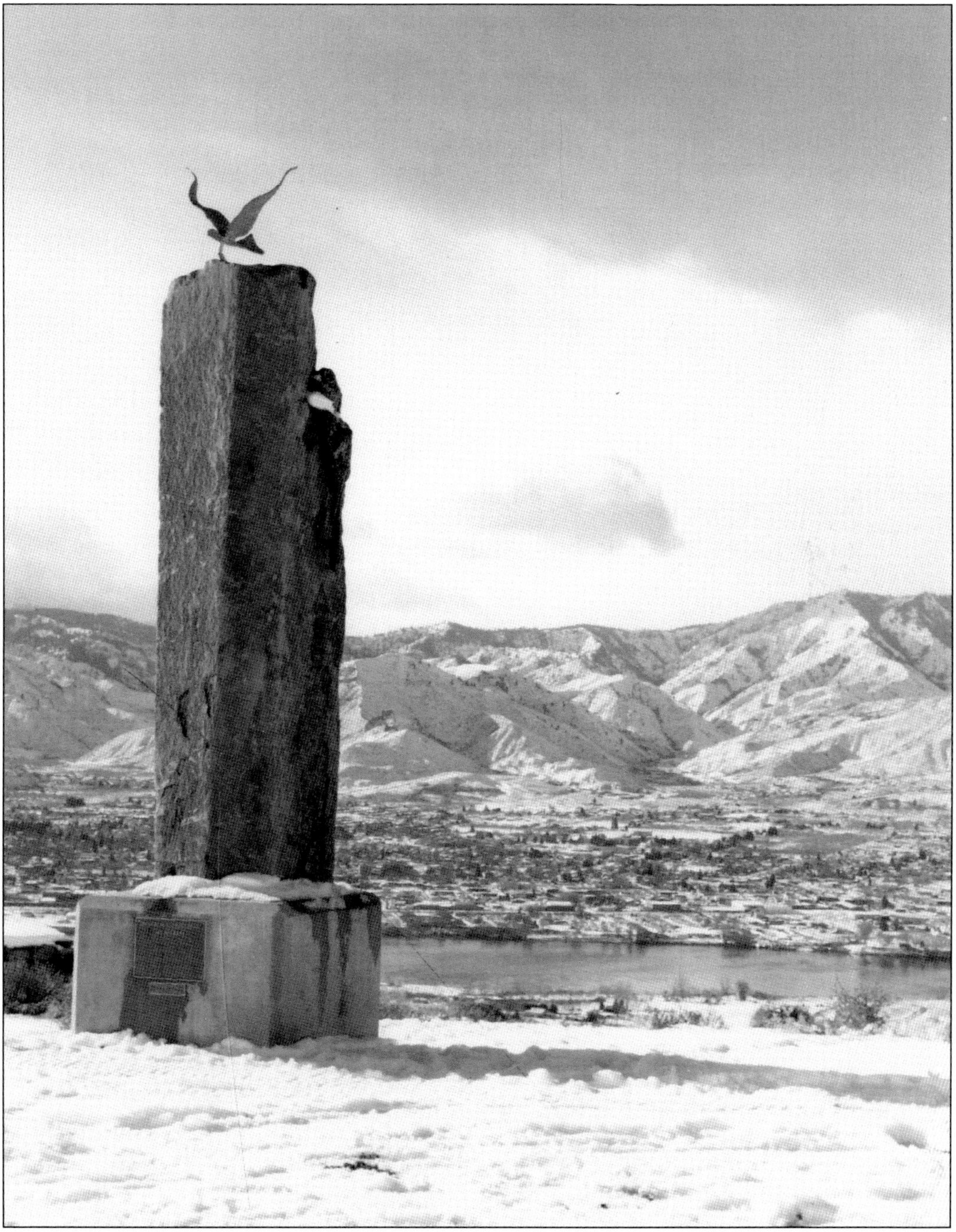

The Pangborn-Herndon Memorial Site northeast of East Wenatchee commemorates the famous flight. Designed by Wenatchee artist Walter Graham, the monument is a column of native basalt that is approximately 14 feet high and three feet in diameter with a three-foot concrete base. Molten aluminum wings grace the top of the hexagonal column. Dedicated May 3, 1969, the memorial is located at 2326 Grand Avenue, three miles up Eastmont Avenue from Grant Road. The view overlooks East Wenatchee, Wenatchee, and the Columbia River, offering a fine panorama from which to appreciate this beautiful valley. (WVMCC 88-108-650, donated by Ileen Taylor.)

INDEX

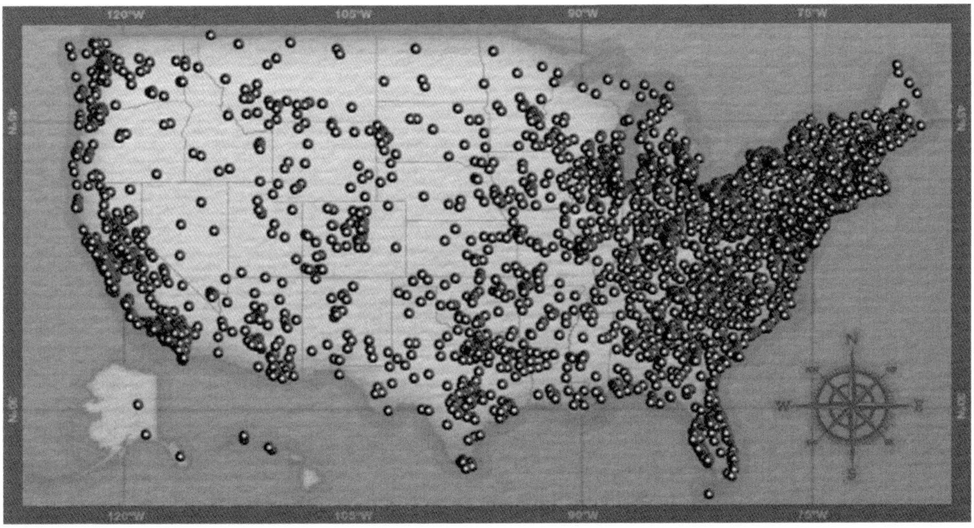